SHOWBIZ
GOES TO WAR

SHOWBIZ GOES TO WAR

ERIC TAYLOR

ROBERT HALE · LONDON

ISBN 0 7090 4616 2

Robert Hale Limited
Clerkenwell House
Clerkenwell Green
London EC1R 0HT

Photoset in North Wales by
Derek Doyle & Associates, Mold, Clwyd.
Printed in Great Britain by
St Edmundsbury Press Ltd, Bury St Edmunds, Suffolk.
Bound by Hunter and Foulis Limited.

Contents

Illustrations

PICTURE CREDITS

Times Newspapers: 1. *West Lancashire Gazette*: 2. US Army Signal Corps: 3, 21 &
22. Douglas Marshall: 4. Fred Harvey: 5–6. Rank Films: 7 & 14. George Scott: 8–9.
Samuel Goldwyn: 10, 13 & 35. Sir Harry Secombe: 11. Ron Rich: 12. Dixey
Collection: 14. Sylvia Wade: 16. Alf Lewis: 17. Ron Rich and Peter Fawcett: 18.
John Topham, *Sunday Express*: 19. United Artists: 20. Dame Vera Lynn: 23 & 24.
Mrs Mercer: 25. Gay Clark: 26–28. Winifred Beaumont: 29. Douglas Marshall: 30.
Eric Taylor: 31. Sir Dirk Bogarde: 32. Frederick Muller: 33. Anthony Quayle Ltd:
34. Air Mail: 36. Daily Telegraph: 37.

Acknowledgements

The recollections and comments of a considerable number of people have been crucial in the writing of this book and it is true to state that it could hardly have been written without their help. Half a century has passed since these people were involved directly or indirectly with showbusiness in World War Two but fortunately the memories of those servicemen, women and civilians have remained remarkably vivid. I am exceedingly grateful to all who have so generously contributed of their time in interviews, and in the writing and tape recording of their experiences.

Without reservation my many requests for assistance have been met with courtesy and candour. I am particularly indebted to Dame Vera Lynn, LLD and her husband Harry Lewis, to Sir Dirk Bogarde, Sir Harry Secombe, Michael Scully and his colleague Mr Cully of the American Embassy, Jane Chilvers of BBC Enterprises, Frank Wappat of BBC North, Mark Seaman of the Imperial War Museum Research and Information Office, and Mr Danny La Rue for their prompt and generous response to my various requests.

I have been greatly assisted in my research by the staff of the Public Record Office at Kew and the National Newspaper Library at Colindale. I give my sincere thanks to the editors of newspapers, magazines and Forces journals who helped me to contact so many of the wartime entertainers.

To all those men and women of service concert parties who communicated with me I gratefully record my thanks and must give special mention to Doug Marshall who let me have his own full account of his activities with the 15th Scottish Division concert party, and to his colleague and compère of that party, Bert Woodfield, to former Nursing Sister Winifred Beaumont, to John Cooper, Syd Whittington, Peter and Tricia Bedford, Freddy Smith, Peter Fawcett, Roger Keyes, and Ronald Rich, all of whom provided such detailed and interesting accounts.

It must be evident that I owe a large debt to all those who wrote to me with significant accounts of their concert party days and sent me programmes yet, because of the limited space, are not mentioned by name in the text. Their accounts were nevertheless most useful in illustrating the vast panorama of showbusiness and the contribution it made to Allied victory in the Second World War.

To all who communicated with me I express again the sincere thanks I have already given privately but meriting further mention are: Arthur Childs, Joan Howse, Bryn Purdy, Hy Schorr, Jacqueline Taylor, Kathryn and Michael Benenson, Robin Cross, Ann Ford, Pauline Smith, L.K. Rewling, T.W. Booth, Jack Lawrenson, Eunice Wilson, Ray James, Alf Lewis, Sylvia Wade, Majorie Kelly, Mollie Urquhart, Lynn Booth Hilliard, Ruth Negus, Edith Viner Owens, G.E. Hardy, David Smith, Jack Grist, Grace Watson Finch, Stan Morrison, Jane Williams, Wyndham Davidson, Frank Cotton, A.S. Jacklin, Richard Roberts, John Stratton, Cyril Risbridger, Rey Gill, Jim Whitehorn, J.T. Philips, Hubert Stanley Haines, W.A. Lovett, L.B. Wheatley, Muriel Clarke, Marjorie Sargent, James Dunnet, Jack Blades, Doug Kneale, Ralph Harrington, Bessie Major Ross, Stan Williamson, James Williams, Bill Marrian, Alan and Sylvia Rusling, Ron Rosonson, S. Thompson, Harold Firman, Catherine Smith, Mikki Godden, Ollie Olsen, Audrey Abbott Hayes, Thelma Holdaway, Mary Osborne, Evelyn Austin, Jose Omahony, Frank Churchett, Tom Taylor, Peggy Cooper, Delma Matkin, James Cullen, Ella Challis, A.J. Whaley, Vera Price, A.J. Clements, Hugh Berry, Arthur Sheppard, Jack Copeland, Cyril Porter, G. Leslie, Jenny Nicholson, Peter Hoy, Brian Piper, L.G. Highley, Peter Jeffrey, Beryl Poulter, Eileen Kisby, Marion Bache, Mostyn Rees, Marion Topping, J.M. Hull, Fred Saunders, Mollie Gale, Audrey Bellenger, Ralph Boyce, David Clark, Jack Lawford, Doreen Royle, G. Hartley, Mae Hawkins, Harry Coutson, Peggy Casey, Dorothy Oates, A. Cragg, Dinty Moore, Jane Wheeler, James Williams, Joyce Beckett, Eileen Cook, Norman Gray, Brian Hawkins, G. Humphrey, Margarette Fisher Page, John Adams, G. and N. Baldock, Regina May, Grahame Waite, O. Longford, Rex Cook, Anne Burge, J.H. Ball, Jane Wheeler, Daphne Guthrie, Alex Stoddart, Barbara Eaves, Cyril Hepher, Marian Carswell, D. Thatcher, Bill Earp, D. Paton, Leslie Flanders, F. Pearman, Charles Landrin, J.O. Crump, Neena Laver, Elizabeth Ballard, Barbara George, Joyce Peake, Jim Davies, Colin Baker, Elizabeth Sealey, Elizabeth Jones, Derek Wellman, J. Cavill, Mrs Wood, Puck Duvall, Arthur Ottaway, Charlie Morris, L.A. Sullivan, Percy Cullum, Edward Astley-Jones, Bernard Howson, J. Ferrier, Les

Sullerby, Neville Gay, Phyllis Beardsmore, Gay Clark, Joan Potter, Leon Monkman, J.D. Roberts, Doreen Horwell, Denys Brown, David Southwood, W.R. Cook, Margaret Finlay, Peter King, Algy Gower, Freda Hemingway, Kathleen Cartwright, Doug Smith, Rusty Russell, Maurice Handcock, Alf Lewis, Peter Selby, A.R. Baker, Hazel Roberts, Kathleen Watts, D.J. Masters, Mrs M. Mercer, Bob Lea, Pat White, Charles White, W. Williams, George Bullamore, Joan Dunhill, William Davies, George Ridd, H. Smith, Gordon Excell, Betty Sleep Tozer, Arthur Jacklin, Marjorie Bogajski, Joan Potter, Reg Humphries, Sidney Munns, Ronald French and Doris Fowler.

There are many others whose support and assistance made this book possible. I must again thank my wife, Sheila, who has organized and collated research, helped so much with the interviews and checked the manuscript so carefully. My thanks once more go to my valued friend and fellow writer Charles Whiting who never fails to produce ideas. Finally I am most grateful for the meticulous way the editor, Susan Hale, has piloted the typescript to port. The responsibility for any shortcomings or errors is, of course, my own.

Glossary

AA	Anti-Aircraft (Ack-Ack)
ARP	Air Raid Precautions
AFHQ	Allied Force Headquarters (Mediterranean)
BBC	British Broadcasting Corporation
BEF	British Expeditionary Force (in France 1939-40)
CEMA	Council for the Encouragement of Music and Arts
ENSA	Entertainments National Service Association
ETO	European Theatre of Operations (American term)
MEF	Middle East Forces
MI5	Military Intelligence 5 dealing with security
MI6	Military Intelligence 6 dealing with intelligence
NCO	Non-commissioned officer
PRO	Public Record Office
SEAC	South East Asia Command
SIS	Secret Intelligence Service
SOE	Special Operations Executive
SS	Schutzstaffel, fanatical elite of National Socialist Germany. They were in charge of the police and the Secret Service and deliberately cultivated fear evoked by their mere existence.

Prologue

In a remote corner within the grimy forbidding walls of the British War Office, one afternoon in the spring of 1944, a bizarre scene was being enacted. At least it would have appeared so to any onlooker permitted to enter that room. It was bare and high-ceilinged, panelled in heavy oak and smelling richly of wax polish. There was about the place a faintly museum-like air.

In this room a small, select group of red-tabbed, senior officers had gathered secretly for a most remarkable purpose. Standing by the bay window was Brigadier Heywood, a tall, thin man with sparse grey hair, next to him was Colonel Lester of Military Intelligence 5, broad shouldered with a close-cropped moustache, trying to look calm and confident but nevertheless tapping his fingers nervously on a narrow table. At the other end of that table stood a choleric colonel, still wearing his red-banded hat.

All three men wore a preoccupied expression, one almost of disbelief, as they watched the antics of a fourth officer whose features were probably better known to the British public than those of any other general officer in history. Most people would readily have put a name to the figure before them, dressed in a well-tailored barathea battledress bedecked with rows of medal ribbons, and wearing a black beret on which were two cap badges. He was a man who stood second only to Winston Churchill as a British folk-hero. His walk, too, was a giveaway; with measured pace, hands clasped tightly behind his back and his whole manner radiating confidence and authority. He was now progressing along a row of wooden chairs lined up diagonally across the room from a large mahogany desk in the corner. Quizzically he looked at each one, then stopped in front of an empty chair and, in that well-known, high-pitched tone of voice, uttered six precisely articulated words: 'Hope we have a good trip.' Then he passed on to the mahogany desk, marked time briefly, turned to face the chairs squarely, and gave the typical Montgomery style, two-stage salute, throwing his arm up slowly, then bringing it down sharply towards his temple.

In the bay window, Colonel Lester shot a glance at Brigadier Heywood, who now for the first time spoke. 'That's it. Salute after the inspection. Then ask for Major Foley. Now, let's run through it once more. Right from the beginning. And concentrate please.'[1]

What was this bizarre charade taking place with, apparently, General Montgomery, the publicity-conscious victor of El Alamein, taking the leading role?

Once again the pantomime performance of inspecting the row of chairs and the final salute was gone through under the critical scrutiny of the brigadier and two colonels who occasionally interjected critical comments.

At last, Colonel Lester released his breath in a long relieved hiss and looked again at his boss. Brigadier Heywood turned towards him, a hint of a smile on his face, as he murmured, 'He'll do fine.' What on earth was happening in that room? Surely the self-centred General Montgomery, notorious for his vanity, egotism and arrogance could not be submitting so tamely to the criticism of his subordinates?

The startling truth emerged soon enough when Brigadier Heywood pulled a cigarette case from his pocket, walked over to the central figure and proffered it, saying, 'You won't be able to have many more of these. Better start cutting them down. As soon as you're Monty you'll be a strict non-smoker.'

'Thank you, sir,' said the 'general' in the black beret, dragging smoke deeply into his lungs. Here, clearly was not the non-smoking General Montgomery who had rocketed to media stardom in the duel with Rommel's Afrika Korps. It was, in fact, the former provincial actor, Clifton James, presently of the Royal Army Pay Corps who had never hit the headlines before but was now cast in a hazardous and momentous drama. He was to be General Montgomery's double.

'I want you to look on this as a play we are going to produce for the benefit of the enemy,' Colonel Lester had explained. 'You, as a professional artiste, have been cast for the biggest role in the history of acting. Our audience are not simple folk, like drama critics. It's the German High Command that we have to hoodwink. Upon your performance will depend the lives of thousands.'[2]

D-Day was imminent. The Allies had built up a mighty invasion force which would soon land in France and battle its way to Berlin. With the south of England packed with troops of all nationalities, it would have been impossible to conceal the build up of such a huge army from the Germans but they did not know the date of the expected attack nor could they be sure where in Northern France the strike would be made. Nor could they rule out the possibility of a surprise assault upon some other front.

Therefore a plan of deception had been drawn up and approved by the Supreme Commander, General Eisenhower. The idea was to feed German Intelligence with evidence that General Montgomery, who would be commanding the British invasion force, had flown down to Gibraltar and North Africa to confer with generals there. The Germans would then be left confused and wondering whether any landing at all was being contemplated in Northern France. So it was that actor Clifton James, was trained to impersonate General Montgomery, flying to Gibraltar. He watched newsreels of Monty, and spent hours being drilled by Colonel Lester in hundreds of details of the impersonation.

To study Monty at close quarters Clifton James spent several days on his staff, this time acting the part of a sergeant in the Intelligence Corps. He attended the full dress rehearsal of D-Day itself at Slapton Sands near Plymouth, watching through the eyes of a theatre director every move Monty made. James was impressed and was later to write: 'What a personality he had! He would have made a fortune on the stage, I thought.'

But then the cue came for James to go on his particular stage. Colonel Lester said:

> Now James, it's time for the curtain to go up. Tomorrow you will be driven to the airport and, in full view of scores of people, you will take off in the Prime Minister's plane. At 7.45 next morning you land at Gibraltar. We have spread rumours all along the African coast that Monty may be coming to form an Anglo-American army for an invasion of southern France. You are going to travel all through the Middle East to give weight to these rumours. Every move of yours will be watched intently by Hitler's agents. Remember from now on senior officers are mere subordinates. There's just one last thing. Here are some khaki handkerchiefs marked with the general's initials, B.L.M. Drop these about as if by accident wherever you think fit. In this game it's the little details that count.

James got off to a good start at Gibraltar, addressing the Governor, Sir Ralph Eastwood familiarly as 'Rusty' and soon was well into his act. He recalled, 'I slipped into my role so completely that to all intents and purposes I was Montgomery. I talked as he talked and faithfully imitated every gesture and vocal mannerism. Even when I was alone I found myself playing the part.'

So well did he play the part that soon signals were flashing

between Spain and Berlin and the Germans were left speculating
whether the expected invasion would be coming into southern
France or the north.

Later, commenting on the role played by Clifton James, General
Sir Leslie Hollis, who attended meetings of the Chiefs of Staff
throughout the war, had this to say:

> By this and other methods, 450,000 German troops were kept
> pinned down in various parts of Europe even after the Normandy
> landings. And the German troops in the south of France were not
> withdrawn and sent north for ten days following this landing. Had
> they been available earlier, then the invasion of northern France
> would have been infinitely more difficult, and the casualties
> greater.[3]

Just in fact as Colonel Lester had predicted, the performance of
Clifton James had saved thousands of Allied lives. Clifton James,
actor and lieutenant of the Royal Army Pay Corps had gone to
war in no small way.

Little in the past has been written about the contribution made
to victory by professionals and amateurs in the entertainment
world. Showbiz went to war in a 'variety' of ways and deserves
credit for the contribution it made to victory. Naturally, in one
book it would not be possible to mention everyone but through
the activities of some of them we can get a better idea of the
unusual tasks they were given, the situations in which they had
to perform, and how much their efforts were indeed appreciated
especially by those in the thick of the fighting.,

We can, perhaps, then see just how magnificently they
responded to the British government's instructions to them in
1939:[4] 'You will serve your country best by staying at your posts.'

Eric Taylor
York
1992

1

War on the Air Waves

The moment I heard the declaration of war on the radio I tore out of the theatre and down the street to the nearest recruiting office.

'What do you want?' asked the sergeant belligerently.

'I want to join the Navy, please,' I said, flushed with patriotism. England for ever. Life on the ocean wave and all that.

'Go away,' he said. 'We've got more than enough men already.'

Utterly deflated, I walked back to the theatre in time to see CLOSED notices going up.[1]

The experience in September 1939 of actor Kenneth More, star of such films as *Genevieve*, *Reach for the Sky* and *The Thirty-Nine Steps*, was not unique. Rex Harrison[2] tried to join the cavalry but was told by the colonel that they were not taking any more recruits yet. He too went back to the theatre where he had been playing to capacity audiences to find that it was closed. Strange things were happening to showbusiness people.

Ninety per cent of them were thrown out of work that day by an edict of the Lord Chamberlain which closed all cinemas, theatres, and places of entertainment where the public might congregate in large numbers. Consequently on that memorable day 3 September 1939 there was only one cinema in the whole of the United Kingdom that opened its doors to the public, and that was on the pier of Aberystwyth. But even there not many people entered. They had already seen pictures of what the German Air Force had done in Poland, and feared the same treatment.

'I fully expected to be blasted to Kingdom-come at any moment,' recalled Kenneth More. But nothing happened.

Instead of Hitler's bombers blackening the skies above every large city, everything appeared much as before, except for a flurry of letters to *The Times* protesting about the closure of places of entertainment. Sir Oswald Stoll,[3] in his letter, questioned the wisdom of closing theatres and reminded the government that in the First World War, showbiz folk played a vital role in maintaining the morale of civilians and servicemen. And playwright George Bernard Shaw wrote to say that the government should open more theatres and cinemas for there soon would be eighty thousand servicemen on leave wanting to be entertained.[4]

This panic measure of the government was soon repealed and on 16 September, theatres and cinemas were allowed to open provided they closed by ten o'clock. The government was now convinced that entertainment was going to be one of the decisive factors in maintaining the morale of the nation and its will to fight. Towards this end, one of the first steps the government did take was to issue an edict that key actors and actresses should remain at their posts as entertainers and be exempt from military service.

It was the beginning of a funny kind of war; a phoney war in which things were happening which would have fitted well into a West End farce. One of Britain's best loved broadcasters, Arthur Marshall, recalled in his autobiography[5] one such absurdity.

He was then a schoolmaster at Oundle in a remote corner of Northamptonshire, a place of negligible interest as a bomb target. He was listening to dance music played by Henry Hall late one night when there was a sharp knocking on his front door. It was almost midnight. Unlikely to be a social call. Turning off the lights of his sitting room before opening the door, because of the blackout regulations, he shone the dimmed glow of his torch upon a small figure standing on his front doormat. It was a woman. Marshall wrote:

> She spoke, and she spoke lugubriously. 'I'm a high explosive bomb,' she said.
> She was, of course, no such thing. I recognised her at once as an assistant in one of the town's two drapery establishments. On that particular evening she was taking part in an Air Raid Precautions exercise organised by the local council. And for this she was a high explosive bomb. I asked if she had gone off, was about to go off or was embedded in the roadway as unexploded. She said that she was sorry but she did not know. 'They' had not told her. Thereupon, her duty performed she accepted an invitation to take coffee, instantly deserting her post, in the carefree and lackadaisical military manner of 1939.

It was a time for mysterious calls. The cheery Liverpudlian comedian, Tommy Handley, received a strange and confidential order from his employer, the British Broadcasting Corporation.[6]

Again, like something out of a silly sketch, the message said: 'Listen to the wireless for the secret signal.'

By this time the government was already into the business of sending messages in code to their Secret Service agents overseas, through the normal broadcast programmes. The signal that Tommy Handley, and other key personnel on the BBC's list, had to listen for would immediately precede the nine o'clock news bulletin. It would arouse no curiosity with listeners who were not privy to the secret but would send those in the know packing their bags. They had been warned that immediately the announcement before the news changed from, 'This is the national programme' to 'This is London', they were to report straight away to designated assembly points. For Tommy Handley this was to be an old parish church in Bristol.

BBC presenter, Wynford Vaughan Thomas, who would later distinguish himself by winning the Croix de Guerre, heard the message at Llandudno where he was about to compere a Sunday evening radio show. It was one of a series when the BBC visited a different popular seaside resort every week to present the show given by the concert party in residence for the season. All was ready for the next evening's performance; the programme was to be opened by organist Wyndham Lewis, on his giant Wurlitzer organ rising from the bowels of the Odeon cinema, and then the mayor of Llandudno was to say a few words.

The secret message put an end to all that.

Vaughan Thomas packed his bags leaving Llandudno's hyped-up performers feeling flattened. Not for long, though. Organist Wyndham Lewis, showing commendable initiative, earned himself the accolade of being the first showbiz stalwart to go to war. He dashed to the house of the local signwriter and had a huge poster painted. He displayed it prominently outside the Odeon cinema. It read:

BE PATRIOTIC. COME INSIDE
AND LEARN THE NEW WAR SONGS!

Meanwhile, BBC Radio was gearing up for playing the most important role in its history, for the Allied Nations at war. It was going to keep its listeners fully committed to the cause, to keep them confident, cheerful, and resolute in its determination to bring down Nazi Germany and restore freedom to oppressed countries. It was going to look after the nation's morale.

So it was that in that first week of the war, key personnel

involved in this task were gathering at their appointed assembly points. Tommy Handley, Mr Itma, duly went to Bristol. By that time his show, *It's That Man Again* had been keeping millions laughing every week, and the BBC was determined to keep them laughing. The show's title, *It's That Man Again* had been headlines in the national press for months heralding every new demand made by that man, Hitler. Handley saw its potential and had commandeered it for his show, which had its first run in the summer of 1939.

Now whatever damage that man, Hitler, and the German Air Force might inflict upon London, the BBC would be keeping the country happy from studios dispersed well away from target areas.

Tommy Handley hurried to his appointed rendezvous, a small regional studio in Bristol. There it was chaos. Hundred of actors, actresses, musicians, and technicians were milling about, all eager to make sure their own show went on the air – as indeed top level orders had ordained they must. But how?

Producers pushed their way from one group to the next, ticking names off lists clipped to a millboard and handing out instructions to those shortly to go into the studio. In their anxiety not to offend any particular section of the public the BBC had a card of brief instructions to be handed to all newcomers and particularly comedians. It read: 'No gags on Scotsmen, Welshmen, Clergymen, Drink, or Medical Matters. Do not sneeze into the microphone.'[7]

At first, artists were thin on the ground. Some were caught up in rail travel delays but the problem of finding talent had been made worse by theatrical impressarios who had drawn up contracts which prevented most variety stars from performing on radio. An added complication came with those performers who, although eager to broadcast and free from contractual obligations, were prevented from being employed by the BBC because they had not yet been 'security cleared'. Military Intelligence 5 was insisting that everyone writing for radio or taking part in programmes must first be thoroughly vetted. Thus it was, for example, that Ted Kavanagh, who wrote Tommy Handley's scripts, found that he could no longer do this until he had been though the vetting process. He explained:

At the beginning of the war, there were many rumours about ingenious systems of getting messages through to the enemy via some innocent item. The stories ranged from simple pre-arranged codes based on words in talks, to involved arrangements whereby a few piano notes revealed the entire movements of the Royal Navy to gentlemen wearing headphones in Bremen. They were all silly stories, but there was, of course, a germ of possible sense in them.[8]

Consequently during that first week, security took precedence over the preparation of morale-boosting programmes and frantic controllers had to resort to filling air time with lengthy news bulletins and request programmes using records and Sandy MacPherson giving marathon recitals on the BBC theatre organ. He actually played twenty-three times in the BBC's first week of near panic and hysteria.

By 19 September, however, commonsense had prevailed and a sense of absurd normality came back to the ears of listeners when the announcer spoke the magic initials, *ITMA*, and, much to the relief of millions of fans, the signature tune by Michael North, sung by Vera Lennox hit the airwaves:

Mother's pride and joy,
Mrs Handley's boy
Oh it's useless to complain,
When trouble's brewing,
It's his doing,
It's that man – that man again.[!]

Tommy then came on speaking into a telephone. 'Hello! Is that Turner, Turner, and Turtle? It is? Then good morning, good morning, good morning. It's that man again. That's right, Tommy Handley.'

Despite Hitler. Despite the war. Britain was laughing again. And *ITMA* was off to a ten year run. From then on, *ITMA* became firmly entrenched in the hearts of millions of radio listeners who were made to chortle and laugh heartily every week no matter how desperate the war news. Everyone profited from 'That Man's' rare gift of making people of all ages feel better.

Dennis Forshaw,[9] then a fusilier doing a pre-Octu course at Number 7 Infantry Training Centre in the forbidding Victorian barracks right on top of the road leading out of Lincoln, recalled what effect the programme then had upon him and his mates.

Though we were all pretty fit in those days, the walk up that hill used to make us pant and sweat like old dogs in a summer heat wave, but many was the time we would all belt back to barracks at a cracking pace just so that we could listen to ITMA. It was not just for the jokes and the laughter though. It was part of a ritual that we did not want to miss for somehow just listening to that programme

linked us with the family back home and gave us all a tonic so that
when the programme finished we'd walk with a lighter step
around the hallowed parade ground to the NAAFI for a mug of tea
and a NAAFI rock cake with raspberry jam inside, feeling good.
That's what Tommy Handley meant for all of us then.

What a way for Tommy to go to war!

His crazy, seemingly spontaneous, quick-fire patter suited the
crazy world of politics and the war that, for most people, was not
yet a war except for the never-ending stream of government
wartime instructions which came from all the new ministries,
urging people not to do this or that: only to have five inches of
water in the bath or to eat carrots to make them see better in the
black-out. Tommy promoted himself to become Minister of
Aggravation and Mysteries (Agriculture and Fisheries) in the
Office of Twerps (Works), though at times he would be His
Lateship the Mayor of the seaside town of Foaming-in-the-
Mouth, unless he was appearing as Governor of the island of
Tomtopia.

The gags in his show were always topical so that people began
to regard their own problems with the same sense of humour.
They echoed the catchphrases used by characters on his
programme as they went about their work: Mrs Mopp's 'Shall I
do you now, Sir?' and they would leave work with her 'Ta Ta For
Now' or 'TTFN'. At night in the pub they would be aping Colonel
Chinstrap with 'I don't mind if I do.' Then there were the polite
couple of workmen who might have come to lay the new
linoleum but found it very hard to start anything because they
would say in their slow, lugubrious voices: 'After you, Cecil.'

'No, after you Claud.'

Those catchphrases served a most useful purpose as well as
amusing the listener. Bizarre though they were, they conveyed
some sense of permanence – of the reliability of things in a world
full of uncertainty and danger. One laughed with a sort of joyous
relief. No matter what was happening outside, these lunatics
were unshakable.

An apochryphal story about these catchphrases but one retold
in the *Daily Telegraph* as recently as January 1992,[10], was about a
young boy buried in the rubble after an air raid, who called out to
a rescuer: 'Can you do me now, sir?'

There was a catchphrase too that took the sting out of those
grim government warnings, 'Careless talk costs lives.' A
gravel-voiced spy's voice came over the telephone in many of the
ITMA programmes. The versatile Jack Train made absurd calls

threatening Tommy Handley in his various roles: 'Zis is Funf, your favourite spy. I haf found out everyzing. Do not leave your office. Your life is in danger. Beware, you haf enemies you do not know.' And so the German secret agent became a figure of fun and not one of fear.

It was Funf too who did a magnificent job for Britain at the time when William Joyce, better known to the British public as the traitor Lord Haw Haw, was making nightly scaremongering broadcasts to Britain in English from Hamburg and Berlin. This harsh-voiced, Irish renegade and former member of the British Union of Fascists, had begun these broadcasts at the outbreak of war in an attempt to undermine morale. His arrogant grating voice was listened to by a surprising number of people. A survey showed that thirty per cent of readers of *The Times* tuned in regularly to Lord Haw Haw's broadcasts. And naturally, there was a time when the government became concerned about the effect these broadcasts might have upon the nation's morale but they soon stopped worrying. Funf, and other impersonations of him turned him into a figure of fun and a full-scale revue called 'Haw Haw' really did make everything about the despicable creature a great joke. Children even made up their own games about Haw Haw and the insidious German Secret Service, in which Funf and his assistant Helga Schwenkwere, were the prized parts they fought over.

What chance had German propaganda after such ridicule?

These were boom times for radio. Robb Wilton made light of the imminent possibility of invasion by poking gentle fun at the newly formed Local Defence Force – the forerunners of Captain Mainwaring's Home Guard so popular later with TV viewers as *Dad's Army*. One of the better known of Robb Wilton's pieces was:

> The first day I got my uniform I went home and put it on. The missus looked at me and said, 'What are you supposed to be?'
> I said, 'I'm one of the Home Guards.'
> She said, 'One of the Home Guards? What are the others like? What are you supposed to do?'
> 'I'm supposed to stop Hitler's army landing!' I said.
> She said, 'What, you?'
> I said, 'No, not me, there's Bob Edwards, Charlie Evans, Billy Brightside – there's seven or eight of us, we're in a group on guard in a little hut behind the "Dog and Pullet".'

Pure comedy such as this was a great antidote to wartime blues. Never had radio showbiz done a more worthwhile job. The BBC Variety Department produced one new show after another.

From the Clifton Parish Hall, Bristol came what sounded like a show from an army barracks. They called it *Garrison Theatre*, and to give listeners the impression they were hearing a show from a genuine military establishment, troops were invited into the small hall and packed in tightly together.

Producer Harry S. Pepper knew that he was taking a risk having boisterous soldiery so close to a live microphone but before every performance, as soon as the heavily studded boots had stopped clumping on the floor, he made a special plea for their co-operation. He ended his little pep talk with a warning, 'Now you can all join in the choruses when the broadcast is on but ...' he paused, smiled and looked meaningfully at the red-capped military policemen standing in the aisles '... anyone singing rude versions will be thrown out.'[11]

Troops, however, proved to be ideal audiences for that show, as Jack Warner recalled:[12]

> The presence of genuine troops proved to be a big asset because having exchanged the cold unfriendly confines of barracks for the warmth of the theatre, and the rigorous parade ground discipline for the comedian's cracks, they were in a relaxed mood and that guaranteed every performer an enthusiastic reception. Furthermore their spontaneous laughter was infectious so that listeners at home joined in too.

Garrison Theatre like *ITMA* and Arthur Askey's very popular *Bandwagon*, followed a regular format, with the same setting and the same cast each week. *Garrison Theatre* had the irascible regimental sergeant major with the booming voice, a man who in World War One had been the RSM to Charlie Shadwell, the Director of the BBC's Variety Orchestra at the show. Jack Warner played the part of a Cockney soldier who was always making daft remarks and interrupting the show. Soon his catchphrases too were on everybody's lips – 'Vereee good, Sir', and 'Mind my bike'. From *Bandwagon*, bus conductors took Arthur Askey's catchphrase 'I thang you' as they took in the money for tram and bus tickets.

What was the point of being downhearted in such exciting times; times when near disasters could become material for comedians' jokes?

There was no shortage of such shows. Another one, typical of this genre, was *Hi Gang*, starring a husband and wife team, Ben Lyon and Bebe Daniels, two Americans who were well known to British audiences through their films. With them too was the comedian Vic Oliver, who was well known by name at least to listeners in Britain through his marriage to Prime Minister Churchill's daughter Sarah, when she was a chorus girl in one of C.B. Cochran's revues. This show had something of the American style about it but still had familiar catchphrases for the audience to latch on to. The show raced along at a whirlwind pace until Ben Lyon called 'time' and said 'So long, Dan' evoking the same response each week from the audience, 'So long, Ben'.

In these strange times, Britain's mood was difficult to fathom. Even war correspondent and Royal biographer, Godfrey Talbot was to comment that 'Making fun of serious things became almost a patriotic exercise. People sang with giddiness and optimism and the worse the situation, the more the people joked.'[13]

Occasionally, though, some jokes were censored by the BBC on the grounds that they might lower morale. Tommy Trinder was furious one day when the BBC prevented him from telling the story of the soldier walking down Whitehall who asked a passer-by, 'Which side is the War Office on?' and he answered, 'Ours, I hope.'[14]

Generally though the British public enjoyed laughing at comedians' jokes about wartime problems, rationing, long hours and overtime, the sergeant major, and of course, the black-out. Here indeed, thanks to showbiz and their own natural inclinations, was a nation nowhere near to despair. A nation determined to fight on despite disasters at sea, air bombardment and the defeat of the British Army in France.

Shortly after that defeat and the evacuation of British and Allied troops from the beaches of Dunkirk, Britain was faced with the enormous problem of how to replace all the military equipment left in France. The British Expeditionary Force had had the pick of weapons before going to France but had left behind almost all its heavy equipment, including six hundred tanks and most of its artillery. So it was that in June 1940 Britain found herself standing alone and also unarmed. America was neither ready nor able to provide weapons for Britain and so Britain's factories were immediately in the front line. Then it was that the phrase, 'The Dunkirk Spirit' entered the English language. Workers just had to work at maximum effort. Days in the factory were going to be long and hard.

Fortuitously the BBC was then about to launch an experiment which was to step up enormously production in factories. On 23 June 1940, a new series of programmes called *Music While You Work* began. Its effect was almost unbelievable. Minister of Labour, Ernest Bevin was so impressed he wrote: 'Britain's army of war workers, an army which is growing daily greater, is untiring in its efforts, but no man or woman can toil unceasingly without relaxation. Consequently the BBC's *Music While You Work*, a daily ration of music, has made the hours pass more quickly and has resulted in greatly increased production.'[15]

Those 'experimental' programmes went on then throughout the whole of the war and surveys over five years showed what an important part that music played in the working life of the community. Hundreds of factories were visited to study reception conditions and to learn the opinions of men and women at their work. To quote from a few of these factory reports, 'The music exhilarates the workers without acting as a harmful distraction. When the wireless set was shut down for a week there was a twenty per cent drop in production.' Another report stated that, 'There was a 22.1 per cent increase in production in the fuse shop over a period of one year after the introduction of *Music While You Work*.[16]

As a result of its popularity with management and workers the BBC was able to report that 'Since 1940 factory installations of radio facilities have increased at the rate of over one thousand a year and now over eight thousand factories, covering more than four and a half million workers, receive programmes daily.'

In addition to *Music While You Work*, the morale of factory workers was improved by a new form of entertainment, the midday works concert in the canteen, called *Workers' Playtime*, which was broadcast by the BBC and relayed over loudspeakers to brighten the long day of factory workers. They were days which often began at eight and finished twelve hours later. It is difficult today to imagine how a workforce could endure such conditions as Priestley described in his novel, *Daylight on Saturday*.

> There are no windows. The roofs are darkened. The factory inside is like a colossal low, bright cave, lit with innumerable mercury vapour lamps that produce a queer greenish-white mistiness of light. In there, three in the morning and three in the afternoon look just the same. Nothing tells you except the rhythm of work whether it is noon or midnight. For this is a cave life.

Spurred on by appeals from Production and Labour Ministers, Beaverbrook and Bevin, factories worked twenty-four hours a day, seven days a week. Hours were long and tedious. The 'normal' working hours for men and women in a small factory in Birmingham which made carburrettors for Spitfire and Hurricane fighter aircraft were set from eight in the morning until seven at night, seven days a week – but almost every worker exceeded them and many kept going until midnight, nodding over their machines, then slept on couches in the office or on sacks in the corner of the toolroom.[17] The same sort of story could be told of hundreds of small-arms factories and of the state-owned Royal Ordnance Factories, where men and women worked ten- and twelve-hour shifts seven days a week. But perhaps the most dramatic story is that concerning the workers of Metro Vickers in Manchester who actually worked at their benches non-stop for forty-eight hours, without a break to dispatch eight special pieces of radar equipment to RAF airfields just before the Battle of Britain.

Workers such as these needed all the help they could get from music and midday entertainment and there was no doubt in the mind of Wynford Reynolds of the BBC,[18] who organized those programmes, that they helped enormously to rouse the whole of the country's work force to great efforts of production when they were so critically needed. They were called upon to 'Go to it!' And they did just that, to music, laughter and song. ENSA and concert parties performed in the factories themselves and the shows were broadcast over the Forces programme.

It is interesting to note that the regular announcement which introduced the programme on the Forces wavelength was aptly symbolic of the link between worker and the fighting soldier – 'Calling all Forces overseas and workers at home.' The BBC was emphasizing the fact that winning the war was going to be a team effort.

The nation's sense of purpose and determination to get on with the war together was bolstered by another feature from radio's repertoire – the inspiring nine o'clock 'Postscripts' delivered every week immediately after Sunday's nine o'clock news, by Yorkshire novelist, J.B. Priestley.[19] Within a few weeks he became one of Britain's favourite broadcasters and his following was so great that *The Yorkshire Post* was asked 'What is it that is giving Mr Priestley a following almost as big as Mr Churchill's?' The answer the newspaper gave was that it was mainly the sound of his voice that the public found so reassuring. He spoke of the courage ordinary people were showing under bombing and after bereavement. He highlighted their determination to fight on, whatever the odds, for a way of life they wanted. Britons in his eyes, were heroes who had stood stoically alone in defiance of Hitler, enduring the destruction of their homes and cities.

This was just the stuff the country needed. But as Priestley's popularity grew even greater, Churchill began to get alarmed. He did not like the way that Priestley was emphasizing the point that heroes needed to be told that out of their bravery and sacrifice would come a new and better world. 'We must not make the mistakes of the past,' said Priestley, alluding to the way that 'the world fit for heroes', promised to soldiers in World War One, never materialized. To Churchill's ears such talk was far too Socialistic. Tory colleagues began asking the questions: 'Are these postscripts just a little too much left-wing?'

Suddenly, without any explanation, Priestley's morale-boosting talks were stopped. The BBC told Priestley it was a decision of the Ministry of Information. Priestley himself thought otherwise. 'I had no direct evidence but I soon came to believe – and friends in the know agreed with me – that it was Churchill himself who had me taken off the air.'

Priestley, though, had given Churchill an idea. He had seen what an effect these talks were having on the public and decided to employ a man after his own heart to do the same thing with the American public. He desperately needed to persuade the 'isolationists' and members of the 'America First' party in the United States that they were absolutely wrong and short-sighted in the war and that now Britain stood alone with all her allies defeated, the New World would have to come to the rescue of the old.

So it was that in June 1940, the Ministry of Information approached a man they considered eminently suitable for this task. He was one of the most admired men in British showbusiness. He was, ironically enough, the man generally regarded as the most perfect example of the Englishman portrayed on the cinema screen. Yet he was a Hungarian by birth, British by nationality, and had spent the greater part of his working life in the United States of America. His name was Leslie Howard.[20]

The Ministry of Information told him that they wanted someone to put over to Americans the British point of view concerning the war. Howard was not only available for this commission but very keen to tackle it. He had left Hollywood as soon as war broke out and had immediately offered his services to Britain. The Director of Military Intelligence, Mason MacFarlane, had asked for him to be sent to the Headquarters of the British Expeditionary Force in Arras and as a result of his work with Intelligence matters, his name was subsequently placed high up on the German Gestapo list of 'Vertrauens Personen', people likely to be in the confidence of the government and deserving to be watched carefully. Henceforth, Admiral Canaris, head of the German Abwehr Secret Service, kept tabs on Howard. His life was from then on, in danger. He would not survive for long.

It was not until 16 July 1940 that Howard was called upon to make his first contribution to Britain's battle against Nazi Germany. At that time its army was massing in the Channel ports for 'Operation Sea Lion' – the invasion and conquest of Britain. Churchill could see that without American help, Britain could not last long. It was then that Howard was asked to make the first of his broadcasts to the people of America and Canada. The brief he was given was simple. He had to coax the American people into believing that Britain was not at all downhearted and certainly not a nation of quitters, but a nation determined to pursue the war until Nazi Germany was defeated. A nation in fact worth backing with American dollars.

This was not an easy task. How could anyone really hope to persuade the United States to gamble on Britain surviving whilst the US Ambassador to Britain, Joseph Kennedy, was painting such a very grim picture of Britain in all his reports to Roosevelt? He claimed that Britain was virtually finished already and that nothing could save her. For the United States to send arms or money would simply be throwing it all away.

Kennedy, though, was not the only source of depressing reports that President Roosevelt had to read. Journalists, working for South American newspapers were just as scathing about Britain's chances against Germany. Film star Kenneth More,[21] who had at last managed to get into Naval uniform as a Royal Navy gun layer on a small merchant ship, found that when his ship put into the Chilean port of Valparaiso, the German controlled newspapers were full of grossly exaggerated reports of the effects that German bombing raids were having on British cities. Liverpool, the port he had so recently left, was, according to the Chile press, razed to the ground. Imagine how the crew of that merchantman felt when they saw those headlines. It took a visit from More to the British consul to reassure them that these reports were completely untrue.

Nevertheless, this was the sort of report which eventually found its way into newspapers in the United States. And they were accepted by the readers as genuine. Consequently it was understandable that most Americans were in no mood to become involved in a war that Britain was apparently about to lose. Historian, Sir John Wheeler Bennett found at that time: 'The predominate desire of every American was an unqualified determination to keep out of the war by all possible means and woe betide those who might be foolhardy enough to try to make them do otherwise.'[22]

The man chosen to be so 'foolhardy', Leslie Howard, knew what he was up against. His own recent experience of American

public opinion was that most people thought Britain had been
stupid to declare war over far-off Poland no matter what the
principle. Many Americans, he knew, particularly in the Middle
West, were people who had earlier in their family backgrounds,
extricated themselves from Europe, or were of Irish stock, and
had no wish whatsoever to be involved in war ever again. Many
of them, like their ambassador, Joseph Kennedy, could recall
reading how in 1939 Britain herself was almost as divided and
defeatist as France. The appeasers, including the Prime Minister
then – Chamberlain – clearly had no stomach for war and had
gone to great lengths to avoid provoking Hitler. And they recalled
too how British left-wing politicians had been positively opposed
to rearmament and, if anything, favoured communist Russia and
Stalin. Those who knew what had been happening on the British
political stage knew very well too that it had not been until 1940
even that a surge of patriotism inspired by Churchill, 'the
Dunkirk spirit' and the Battle of Britain, that the country had been
really united in its resolve to pursue the war. Kennedy had been
able to play upon these divisions in Britain to strengthen the
claims of the isolationists and the America First party members
who were hampering those other groups of US citizens who
wanted Roosevelt to provide more positive help for beleagured
Britain.

Once Howard's talks began, however, he attracted an
enthusiastic body of support. His popularity as a radio speaker
grew from the way that he understood America's suspicious
attitude to Britain and he also had an ace up his sleeve when it
came to persuasive oratory for his name was a household word in
America because of his films, and he could therefore talk to his
listeners as one of themselves and, furthermore, he could be quite
honest with them by reminding everyone that he too was a
person with divided loyalties, coming from Hungarian stock and
having spent most of his working life in the United States. He was
almost as American as many of his listeners.

Nevertheless it was with some trepidation that he tackled his
first few broadcasts. Fortunately his enthusiasm for what he was
talking about hid any anxieties he might otherwise have
displayed. Cunningly, in his early talks especially, he made
frequent references to American themes; he talked of Jefferson,
the American constitution, presidential elections and other
topical matters which put himself on an intimate fireside footing
with his radio audience. His voice, from the pear-shaped wireless
sets, came to them almost as from a neighbour, a fellow
American.

Those talks had a wonderful effect. He reminded people of their common heritage and coaxed them gently and slowly towards the belief that perhaps, after all, as a matter of conscience as well as logistics, America should give more practical help to Britain.

Perhaps the impact of Howard's talks was somewhat greater when listeners realized that whilst he was addressing them London was enduring the worst of the Luftwaffe's blitz. For fifty-nine consecutive nights they plastered the capital city but Howard, sleeping on mattresses on the floor of a hotel cellar, was not put off. During the evenings he worked on the scripts for each talk himself and during the daytime he was busy making films, as we shall see, to present Britain's case for fighting against Nazi tyranny.

His performance brought him no Oscars except one from the Gestapo who promoted him to a higher place on their black list of people who would be eliminated after the German conquest of Britain. It was Lord Haw Haw who gave Britain the news: 'This sarcastic British actor will be liquidated along with the Churchill clique, if, of course he is still alive after the Luftwaffe has finished with London.'

Broadcasting House was absolutely in the thick of it then as newsreader, Robert Dougall recalled:[23]

From September 1940 until Sunday 11th May 1941, there were very few nights without German bombers. Around Broadcasting House, it began to look very different. Queen's Hall, the home of the Proms, and St George's Hall, Headquarters of BBC Variety, were both totally destroyed. And so was the Devonshire pub. It was just a fluke that I wasn't there – something had cropped up in Broadcasting House to prevent my going for my nightly tipple. The last of the big raids before Hitler turned against Russia was the worst though. On that May night more than 500 bombers came over and 1,500 Londoners were killed. Westminster Hall, the Abbey, and the Houses of Parliament were all hit. Every mainline station except one was out of action, and the Thames bridges blocked. When daylight came, hundreds of acres of the city were still burning. The capital had had about as much as it could take. I really felt that a few more nights like that and London might have cracked.

What then were the Americans thinking about Britain's chances of survival? They were getting stories from their own correspondents in Britain. One of them, Ralph Ingersoll,[24] was based in the deepest shelter of Broadcasting House. Along with Edward R. Murrow of Columbia Broadcasting System he recorded his observations about how Britain was coping and reported at length on his visits. The BBC and Ministry of Information officers looked after him well, giving him every facility. And more! In a report to *PM*, New York's newest newspaper, he wrote:

> I have just returned from London, flying through the Nazi aerial blockade to Lisbon, thence to New York by Clipper. I was mostly in London, spending the nights going from shelter to shelter and the days talking to government officials and cabinet ministers, and going over the city and its defences on foot and by car. I was given complete freedom of action and used it as best as I knew how.

Some strange stories were being fed to him. Of necessity. After one visit to an RAF station he wrote:

> I visited the field from which the most mysterious and terrifying of Britain's secret weapons is launched, the dread night-fighter that is striking down five enemy bombers a night from 20,000 feet in the air, at 300 miles an hour, in the pitch black dark. I spent forty continuous minutes looking through the wind-shield sights of British pilots, plastering Nazi planes with machine gun fire in actual combat in the air.[25]

After the Battle of Britain was over this same correspondent, Ralph Ingersoll, wrote: 'The Luftwaffe over England has never been the same since. Its morale in combat is definitely broken, and the RAF has been gaining strength with every week.'

Heartening words indeed coming over the US airwaves to those people in the United States who supported Britain's cause. But at the end of September came even more reassurance from Ingersoll for his American listeners and readers:

> In the month of September, Hitler failed to follow up his initial advantage and lost his opportunity to win the kind of blitzkrieg that took Poland, and Norway, and Holland and Belgium and France for him. The RAF that beat him on 15th September, and kept him beaten on the 26th and 27th, would like to see him try! From now on he must find some other way to win his infamous war.

Now most Americans could believe that Britain was not going to give in. They were going to fight on and they were worth helping. As Ingersoll said in one broadcast:

> The Londoners stuck it out without panic, each day burying their dead and binding up their wounded, each day going back to their businesses, unloading their boats in the middle of it all on the

bombed docks, opening their shops, putting out their fires, and repairing their telephone lines and water mains, shovelling out their streets, going back to their factories.

With all his reports, Ingersoll could not help retelling stories of how Londoners made light of their problems. He was at first puzzled by it all and reported on it as follows: 'This phenomenon produces a standard London joke about the young lady who has just come to town and whose guide pointed to a break in a row of buildings, explaining, "That's where a bomb dropped last night." Said the young lady, "Oh, but wasn't it lucky that the bomb missed all those houses and fell in that vacant lot."'

And so, in one way or another, through the spoken word and the written, the sombre and the humorous, showbusiness men and women together with the BBC got the message across to both British and American listeners that this war was going to need the combined efforts of all freedom-loving people. Sooner or later, America would have to become fully involved.

But there was still work to be done in that direction. They would not only have to hear from their correspondents about what was going on but also see it for themselves. This they would soon do.

2

Not a Dry Eye in the House

It was an unforgettable sight. The whole of London was erupting in flames and sparks, steam and smoke. A wind which had sprung up through the heat of the fires, momentarily parted the clouds of smoke revealing in all its majesty, St Paul's Cathedral, a hauntingly beautiful yet bizarre picture.

From a factory to the right of St Paul's a gigantic explosion threw a basketful of flaming balls into the sky and nearby to that, another factory was blazing fiercely with what looked like flaming glue or paint pouring like lava down the front of the building. Further away still, a balloon of fire enclosed in its own shroud of thick smoke, rose into the sky, then it fell downwards leaving a comet-like trail of bright streaks.

In the midst of it all, the long bright beams of searchlights probed and the anti-aircraft guns barked incessantly. And in the intense heat firemen were fighting a losing battle. From time to time the water from their hoses dropped to a pathetic trickle and then suddenly it would gush forth again lashing the pipe end viciously from the fireman's grasp.

In the midst of the conflagration and chaos, women could be seen carrying half-asleep children, lolling limply in their arms, and old people stumbling with blankets and bags. All had the blank look of fear on their faces.

This was London at the height of the blitz in 1940.

Watching all this in the film *Christmas Under Fire*, were citizens of former US President Thomas Jefferson's home town of Charlottesville, Virginia. The elegant Paramount cinema there – now the subject of a conservation order – was packed.[1]

For several nights the peace-loving inhabitants of this town, where but sixty years earlier civil war had raged, and where now Jefferson's tombstone carried merely the simple inscription: 'Author of the Declaration of Independence', had flocked to see a war film. But they had come with mixed feelings. They did not want to be involved in yet another war in Europe. Too many lives had already been lost fighting Europe's battles was the way that most families talked. But they had heard that this particular film was exceptionally good entertainment and what was persuasive too was that their own war correspondent for *Time* magazine, Quentin Reynolds, featured prominently in the film.

His voice replaces the noise and crackle of the burning city as the camera switches to the platform of a London underground station where people huddle closely together, and then on to a small Christmas tree by the side of which three or four very young children are sleeping. As a quiet background to his low voice, a choir is singing, '*In Excelcis Deo.*' He begins:

> It's not a very large Christmas tree. There's no demand in England for large trees this year. They would not fit into the shelters or into the basements and cellars with their low ceilings. This year, England celebrates Christmas underground. The first Christmas since that first Christmas, that the day will be celebrated underground, because the stable in Bethlehem was a shelter too.
>
> The nation has made a resolve, that war or no war, the children of England will not be cheated out of the one day they look forward to all the year. So, as far as possible, this will be an old-fashioned Christmas in England, at least for the children.

Those last few words had to be explained.

Reynolds went on to tell of the serious business of survival that the adults were involved in, protecting their families in that year of the blitz when the German Luftwaffe dropped their lethal cargoes of bombs over London.

As he is speaking, calmly presenting the facts, the film shows vivid contrasting images of Christmas decorations, sprigs of holly over an entrance to a garden shelter, paper streamers dangling from the empty shell of a terraced house in London's East End dockland and of guns and barbed wire. But the most vivid and moving of all these images are those of small children in a nursery school. This provides Reynolds with the link between Britain and his American audiences, when he goes on to say: 'Christmas here this year will not be the same as the Christmas children in America will be lucky enough to enjoy. England is fighting for her life and even the smallest child understands that.'

If the smallest child knows that Britain is fighting for freedom against the evil might of Nazi Germany, then the implication is that surely adults must see that too.

In the closing stages of the film when the choir of King's

College, Cambridge, are singing '*Adeste Fideles*' – 'O Come All Ye Faithful', Quentin Reynolds concludes:

> There is no reason for America to feel sorry for England this Christmas, England does not feel sorry for herself. Destiny gave her the torch of Liberty to hold, and she has not dropped it. She has not allowed the stormy waves of terrorism, which are sweeping over the world from Berlin, to let that bright light even flicker. She is thankful that when the test came she had the high courage to meet it. And today England stands, unbeaten, unconquered, unafraid. On Christmas Eve England does what she has done for a thousand years: she worships the Prince of Peace.

As soon as Reynolds has finished speaking, the sound of the choir and the organ takes over and the camera pans across the platform of the underground tube station shelter picking out significant images: mothers and fathers carefully opening blankets and covering their children, a mother is holding a baby in her arms, the baby's innocent-looking face is peaceful and lovable, then there is a long shot of the whole platform showing people settling down for the night.

Slowly then, with the choir now singing softly, the film comes to its close. There is not a dry eye in the house.

Finally, as the audience in Charlottesville's Paramount cinema pocket their handkerchieves, the youngest chorister's unbroken voice soars aloft with the Christmas message: 'O Come All Ye Faithful'. O come all ye faithful indeed!

Were Americans going to stand by and do nothing? Were they going to walk by on the other side of the street whilst a bully stood over a bruised and weakened adversary? The film does not directly ask that question. But it was there in the minds of all who left the cinema after the show.

The film had used highly evocative music and emphasis upon children, religion, and the sentimentality of Christmas to make a direct appeal to the American people to support British mothers and fathers protecting their children.

What is also remarkable in the film is the subtle way that words and images are linked to the American way of life as if to emphasize the act that this war was not one that just concerned Europe but America too. For example, when Quentin Reynolds said that 'Destiny had given Britain the torch of liberty to carry', the words immediately conjured up the image of the Statue of Liberty and how in every American's mind it stood for the greatest single symbol of American democracy.

Films such as *Christmas Under Fire* and its forerunner *England*

Can Take It, a ten-minute picture of life in London during the day and night raids of the Battle of Britain made by the Ministry of Information, were soon making their impact felt all over the United States.

But that was not surprising for it was part of an overall plan which Prime Minister Churchill had set up. It was in 1940, when Britain was in that life and death struggle with Nazi Germany that the beleagured British Prime Minister called upon the film industry for help.

With all her allies defeated, Britain stood alone facing the might of the German war machine that had smashed its way across Poland, Holland, Belgium, and France to build up a reputation of being an unstoppable juggernaut. American help was urgently needed.

But it was not just a matter of persuading the American people and its president to send weapons. Unfortunately, President Roosevelt, though sympathetic, was in no position to provide that help. The Neutrality Laws passed by Congress in 1935 prohibited America from exporting arms to any belligerent nation. Those same laws also made it illegal even for an American ship to carry arms to any country at war.

Even if the US had arms to spare, which she certainly did not in 1940, Roosevelt did not want to upset the country by an act which suggested that the nation might become involved in a war, for this was the year of the presidential election and Roosevelt did not want to risk losing it by alienating those who feared American involvement in a war.

He knew that any step he might take towards helping Britain had to be taken against the wishes of a formidable body of isolationist opposition. Its most vocal organization was the 'America First Committee' which continually stirred the masses against the idea of being dragged into another European war.

Consequently, something drastic had to be done to win public opinion over to the British cause. This is where the film industry came in. Churchill had long had ideas on what to do. First, though, he called Military Intelligence and the Special Operations Executive to a conference. He had in mind a special assignment for Britain's foremost film maker. He was a man Churchill knew he could rely on, a man who in the past had already shown his mettle in the hazardous world of espionage. His name was Alexander Korda.[2]

He was born Sandor Kellner, on 16 September 1893, in a remote Hungarian village and as he grew up proved himself to be one of nature's survivors. He survived the early death of his father, which left the family penniless, he survived the Hungarian revolution and the counter revolution with their accompanying 'terrors' and emigrated first to Vienna and then, with little money in his pocket, to Hollywood and worked his way to the top of the film industry there.

Despite such a hectic and busy life he still had found time to undertake tasks for the British Secret Intelligence Service, and as a result of these 'hush-hush' activities he featured prominently on the German *'Sonderfahndungsliste'* – a death list similar to the one upon which was Leslie Howard's name.

Briefed by his Intelligence Service, Churchill sent for Korda and gave him instructions to leave the country immediately without telling anyone why, and go to California. This hurried departure, Korda knew, would leave him open to criticism in the press. The cheaper tabloids were already vilifying those actors who had gone back to the States as 'Gone with the Wind Up', parodying the title of the popular film. Korda was unable to defend himself because his brief was secret. He was to start immediately making films which would present the British attitude to the war in a way that the American public would appreciate. Though these films were to be patriotic they were not to be obviously propagandist nor was there to be any hint of official backing.

In addition to this wartime role, conferred upon him by Churchill, Korda had further Secret Service duties to perform. He was to set up offices in both New York and Los Angeles which would be linked to a worldwide motion picture corporation. In this way, British agents working in neutral America would have a safe cover from which to operate and so give Churchill an independent source of information on American policy and strategic realities. As Michael Korda, his nephew later recalled: 'Alex was not only providing cover for the attempts to spy on German activities in the USA, but he was also involved in the British efforts to discover whether or not they were receiving accurate information from President Roosevelt and his emissaries.'[3]

This was going to be a risky business for Korda. The American Bureau of Investigation, heavily influenced by the isolationists, had already made it difficult for British Intelligence agents to operate as freely as they would have liked. Anyone discovered operating clandestinely was assured of harsh treatment by the American Secret Service, but more hazardous still was the risk of being discovered by the German Secret Service who would not think twice about having an opponent killed.

'Those were the most difficult years of my life,' said Alexander Korda. 'Only four people knew what I was doing, Brendan

Bracken, Max Beaverbrook, Churchill and myself.'

Korda appreciated fully the risks he was running but nevertheless he accepted his new responsibilities in complete secrecy. He was grateful to Britain, it had made him welcome, given him roots, riches and an honoured place in its hierarchy of famous people.

Now he would repay that hospitality.

Before leaving Britain he conferred many times with the Secret Intelligence Service and the Special Operations Executive. They gave him as much information as he needed to know about a certain camp 'X', situated just across the Canadian frontier along the shore of Lake Ontario near the Toronto-Kingston highway. There it was that special agents were trained and guerilla devices tested. It was a convenient point for agents to slip across the frontier without attracting too much attention. The 'Hydra' radio transmitter at Camp 'X' linked British Intelligence stations around the world. Its tall aerial masts were explained away to local people as part of the Canadian Broadcasting Service.

Such was the nerve centre with which Alexander Korda, his brothers and showbusiness team, were linked. The talent of Alexander's brother, Zoltan, usually expressed at that time in the building of spectacular film sets, was quickly employed in building mock-up replicas of Nazi buildings which were either to be burgled or attacked by special forces. The buildings were constructed from details gleaned from picture postcards, old holiday photographs or clips from old movies which Korda had recalled, showing details of areas occupied by German troops.

One of Korda's chief contacts in Canada was Sir William Stephenson, who headed British Security Co-ordination (BSC), an umbrella body for British Intelligence operations in America. Korda helped Stephenson to set up a branch of BSC in New York, under the aegis of London Films.[4]

Another key figure in Korda's spying activities was Sir Claude Dansey, a director of London Films, who was also deputy head of Britain's Secret Intelligence Service.

Korda worked closely too with the US office of Strategic Services (OSS) which also made propaganda films through its subsidiary, the Field Photographic Unit, headed by film director John Ford.

One can easily imagine the 'Scarlet Pimpernel' life that Korda had to lead in those early war years, making frequent flights in unheated Liberator bombers to the cold Camp X to help with the Intelligence programme and then flying back to the warmth of California for his cunningly crafted propaganda films.

There is a strange story about one of those films. It was shot mainly in North Africa and called *King Pausole* and the footage of it disappeared without trace. Rumour has it that Korda was simply shooting desert terrain in anticipation of North Africa becoming a crucial battlefield of the war.

One of the best remembered of the propaganda films Korda made at that time is *Lady Hamilton*. It is typical of the many films he produced deliberately to foster pro-British feeling in the States. He used historical settings to bring out the significance of the present war situation – a country in peril from an evil aggressor. Korda dare not make any films which were too obviously pro-British and in a present day setting for fear of being attacked by isolationists, Congress, and the press. Thus he chose historical situations with parallels to the present. *Lady Hamilton*, with its romantic element adding to the excitement of the battle with Napoleon, fitted the bill admirably. Nelson's efforts against the French, in fact, became an open metaphor for Britain's current war with Germany.

Korda was able to make the film in the very short time of six weeks because of the availability of a special pair of British exiles in America then – Laurence Olivier and Vivien Leigh, currently considered to be the most romantic couple in the world (after perhaps the Duke of Windsor who had given up a kingdom for love, and his bride, Mrs Wallis Simpson). But Olivier did not just 'happen' to be there. Shortly after Britain went to war, Olivier telephoned from America to the Minister of Information in Britain, Duff Cooper, and offered his services with a view to joining one of the fighting services. He was told to stay where he was because he would be far more use to the country there and that Korda would be contacting him.

In that hastily produced film there was however one embarrassing and amusing cause for delay. One morning, Korda arrived on the set to find Olivier only half dressed, standing holding his jacket. Korda asked him what was the matter. Olivier replied with his own question. 'Which eye and which arm did Nelson have missing?'

No one knew.

It was Sunday. Libraries were closed. To wait another day would have added greatly to the expense. Korda had a flash of inspiration. An old Hungarian living nearby had played Nelson in an operetta years ago in Vienna. A studio car was sent to bring him to the set. The old chap, excited, surprised and flattered at the possibility of being offered another part arrived breathless to answer the crucial question Korda fired at him: 'Which eye and which arm was missing?'

The old man scratched his head and then replied seemingly confident enough: 'Ah, I remember now. It all comes back to me. It got so boring doing it always the same way, so one night I would cover the left arm and the right eye and the next night I would do the opposite.[6]

Olivier played Nelson minus his right eye and right arm. The film was a tremendous success in America and Britain and it did much to further British and American relations. Nevertheless the film earned Korda a subpoena from a committee of isolationist American senators who charged him with making the American branch of the company a centre for British propaganda.

That same committee had already laid complaints about the propaganda element in Korda's earlier film, *The Lion has Wings* in which Korda's wife, Merle Oberon, played a fervently patriotic nurse. Despite being a rather jingoistic film about events leading up to Britain's entry into the war and the RAF's disastrous raid on the Kiel canal, American audiences were, in general, impressed and the majority of people watching the film seemed convinced that Britain really did have an airforce that could take on the mighty Luftwaffe. A country which was, perhaps, worth supporting after all.

Nevertheless, after *Lady Hamilton*, attacks on Korda came from all directions. The isolationist complaints were backed by vociferous ones from the German Embassy in America. They claimed that Korda was deliberately using films as a vehicle for anti-German propaganda. Surprisingly, too, British newspapers harshly and unjustifiably criticized Korda for having deserted Britain for Hollywood. They were not to know until many years later that Korda was making frequent trips across the Atlantic acting as a courier for the Secret Service. Those critics were, however, silenced when King George VI knighted Korda in 1942. He was the first film personality to be so honoured.

Meanwhile, another celebrated film maker, Alfred Hitchcock was playing an equally important part in the campaign to counteract the arguments of the isolationists and swing American opinion behind Britain.

Hitchcock, like Korda, had received precise instructions from the British government about what he was to do when war broke out. He was to stay put in Hollywood and make films portraying the evils of German National Socialism. Hitchcock relished the challenge and was quick to respond. In the summer of 1940 when Britain was reeling under the German Air Force's attempts to pulverize it into surrender, Hitchcock released the film, *Foreign Correspondent*, a film deliberately scripted to bring home to

American cinemagoers the real threat facing them should Germany be totally victorious in Europe.

The film was set in the Germany of 1938-9 and its hero is a rather naîve American newspaperman, Joel McCrea, who falls in love with the attractive daughter of German master spy, Herbert Marshall, currently masquerading as the president of an international peace organization. Gradually young McCrea gets involved in a web of Nazi intrigue whilst trying to be objective in his task of covering political events in Europe. He becomes disenchanted with what he sees of Germany, survives several attempts on his life and after a series of exciting episodes culminating in a spectacular fight on the top of Westminster Cathedral tower, he gains the safety of the BBC's Broadcasting House. There, in the middle of an air raid, he makes a fervent appeal on behalf of a Britain beseiged, for fellow Americans to wake up and arm themselves to fight this evil of German National Socialism. Passionately he cries in the closing sequences: 'The lights are going out in Europe. Ring yourselves around with steel.'

The film was a great success as a thriller, a classic example of Hitchcock's special brand of seat-gripping suspense, through which he exposes the terrifying realities of rule under a ruthless Gestapo. So good was the film, in fact, that even Germany's propaganda Minister, Dr Goebbels, himself a film buff, was said to have enjoyed it!

That last appeal made by Joel McCrea in the film was tremendously dramatic in more ways than one. Undoubtedly the emotional appeal caused many isolationists to back away from their old neutrality stance and Roosevelt himself, soon afterwards, risked ruining his chances in the forthcoming presidential election, by releasing fifty over-age destroyers to help Britain in its battle against the U-boats in the Atlantic.

It was about this time too that Britain's Ministry of Information sponsored a full length feature film deliberately made to stir the American conscience and bring the country into the conflict. The film, written and produced by Michael Powell and Emeric Pressburger, was given a Canadian setting and called *The 49th Parallel*. It featured Laurence Olivier again, with Eric Portman, Leslie Howard, Raymond Massey and Anton Walbrook, in a story about six German submariners who scrambled ashore in Canada after their U-boat had been sunk in the Gulf of St Lawrence.

The leader of this group of ruthless committed Nazis is Eric Portman. He takes the group first to a settlement of 'Herrnhuters' – refugee Germans who fled from the Nazi terror of pre-war

Germany to make a new life in Canada. When the German U-Boat survivors make plans to hide in the settlement the Herrnhuter's leader, Anton Walbrook, will not have this at all even though they are fellow countrymen. He has had as much as he can take from the Nazis and he tells the U-Boat crew just what he thinks of them and their National Socialism and the way it is governed by fear of the secret police. In a very moving speech, presumably for the benefit of American cinemagoers, he roundly condemns the brutal Nazi doctrines and extols the virtues of living in a country with free speech where the Gestapo's knock in the middle of the night is not known.

So convincing is this speech that one of the less committed submariners in the film shows signs of agreeing with the ideas of the Herrnhuter's leader. For this he dies. He is the first of six to go. The others fall one by one until there are only two survivors left. These two men then meet the quintessential English academic, Leslie Howard, who appears to be living in a world of his own, specializing in the study of some abstruse Indian culture.

Here, Howard deliberately presents, and almost overplays the parody of a soft decadent Englishman which many Americans had grown to accept as the typical English gentleman. When he is dealing with the submariners, Howard is unruffled, generous and polite in the extreme. He offers them accommodation and in his most genteel manner behaves as the perfect host. Somehow this is just too much for the hard-nosed Nazis who are uncomfortable in the presence of such a polite man. Consequently they begin to take advantage of him, to bully and taunt him as a 'softie'. But to the delight of the cinema audience, they push him just that bit too far. The worm turns. Howard is roused to a controlled fury at their wanton vandalism and the man who had been a docile pacifist becomes unexpectedly aggressively tough, determined to teach his arrogant guests a severe lesson. This goes down so well with the audience that one film critic was moved to write: 'It is a likely bet that Howard's knock-out of the Nazis will be a good propaganda stroke in the USA.'

The sole surviving Nazi, Eric Portman, jumps on a train heading for the 49th Parallel and thence to the neutral United States. But he is in for a shock, for when the train does reach this frontier, the US customs officer will not allow Portman to pass through. All arrogance gone now, Portman pleads for political asylum. In vain. The customs officer locks the carriage door and orders the carriage to be shunted back into Canada.

No doubt is now left in the minds of those sitting in the cinema. The message is absolutely clear: America has no time for Nazis.

As pure entertainment this film is one of the finest of its time. It is grippingly exciting, yet coincidentally it was a most effective piece of propaganda, making the point that freedom is worth far more than fanatical political dogma. The merit of a good film is often said to lie in the effect it has upon the audience as they walk out and travel homewards. More than a few of those Americans leaving the *49th Parallel* would no doubt be wondering whether or not 'the sitting on the fence policy' of the United States was the right one, in view of the threat which the Nazi mentality was then posing to the democracies of the world.

The German Embassy was quick to complain once again about the way films with a pro-British bias were being distributed.[7] The Ambassador claimed too that these anti-German films had obviously been made with Jewish money and influenced by British agents. Little did he realize perhaps just how well-founded were those complaints! Dozens of former German, Austrian and Polish actors, many of them of Jewish extraction, who had fled to the sanctuary of Hollywood in 1938, were now putting their hearts and souls into playing the parts of Nazi thugs and German officers in those wartime films. Conrad Veidt, for example, in *Nazi Agent* and Eric von Stroheim in *Five Graves to Cairo*.

All the complaints piling up against Korda eventually brought the day of reckoning. He was summoned to appear before a senate committee enquiring into his activities, which was to meet on 12 December 1941.

Meanwhile many other showbusiness folk had also been actively crusading to mobilize a sufficient body of public opinion to support Roosevelt's tentative measures to help Britain. Prominent amongst these strenuous campaigners was a face well-known throughout the world of cinemagoers, the dashing debonair Douglas Fairbanks, jun.[8] Famous then for his star roles in such films as *Gunga Din* and that classic film of the exploits of the Royal Flying Corps in World War One, *Dawn Patrol*, Fairbanks joined an organization in California dedicated to rallying public opinion behind the move to repeal the Neutrality Act arms embargo. For this cause, Fairbanks campaigned persuasively at public meetings. He put the weight of his celebrated name behind a campaign for getting members to persuade their neighbours and friends to bring up the matter with their clubs and professional organizations, who would then wire or write to their congressmen and senators. It was a highly successful ploy and under such a barrage of messages the arms embargo was repealed. Aid could now flow freely to Britain.[9]

Having witnessed what could be achieved by a well-known and energetic public speaker, the Ministry of Information turned to Fairbanks in the autumn of 1941 and asked him to help boost British morale which was then at a low ebb, by giving a weekly transatlantic talk to the people of Britain.

Fairbanks readily agreed and his encouraging voice was soon giving British listeners hope for the future – the hope that, as Churchill once put it – the New World would come to the aid of the Old. These sentiments were repeatedly presented by Fairbanks and on one occasion he gave British listeners a real boost to their morale, saying:

> We in America, are becoming increasingly aware that again, like most families, we need each other and that our respective fates are indissolubly joined. There is, thank God, a common independent connection between English speaking countries. Without impugning so much as a breath of our loyalties to our native land, or the pride we take in our national sovereignties, we must now admit that so far as our cultural, economic and military affairs are concerned, ours is a hyphenated destiny.

This was becoming increasingly obvious to Americans anyway. Like it or not, war was coming. Events in Europe were soon going to affect the lives of everyone in the United States and Roosevelt began to say more openly that it was time for the United States to give more aid to Britain. A succession of films continued to rally support for this idea.

Tentatively, at first, Warner Brothers brought out a few short patriotic films like *Here Comes the Navy* and *Rear Gunner*. The latter film was really nothing less than a thinly disguised recruiting device and its interest now lies in what was behind the making of that film. The US Air Force General Arnold, who later would command the US Air Force in Britain, was worried about the lack of volunteers for rear gunner duties, the tail-end Charlies. He asked film maker Warner to give the film a romantic interest centred on a handsome rear gunner. Warner duly obliged. 'Rear gunnery in the film seen to be an extremely sexy occupation, and the airforce suffered an almost embarrassment of applications,' commented film critic Barry Norman.[10]

Now Britain's message was really getting home to the people in the United States and this resulted in more support rallying behind President Roosevelt's opinion that the USA should be giving much more help to Britain. Encouraged, Hollywood promptly produced more pro-British films.

In a more overtly propagandist way, Warner Brothers featured

Errol Flynn in *The Sea Hawk*. Trailers advertising the film presented it merely as the exciting story of how Sir Francis Drake repelled the Spanish Armada, but as people left the cinemas they could not fail to realize that Philip of Spain and his Armada were little different from Hitler and his Luftwaffe. But just in case some people failed to recognize the similarity, the message of the film was spelt out plainly in its closing shots, when Queen Elizabeth, played by Flora Robson, spoke the poignant words:

> We have no quarrel with the people of Spain or of any other country. But when the ruthless ambitions of a man threaten the world, it becomes the solemn obligation of free men, wherever they may be, to affirm the earth belongs to all men and that freedom is the deed and title to the soil on which we exist.

To sensitive Americans in the audience it seemed as if those last few words were given a special emphasis. And well they might. Who in America could fail to respond?

Shortly after this film was released, yet another one made an even greater impact upon American public opinion. It was *Pimpernel Smith*, directed by Leslie Howard and set in pre-war Nazi Germany. Professor Horatio Smith, played by Leslie Howard himself, is another archetypal Englishman whose vague mind seems preoccupied with dusty archeological objects, but beneath this deceptively placid exterior however, there lies a quick brain, contriving ways of smuggling Jews out of Nazi Germany.

Though the film has none of the violence of war, it is probably the most virulent, anti-Nazi film of all those produced during the Second World War. It explores the rigid, brutal and sadistic mentality of senior Nazi officers and shows them up as a terrifying threat to any decent and democratic nation.

The way that Professor Smith and his troops of undergraduates take on and outwit the German Secret Service chief and his henchmen, is not only exciting and amusing but a sheer delight for both British and American audiences. German cinemagoers were not allowed to see this film which the German press said was a grossly insulting caricature of Nazi officialdom.

After the film was distributed in neutral countries, Spain, Sweden, and Portugal, Leslie Howard's name moved into an even more prominent position on the German black list.

On 1 June 1943, Leslie Howard, at the peak of his career was to die, a victim of German bullets off Cape Corunna in the Bay of Biscay. He was aboard a KLM airliner, in flight between Lisbon and London, and once again he was in the service of his country.

Could it have been merely coincidence that barely a week before his flight took off from Lisbon, the film *Pimpernel Smith* was shown in the Estrella cimema there?[11]

Now all is a matter of speculation but investigations subsequently suggest, as his son points out, that Howard 'had played the part of a man who was tricking the Germans and possibly he was doing the same in real life'. What is not a matter of speculation however, is that Leslie Howard, along with many other members of the showbusiness profession, too numerous to mention here, played a vital role in swinging American help to Britain's cause when she was standing alone against Germany.

That campaign, though, became merely a matter of academic interest on the bright sunny morning of 7 December 1941 when, at precisely 7.55 a.m. ahead of any declaration of war, the first wave of 350 Japanese bombers delivered a shattering attack upon row after row of United States battleships forming the Pacific Fleet, riding proudly at anchor in the sleepy Hawaiian base of Pearl Harbor.

The stunned Americans, barely over the shock of that first attack, were caring for the wounded when the next wave came in, and the next, and the next as horizontal bombers, dive bombers and torpedo bombers pressed home their attacks.

It was at 9.45 a.m. that the last attacking Japanese plane turned northwards to rejoin the carriers of Nagumo's fleet. In one hour and fifty-five minutes, the Japanese reduced the mighty US fleet, which had boasted mastery of the Pacific, to a mass of blackened, twisted metal.

Like it or not, America was now at war. Soon she too would be having men killed, wounded and put behind wire as prisoners of war. But even there, showbusiness was already at work.

3

Burlesque and Barbarism Behind the Wire

On 6 December 1941, the popular British weekly magazine *Illustrated* made a surprising gift to the German Propaganda Minister, Dr Joseph Goebbels. The magazine published two pages of text and pictures showing what a cosy and cultured life British prisoners of war were leading in a Bavarian castle.

The story was about a certain Hugh McGoverne, a man who had graduated from Oxford University with a degree in history and had a passion for films. Instead of pursuing an academic career when he left Oxford, McGoverne had taken employment in a film studio. Soon he was acting in such box-office successes as *The Outsider*, and the thriller, *The Passing of the Third Floor Back*. But although he occasionally stood in for famous actors taking the leading roles, he never quite made the big time himself, and so he eventually went back to his academic role and became a professor at the British Institute in Prague.

Surprisingly, for a man who worked in an institute which had the latest news of political trends, he was caught napping when war broke out and he actually left it as late as the morning of 3 September 1939 before going to Prague railway station to buy a ticket home to London. There, one of those men seen so often in films, wearing the black trilby hat and buckled raincoat affected by the Gestapo, asked for his papers and immediately placed him under arrest. Within hours he was amongst 250 other British civilians, who had also buried their heads in the sand believing Britain would never be daft enough to go to war, and confined in the castle of Wulzburg, Bavaria, designated as Ilag XIII.

Now the would-be film star really did have a captive audience. He wrote the scripts of plays he had once acted in, improvized where necessary and took the leading parts in those plays too.

The first play he put on was *The Bells*, an old melodrama. All the female roles had to be taken by men and they made a very fine and convincing job of it though the make-up had to be concocted from a variety of powders and colours from a children's water colour paint box. Dresses were made by the men themselves and so was the scenery.

'The play was a great success and McGoverne scored a personal triumph. He was congratulated not only by the British Camp Captain but also by the German authorities. So good was *The Bells* and so sincerely appreciated, that *The Lyons Mail* is now in course of production,' reported *Illustrated* magazine.

So it was that as General Sir Claude Auchinleck, Commander in Chief of Middle East Forces, was fighting the 'Second Battle of Libya' – as the magazine called Auchinleck's campaign, *Illustrated* was incidentally telling the British public and the troops back in Britain training for their own battles in the future, what a nice, easy life they could have if captured. An open invitation to be taken prisoner.

No wonder the German High Command took special care that Hugh McGoverne had a good supply of photographs to send home to his mother who sent them off to the *Illustrated*. Captions beneath the pictures said:

> *Illustrated* is glad to be able to put the case of Hugh McGoverne and his fellow prisoners before its readers. It is good to know how our compatriots are making the best of their misfortunes. It is encouraging to hear that these prisoners at Ilag XIII are permitted to produce their own plays; are not receiving unkind treatment from the Germans. We hope that these pictures will encourage the relatives of all the men shown proving that they are fairly well treated and that their morale is high.

How misleading this article was, can be readily appreciated from the reports of soldiers who were captured in France in the retreat to Dunkirk.

Sergeant Cameron Simpson[1] recalled:

> I was captured near the Belgian frontier on 24th May 1940 and was taken to the French civil gaol of Doullens. About a thousand British soldiers were there, and men were being shot down by the guards for the slightest movement or protest. We were forced to march all the way from Doellens to Trier and that took us three weeks. At night we were penned in open fields ringed by barbed wire and we were fed on black bread which had green mould on it. At Trier we were loaded onto cattle trucks, 26 in each, and for three days we travelled across Germany to Poland. One of the most impressive

moments for me occurred in that truck. We were all in low spirits and in the corner was a youngster of the Gordon Highlanders, a lad from Aberdeen. He was in great pain, and he knew, as we knew, he was dying, but as the discussion grew more gloomy, he called out to me: 'Sarge, prop me up. I want to have my say.' Slowly he then looked round and said steadily and distinctly, 'Never mind boys, Britain will win this war.' That was all. But it stopped the discussion. Men turned away with tears in their eyes. That lad died in the night but a new spirit was born.

On a lighter note, Sergeant Simpson recalled another memorable occasion about their capture and imprisonment. 'We had been in the POW camp for about seven months when the first consignment of Red Cross parcels arrived in Stalag XXA. The camp went mad. It was a pandemonium of pleasure.'

Understandably, for those parcels contained more than just nourishing food, they also had chocolate, coffee, and cigarettes. All these items were already in short supply for German civilians and servicemen and so they were an excellent form of currency and means of bribing German guards. These guards were just soldiers like themselves, men with wives and girlfriends and children. After a time the guards became more and more familiar. One of Sergeant Simpson's men, Fusilier George Mitchinson, of Morpeth, Northumberland, had other ideas about what to do with his parcel though. He raffled it and with the money he raised by selling tickets to British and Germans, he bought an accordion so that he could give his fellow prisoners some music.

George Mitchinson[2] knew just how well music could raise the spirits of despondent men. He had seen in his short life amongst the unemployed, deprived men of the North East, just how well a tune could take men out of themselves, voyaging back to happier times, even deriding what they were getting out of the world and to thumb their noses at what fate had offered them.

Corporal Robert Johnstone,[3] of the Royal Corps of Signals recalled how it was too:

As long as there was just one trumpet or accordion or even a mouth-organ to start us off, we would sing and pretend that we didn't give a toss what the so-and-so's at base had in store for us. We were singing the same songs we sang back in Perth, Corbridge, Carlisle or wherever we had done our square bashing. And in our minds we would be back in the same local pubs, sitting at those round beer-slopped tables with iron legs which weighed a ton so they could not be picked up and thrown in a fight, and we'd be raising our frothy pints singing, 'We don't want to join the army', or 'Here's a toast to the dead already, three cheers for the next man to die' ... and whilst the words were coming out of our mouths we were no longer afraid, we were acting a part and almost believing it.

Once George Mitchinson had his accordion in Stalag XXA, music flourished. Magically musicians came forward, instruments were begged or 'bought' with barter and bribery, using Red Cross parcel items, until a small band got together. And so it was that whilst the Council for the Encouragement of Music and the Arts was keeping music alive and accessible to vast numbers of people in Britain during the worst days of the blitz in 1940 and 1941, Fusilier George Mitchinson and his fellow musicians – some on home-made instruments – were doing the same in Stalag XXA.

Those first few weeks of captivity were very difficult for troops captured on the retreat to Dunkirk in May and June 1940. Company Sergeant Major James Fulton of the 2nd battalion Seaforth Highlanders, 51st Highland Division, in nearby Stalag XXB, recalled:[4]

> It was far from an easy number. All we possessed was the clothing we stood up in. Ten of us shared two towels, one handkerchief and three razors. We were given billets in the unlit garret of the village school and had hay to sleep on. The working day was from five am to seven pm, and in the winter we used to arrive in the fields in darkness and await daybreak before starting to dig potatoes and dress turnips.

Eventually Sergeant Major Fulton recognized the fact that if the morale of the troops was to be maintained then some form of link would have to be made between them and the German guards. As it happened, by this time, both the Germans and the prisoners saw Fulton as a man they could rely upon and he became the *'Vertraudeman'*, a trustworthy man of confidence. He administered the distribution of Red Cross parcels and was the go-between on all matters concerning the prisoners and the camp commandant. The arrangement worked so well for everyone that co-operation was established and concessions granted. Prisoners dug their own swimming pool, and built their own concert hall and theatre.

Soon too instruments were brought and borrowed from the town nearby and an excellent twelve-piece band developed. Time for rehearsals was never a problem! Over the next few years many plays and musicals were produced by Norman Wylie, who had worked pre-war in an Aberdeen theatre, and James Fulton. And so, in one way and another, the men of the 51st Highland Division adjusted themselves to life behind the barbed wire.

Preparing for a concert was a great morale booster. There was always the busy period of preparation, the challenges to prisoners' skill and ingenuity, the making of scenery, costumes, stage lighting, scriptwriting, and rehearsals of the programme itself.

But in addition to the entertainment value of the theatre and concerts there was another considerable bonus that came from being able to use 'concert party' work as a cover for preparation of items needed for escape plans. Lieutenant John Hamilton Baillie of the Royal Engineers, for example, made a wooden sewing-machine ostensibly for the making of theatrical costumes but was in fact more often used for the making of civilian suits or German uniforms for escapers.

Buttons and badges were moulded from melted down lead piping and gramophone records, leggings and belts fashioned from boot-polished lino and cardboard, gold braid for epaulettes was plaited from stripped electrical wiring.

The fate of men who made repeated attempts to escape was to be despatched to a maximum security prison such as Colditz, Oflag IVC. This was a majestic but forbidding-looking castle built on the edge of a cliff and towering about the village of Colditz. There the most troublesome and escape-happy prisoners were assembled in one 'escape-proof' place. But the prisoners immediately took this as a challenge designed to test their mettle. Consequently and paradoxically, there were more 'home runs' (thirty) from Colditz than from any other prisoner of war camp. In many of these escape attempts the theatre and concert party featured prominently in one way or another.

Young Lieutenant Bouley[5] for example, tried out his luck as a drag artist. His blouse, checked jacket, skirt, shoes and hat were all made in the theatre props workshops and when all was ready he donned his overcoat on top of his outfit and walked down to the exercise ground with his comrades. Once round the corner he quickly whipped off his coat, donned a curly wig, a wide brimmed hat, put his false bosoms in place, powdered his face, reddened his lips and set off back along the path he had just walked down. All was going well and he was well past one guard when his wrist watch fell to the ground. An English officer who was walking behind and not knowing that the 'lady' was on an escape attempt, called out loudly for the *'Fraulein'* to stop and retrieve her watch. The guard he had just passed, hurried up, took the watch from the British officer and hurried after the 'lady' who was now walking primly towards the main gateway which led out of camp.

When he caught up with the 'lady' the guard stopped her, and, recalled Pat Reid, 'became affable, looking no doubt deeply into her eyes from which, unfortunately, no tender light responded! "Hm!," the sentry reflected as she did not reply to his cajoling. She is dumb or very haughty or just plain rude. He looked at her again and suddenly grabbed her hair which came away in his hand.'

The attempt, which was the result of months of patient effort on the part of wardrobe staff in the camp theatre failed but at least it had kept prisoners busy and given them hope. The clothes Lieutenant Bouley wore went into the theatre costume cupboard. They were often needed for plays and revues. Dresses were difficult to make and usually the problem had to be solved by taking to pieces the blue and white check sleeping bags issued to officers. Sometimes, though, the costumes were made out of crepe paper, as with one of the most successful of all the Colditz concerts – *Ballet Nonsense*. The underlying theme of this concert was a *corps de ballet* comprising the toughest looking, heaviest moustached officers available, who, wrote Reid, 'performed miracles of energetic grace and unsophisticated elegance upon the resounding boards of the Colditz theatre stage attired in frilly crepe paper ballet skirts and brassières'.

This theatre, on the fourth floor of the castle was a crucial element in one of the most celebrated of all the escapes from Colditz. The prisoners had discovered that leading down from under the theatre stage on the fourth floor of the castle was an air shaft which came out in the kitchens on the ground floor. Furthermore, the escape committee had kept watch on the doors leading to these kitchens and found that after the meals were finished and the kitchens cleaned each day, nobody seemed to go into the kitchens at all. Doors from the kitchens led into the open courtyard close to the main gate.

The plan was that towards the end of the *Ballet Nonsense* and whilst the band was reaching a thunderous finale the escape party would crawl under the stage in their theatrical outfits, climb down a four-hundred-foot rope to the kitchens, and there change into their escape disguises. Two men were to dress as painters with their official yellow arm bands; Airey Neave and his Dutch companion, Toni Luteyn, were to dress in their carefully tailored German army officers uniforms and walk out from the kitchens, chatting confidently away in German. Toni, being Dutch, had a fluent command of the language.

Getting hold of the right material for those German Army uniforms had tested their ingenuity to the full. But the theatre wardrobe tailors had done wonders. Neave's belt was of cardboard painted brown from a box of water colours, his revolver holster was also of cardboard filled with newspaper, epaulettes were made of linoleum finished with a gold numeral denoting the infantry regiment and the uniform itself was made from a uniform of similar colour worn by the Dutch army. One piece of good fortune was that when Neave stripped the khaki material from his own Service Dress cap he found to his surprise that there was a shiny black peak just like that worn by officers in the army of the Third Reich. The familiar eagle's wings and swastikas were carved from lino and the finishing touches to the cap were completed by sewing white piping to the edge of the brim.

Neave was acting in the performance, taking the part of Dr Calomel and through that icy December he was busy rehearsing, helping with the production and at the same time getting ready his own escape gear and that of Toni Luteyn's.

The night of the 'ballet-cum-pantomime' arrived. Snow carried in the wind, plastered itself against the castle's wall. It was bitterly cold. German officers in the audience arrived with coat collars buttoned up, and breathing steam. Inside the auditorium the atmosphere was warmer and an air of expectancy was evident.

Suddenly, with a roll of drum beats, clashing of cymbals, and fanfare of trumpeting the show opened. On to the stage pranced a bevvy of frilly skirted ballet dancers with nothing above the waistline save for a bulging round bra. Following this dramatic opening there came a play, *The Mystery of Wombat College*, several individual acts leading to the grand finale, a noisy musical scene in which the praises of the 'Rose and Crown', were sung in typical bar-room style.

Whilst all this noise was going on, the boxes containing disguises for the escape party were dragged beneath the stage and lowered down the rope to the kitchens below.

Unfortunately for Neave and his companion, Luteyn, parts of their escape uniforms had been discovered and confiscated. Fate had decreed that Neave's moment of glory was yet to come and in a much stranger situation.

For the others in the escape attempt, everything was going according to plan. The first two to go were the pseudo painters dressed in civilian clothes. Without any hitch, they descended the rope, changed into their civilian clothes and boldly strode forth from out of the kitchen into the courtyard where several people were moving about. The two 'painters' walked towards the park gate where there was a sentry who did not carry a check list of passes, no brass disc was required either. There was a lot of coming and going through that gate and in the intense cold of that night the sentry did not bother much with the two civilians with their yellow arm bands. But someone else noticed these two painters leaving. The laundry man from the town. He prided himself on knowing everybody who worked in the camp and he did not recognize the two men now leaving the camp. For the next hour his mind kept coming back to the two men. Who were they? They were not from his village, that was for sure. In the end he went to the security officer and asked him who the two men might have been. The security officer was puzzled. He knew of no painters working in the camp. He called out the dogs. They set off at such a pace that only guards on cycles could follow them. Six miles later, the two men were caught and brought back to the castle for a spell of solitary confinement. No more than that, yet. The horror was still to come. It would not be at Colditz though, but at Stalag Luft III, Sagan.

There, concert party work was always in full swing. The notorious Stalag Luft III camp had been built in the spring of 1942 as a 'completely escape-proof' prison especially for Air Force prisoners. It was to this camp that men like Warrant Officer George Grimson[7] was sent after several break outs from other camps.

It was sixty-three days before Christmas and already the concert party was rehearsing for the big festive show, when Warrant Officer George Grimson paused in his amble around the camp to watch what was happening on the makeshift stage.

Because of his previous history of escape attempts, Grimson was a marked man. He had almost got away from Sagan on two occasions in the short time since his arrival but fortunately for him the Camp Commandant, Oberst von Lindeiner-Wildau, was a military man of the old school who believed that it was the duty of every soldier to try to escape. Consequently he dealt scrupulously fairly with any man who was caught and brought back to the camp after a day or two of freedom. Each time that Grimson was caught, he was given the usual fourteen days solitary in the cooler and then received the commandant's characteristic congratulations on a brave attempt to escape. Grimson then returned to the boring routine of camp life.

It was to help alleviate this boredom that the concert party was presently rehearsing and attracting the usual knot of casual onlookers. Amongst these there were one or two German guards who were amused by the antics on stage.

On this particular morning when Grimson was gazing
indolently around, one *Gefreiter* (corporal) paused longer than
usual on his patrol to chuckle and smile at the airmen acting parts
of older men and younger women. Clearly he was intrigued and
fascinated. He had never seen anything like it in his own
company, although he had heard that men made up as glamorous
women were well-known participants at late night SS and SA
parties – particularly in the days of Ernst Rohm's Brown Shirt
brigades.

Whilst this *Gefreiter* was lolling entranced for several minutes,
George Grimson's gaze fell upon him, idly at first and then with
increasing excitement his eyes began to focus upon every detail of
the *Gefreiter's* features, physique and posture. It was then that
Grimson suddenly realized what it was that had aroused his
interest. There was his double! An almost perfect 'look-alike'.

Whether or not it was the association of ideas presently in his
head, the proximity of the actors, and the never absent thoughts
of escape that gave him the idea, Grimson did not pause to
consider. What had come clearly to him was that if there on the
stage before his eyes now, his pals could be impersonating old
men and young women, he could quite easily impersonate this
Gefreiter who already looked very much like himself.

And so, sixty-three days before Christmas 1943, the beginning
of yet another escape plan formed in the mind of Warrant Officer
George Grimson. His first action was to seek out his friend,
German speaking Alan Morris, another aircrew NCO. From this
initial conversation two quite surprising coincidences emerged.
The first was that Alan Morris, had also spotted a 'look-alike' – his
own, in the shape of another *Gefreiter* who, by a strange bit of
serendipity, was a close colleague of Grimson's look-alike. Every
night they walked out through the camp gates together.

This being so, what was there to stop Grimson and Morris
impersonating them? Now there was work to be done. A fellow
prisoner then was John Dominy[8] who recalled how all prisoners
had impressed upon them that it was their duty to help all
would-be escapers. Jobs were handed to those who had the skill
to execute them. Under the pretext of hobbies or of making props
for the concerts, the tailors, forgers and map-makers got to work.
By the first night of that Christmas show all was ready. The camp
commandant and many of his officers were invited and were
comfortably seated in the first few rows.

'It was a roaring success,' Dominy recalled, 'for the surprise
opening to the show was a well-drilled chorus line coached by a
one-time chorus boy and later an aircrew NCO with 34 bombing

missions to his credit. In a camp starved of women, the sudden appearance of a line of high-kicking, and lightly clad "girls", was devastating.'

It did not matter a jot to the audience when their loud applause so drowned the band that the chorus lost its step, nor that their breasts were false and that one or two of the chorus had all too revealing trouble with their panties. 'The Germans were as tickled with the show as we were,' wrote Dominy. 'Consequently applications for seats, from "the other side" increased. This was all to the good. The more guards there were in the theatre, the fewer there would be patrolling. Everything seemed to be going too well to be true.'

For each of the three nights the show was on, Grimson and Morris, dressed in their newly made German uniforms and holding their escape kits, crouched in a dark corner of a nearby barrack-block waiting for the signal to make their break. On the first two nights, no opportunity arose for their escape attempt. Then, on the third and last night, there came an unexpected bonus. The two 'look-alike' *Gefreiters* were seen entering the camp together. By eight o'clock, they were lolling back in their theatre seats, smiles of anticipation on their faces, as they waited for that already much talked about opening chorus.

Item by item the show then went on. Still no signal came for the two waiting men. Then when the show was just ending, the signal came: 'Go now'. The two men rose and walked casually towards the gates, just before the main body of the audience would be filing out.

Confidently, Grimson and Morris trod purposefully towards the gate, Morris doing all the talking in German. Through the first of the two gates all went well but then at the second gate it looked as though all the efforts of the two men and their colleagues were to be of no avail. The sentry asked the two men for their numbers. Unknown to them, a new security officer had arrived and had brought in a new system of issuing numbers to all men entering the camp. Morris thought quickly. He had no idea what range of numbers might be in use. There was only one hope – to bluster and shout. He raved at the sentry, this was Christmas, they had left the theatre early because they had other service commitments and in any case they had wasted enough time already that evening on the decadent entertainment served up at the theatre.

'Overwhelmed, the sentry unlocked the gate, froze to attention and let them through,' wrote Dominy.

Grimson and Morris walked on, into the black night leaving behind them the sound of a small band and the raised voices of the prisoners, rendering in best Albert Hall style, 'Land of Hope and Glory'.

That really would have been a satisfying end to the story but it was only the beginning. It was the beginning too of a shameful saga of events which shook not only the prisoners of war throughout Germany but eventually, the world at large.

Less than an hour after the escape of Grimson and Morris a general alarm was sent out and the pair of escapers were just approaching Leipzig station, when a suspicious railway policeman arrested them.

Back they came to the cooler. But by now the benign Oberst von Lindeiner-Wildau was forced to take sterner measures against escaping prisoners. He received a warning from High Command together with notices which were to be displayed prominently throughout all prisoner of war camps. It read:

TO ALL PRISONERS OF WAR

The escape from prison camps is no longer a sport!

Germany has always kept to the Hague Convention and only punished recaptured prisoners of war with minor disciplinary punishment.

Germany will still maintain these principles of International Law.

But England has, besides fighting at the front in an honest manner, instituted an illegal warfare in the non-combat zones in the form of 'Gangster' commandos, terror bandits, and sabotage troops even up to the frontiers of Germany.

They say, in a captured secret and confidential English military pamphlet,

THE HANDBOOK
OF MODERN
IRREGULAR WARFARE

'... the days when we could practise the rules of sportsmanship are over. For the time being, every soldier must be a potential gangster and must be prepared to adopt their methods whenever necessary.

'The spheres of operations should always include the enemy's own country, any occupied territory, and in certain circumstances, such neutral countries as he is using as a source of supply.'

ENGLAND HAS WITH THESE INSTRUCTIONS OPENED UP A NEW NON-MILITARY FORM OF GANGSTER WAR

Germany is determined to safeguard her homeland, and especially her war industry and provisional centres for the fighting front.

Therefore it has become necessary to create strictly forbidden zones, called death zones, in which all unauthorized trespassers will be immediately shot dead on sight.

Escaping prisoners of war entering such death zones will certainly lose their lives. They are therefore constantly in danger of being mistaken for enemy agents of sabotage groups.

Urgent warning is given against making future escapes!

In plain English: Stay in the camp where you will be safe! Breaking out of it is now a damned dangerous act.

The chances of preserving your life are almost nil!

All police and military guards have been given the most strict orders to shoot on sight all suspected persons.

Escaping from prison camps has ceased to be a sport!

So it was that when, eleven weeks later, 76 'terror fliers' – as Germany called Bomber Command aircrew – escaped from the camp at Sagan the full venom of the Gestapo was unleashed upon the whole camp, from the commandant downwards. It was the time when they had been on the alert in occupied countries and harassed by Britain's Special Operations Executive agents carrying out Churchill's express orders 'to set Europe ablaze'. These agents were blowing up the bridges and troop-trains and getting away with it more often than not.[9]

When Hitler heard the news of the 76 escaped prisoners of Sagan, he flew into an uncontrolled rage. Savagely he gave orders. All those 'terror-fliers' who had escaped would be shot. His generals tried to dissuade him, fearing reprisals upon their own men. But Hitler was adamant. They would be taught a lesson and others like them in Germany's prison camps would never forget.

A top-secret document was sent to all Gestapo chiefs in all those areas where those escaped prisoners might be caught. The uncompromising order gave precise instructions: prisoners would be taken by road towards Sagan and shot on the way – ostensibly 'while attempting to escape'.

Ironically it was precisely during this same week that in London crowds were gathering in the grounds of Clarence House to hear the Duke of Gloucester open *The Daily Telegraph* prisoner of war exhibition called: 'Stalag in London'[10] which was designed to show men and women of the Services the 'realism' of a prisoner's life of guarded monotony. For half an hour, people met in the replica forecourt of a German prison camp. A Nazi guard in a lookout post glowered down at them and the drab huts formed a rectangle of unrelieved monotony.

The *Telegraph* journalist reporting the occcasion, ended his piece with these comforting words. 'But behind the barbed wire, behind the lookout posts and behind the bayonets was evidence of how the spirit of British prisoners of war had conquered the turgid Nazi regime. The evidence was in the pictures painted, the scale models of machinery, the carvings and the stage settings for elaborate dramatic performances.'

Whatever comfort the onlookers might have drawn from that exhibition, it would surely have been shockingly removed by an article in the same newspaper a few days later, 19 May 1944 which read:

'Intense feeling has been roused by Mr Eden's statement in the House of Commons today, that forty-seven officers of British and Allied Air Forces have been shot after escaping from Stalag Luft III. The Nazis allege they were shot while resisting arrest or while making a fresh attempt to escape.'

It was surely fitting that one of the principal roles in the last act of the sad prisoner of war saga was played by the former concert party actor, Airey Neave, who had failed in his first attempt to escape from Colditz during the *Ballet Nonsense* concert. He escaped later and during the years after his escape he served in many capacities earning the MC, DSO, and the OBE. And the next time he went to prison was to be on the right side of the cell doors at Nuremberg. And the man he had come so far to meet, the man under whose command once were all German prisoner of war camps, was General Field Marshal Keitel. He stood to attention as former Lieutenant Airey Neave entered the cell and he listened attentively to the words the now Major Neave spoke clearly to him:

'I am the officer appointed by the International Military Tribunal to serve upon you a copy of the indictment in which you are named as the defendant.'[11]

Poetic justice indeed.

But what about the justice meted out for the shooting of forty-seven Air Force officers? And what really did happen to them?

It was all pieced together from evidence given at the war criminal trials. Briefly, the fates of Squadron Leader Roger Bushell and Squadron Leader Bernard Scheidhauer serve to illustrate how the cold-blooded murders were carried out. In his testimony at the trials, Driver mechanic Walter Breithaupt, on oath, told his version of events.

I went back to the car with Spann, who told the two prisoners that they could get out of the car to relieve themselves. They got out and went into the bushes to the right and rear of the car. Spann and Schultz followed, each carrying a pistol, Spann saying as he walked behind them: 'You will be shot if you try to escape.'

I stood next to the car and I could see everything. Both prisoners were just unbuttoning their trousers, while Spann and Schultz stood a metre behind them with their pistols in their hands. Spann gave a sign and Spann and Schultz each fired one shot at the same time in the neck of one of the prisoners. Both prisoners dropped to the earth at the same time.[12]

For the record, the perpetrators of those forty-seven shootings were brought to justice. Twenty-one Gestapo officers were executed, eleven committed suicide, six were killed by air raids and in the last days of the war, seventeen received long sentences of imprisonment, and one died in Soviet hands. All claimed they were only obeying orders.

Though the news of the shootings soon reached prisoners in other camps, the interest in escaping was already waning, and by the time Christmas arrived, the sixth Christmas of the war, the prisoners were often living far better than their guards. As German Security Officer, Reinhold Eggers was later to write:[13] 'The supply of Red Cross parcels of different kinds was regular enough to keep at least all the British prisoners decently clothed, and sufficient also to provide one food parcel per week for each prisoner in their ranks, as well as fifty cigarettes a week.'

Now it was the morale of the German guards that was so low. Eggers again said: 'It would be true to say that most of the Colditz prisoners were better fed than the German civilians in the town, at least as far as calorie intake. The morale of guards and civilians was reduced to mere stoicism. Thousands were buried every day under the bombed ruins of their houses.'

For guards and prisoners alike now, the concert party shows came as a blessed light relief, just as they had been also for those who had been enduring the horrors of fighting in the driving snowstorms of Russia or in the blazing heat of North Africa.

4

Carmen Miranda Saved My Life

The fighting had gone from the dry, lonely and unfriendly Western Desert, leaving behind the pathetic relics, the debris of battle, rusting helmets, broken rifles and shell fragments. No longer now from the Tunisian skyline came the flashes of gunfire, fretting the edges of the night; no longer did the six-barrelled rocket launching Nebelwerfers scare the living daylights out of anyone within range of their terrifying chromatic braying, and no longer, thank God, did jagged bits of metal tear and whirr into the heaped up earth round holes in the ground in which men crouched.

Slowly, to those infantrymen, sitting out the night in front-line trenches, to those sappers clearing mines, to the tank crews grinding forward in the dust came the news which explained it all. At eight minutes to eight on that morning of 12 May 1943, the German Army in North Africa had officially ceased fighting.

The Wehrmacht had suffered a defeat far greater than that of Stalingrad on the Russian front the previous January. Eleven German and twenty-six Italian divisions had been wiped out; a quarter of a million prisoners captured.

Tunis had fallen. Its streets were lined with people, shouting, cheering, throwing flowers and thrusting open bottles of red wine at the troops marching into the city's suburbs. All over the Tunisian front, dazed and bewildered German troops were wandering about, their hands over their heads, trying to find someone who could be bothered to take them prisoner.

War correspondent, Alan Moorehead came across a bizarre situation in the suburbs of Tunis where a mass of German prisoners, apparently unattended, had gathered.[1]

> Two days earlier these German soldiers were concentrating all
> their minds and bodies on killing British and American soldiers [he

wrote, as he surveyed the German soldiers standing near their abandoned vehicles which British troops were eyeing covetously, climbing behind the steering wheels and feeling like millionaires for a day]. At that moment, they were entirely free to pick up their rifles and shoot us. But these prisoners did not seem morose or resentful. They were eager to be pleasant. In dozens they came up explaining the workings of the Volkswagen to us. Their attitude was 'Well it's finished for *me* now. *I* can relax a bit.'

These Germans were not worrying about the future. 'The whole astonishing spectacle was more and more like an army manoeuvre. They were simply going off to another place, America, they hoped. They had heard how well people ate there and they had always wanted to see America,' wrote Moorehead.

What was perhaps even more surprising, was that whilst the German prisoners were waiting for their next move, they were quite happy to help in a variety of ways, in maintaining the morale of British and American troops, who still had a lot more fighting ahead of them.

This writer well remembers, for example, turning out to play football for the 5th Northamptons against the East Surreys in the local town stadium and finding a complete German regimental band in the centre of the pitch – Wembley style – playing popular music to spectators singing 'Lili Marlene' and 'Roll out the Barrel', both of which songs had German origins.

But nothing surely could have been more bizarre than a performance witnessed by the then obscure Lance Bombadier Harry Secombe[2] that week too. Those same musicians, now identified as the band of the crack Hermann Goering Jaeger Division, were playing in a roped off area on the beach near Carthage, guarded by red-capped military police. Secombe, now Sir Harry Secombe, recalled: 'There they played selections from Strauss and 'Roll out the Barrel' and 'Mademoiselle from Armentiers', while we stood around in drawers cellular, short, clapping their efforts. We threw cigarettes into a couple of hats that the Red Caps had set down in the sand, and none of us could really believe it was happening.'

That was not all though. In many unit locations, German craftsmen were sawing wood and hammering it together to make stages for visiting concert parties. And how they were enjoying their work! As Moorehead was to write: 'They were all sick and tired of army life. They looked forward to having a rest. For the moment, the escape from the terrible bombing and shelling was all they asked. These men were not soft. They simply felt: "I have done my bit. Let someone else carry on now." '

It was not surprising that similar thoughts were going through the minds of front-line Allied troops, particularly those who had been in action for close on three years. The 7th Armoured Division, for example, had moved into the Western Desert when France fell, way back in May 1940, followed by the 50th Northumbrian Division, 'Tyne and Tees', and the 51st Highland Division – 'the Highway Decoraters' as they were called because of their habit of painting 'HD' signs wherever a wall on their route was left standing. What did troops like these, the veterans of El Alamein and subsequent battles through to the Mareth Line before Tunis itself, think about the situation?

Realization came slowly to them as they emerged from their trance-like battle mentality which had anaesthetized their emotions when under fire. They found it difficult to believe that they had come to the end of the road which stretched over two thousand miles behind them to that insignificant coastal railway station fifty miles from Alexandria, named after the ridge between the railway and the sea, the hill of the twin cairns, Tel el Alamein.

Slowly, ever so slowly, to those men in faded khaki jackets, torn and sweat-stained, the rhythm of 'normal' life returned. It took some days before the possibilities of the new situation sank in.

So, Tunis had fallen. So what?

There would be other new battles. There always were. Meanwhile though, the men of the First and Eighth Armies could celebrate, get spruced up for trips on 'passion wagons' to Tunis, to see an ENSA show, get drunk on the thick red Tunisian red wine and chase smartly dressed French colonial girls, who, but a few hours earlier had promenaded happily upon the arm of German soldiery.

But even as they celebrated, a more sombre mood began to grow among their ranks. Where would they be sent to fight next? Rumours abounded.

The word went round they'd be shipped back to Blighty to form a battle-experienced core for that army now training for the invasion of France. That possibility did not worry anyone too much. After all, the eventuality of that long talked of Second Front with its accompanying communist-inspired placards in Britain of 'Strike now in the West' still seemed a long way off and a period of retraining in the UK, many had not seen since 1940, seemed an attractive option.

But then came other rumours; tales about going to invade another island or the south of France. This was not at all as pleasant a prospect. A feeling of resentment developed, fertile ground for new rumours.

'We heard stories of a battalion flinging down their rifles and walking off their sandy parade patch shouting, "Fuck the Colonel, fuck the adjutant, fuck the RSM and fuck the bloody war!",' recalled James McGrath formerly with the Highland Division.[3]

It was about that same time that the poet, Vernon Scannell, then a soldier serving with the Seaforth Highlanders, had already had enough.[4] He too was sick of the war, of seeing dead bodies scattered over the desert battlefield like broken dolls, of the meat wagons taking away the wounded, and of soldiers in his own platoon scavenging among the dead bodies, those of their own battalion as well as those of the German army. 'They were turning them over with an indifferent boot before they removed watches, rings and whatever valuables they could find,' he wrote. War revolted him so much that there came a time just before the end of it all in Africa, when he just walked away. Deserted, like so many others and when caught by military police, sentenced to three years penal servitude in Egypt's Number 55 military prison and detention barracks. There, manic bullies and dedicated sadists, dressed in crisply ironed khaki drill and caps with the peak forced down on to the bridge of the nose, as if they were in a regiment of the Brigade of Guards, took a delight in meting out 'punishment diet number one' – solitary confinement with eight ounces of dry bread at 0730 hours and a further eight ounces at 1600. These men who had never even heard a shot fired in anger, could sneer self-righteously at their 'soldiers under sentence', calling them yellow and soft, provoking them into retaliation which resulted in strait jacket restraint allowing for further beatings and kickings to smash any spirit left in men already broken by battle fatigue.

Tales of the horrors of such detention barracks got to the men at the front who came to the conclusion that desertion in the Western Desert was not a viable option. There was nowhere to hide. Discipline, though, was showing signs of disintegrating. General Sir Ronald Adam of the War Office's morale committee was handed the problem. He sent out his military assistant, Coldstream Guards officer and classical scholar, John Sparrow, to report on the situation. The infantrymen did not see him. Nor did they have the opportunity of telling him what they thought. Commanding officers were not too eager to tell him that morale in their own regiments was a problem either. That would reflect upon their leadership, of course.

For the infantryman, the victory in North Africa was a barren one. They were getting nothing out of it. James McGrath had his own view of the situation: 'It was all right for the Jerries. For them the future was assured, their lives and limbs were no longer threatened. They smiled and shrugged their shoulders as they carried out their chores, teasing us, taunting us even with that old chestnut "For us ze war is over." '

Neil McCallum, a young officer who would later be wounded in Sicily, recalled in his book, *Journey with a Pistol*[5], what the situation was like in his own battalion:

> Discipline, while not breaking down, showed signs of wear and tear. NCOs approached officers with their hands in their pockets, cigarettes in mouth. Drunks strode through battalion lines at night shouting defiance at all and sundry. 'Muck the bloody muckers, we're doing no more fighting.' At times the camel's back was nearly breaking and it seemed that mutiny and disorder were but a hair's breadth away. Had we been in a country of easy communications or near a large city, desertions would have been numerous.

Unit commanders were worried but tried to keep their problems under close wraps for they feared others in authority reporting upon their own capabilities. Consequently, as McCallum recalled, 'Licence was tolerated up to a point, and for the rest, a rigid programme, of exceptional physical severity, occupied a fixed number of hours each day ... a large marquee was erected and a wet canteen opened and battalion orders carried the amazing instruction that all ranks might get drunk, provided they stayed within camp lines.'

Strange rumours about mutinies were circulating. It was said that the Mediterranean Fleet was near mutiny. There was talk of a battalion of the Rifle Brigade having walked off their training lines into an olive grove because they had heard they were not going home. The story went that the CO and other officers had apparently walked out on the mutineers and had left their senior NCOs to sort it out. It had taken several days of hard talk, threats and some physical violence to get the riflemen to 'soldier on'.

To put an end to uncertainty and rumours, the waspish General Montgomery, who preached that 'the real strength of an army was provided not by the sum total of its parts but its morale, fighting spirit and mutual confidence between leaders and the led,' decided to take immediate action. He toured all units, gathering men and officers together in small groups and talking to them, telling them all what was going to happen.

Young Gunner Harry Secombe was there in the front rank when Montgomery came to talk to his regiment.[6] It was, for him a memorable and almost farcical occasion:

He arrived in style, the great man, wearing his famous beret and carrying a fly whisk, and sitting in the back of an open staff car. We were all standing to attention in a three-sided square when his car came to a halt in the middle of us.

He stood up and called: 'Bweak wanks and gather wound.'

Secombe found himself pushed so far forward that he was hard against the rear wheel looking right up into Montgomery's face when the General said: 'Take off your hats. I want to see what you chaps look like.'

Secombe was not looking so good. At that time he was feeling well below par too for he was just recovering from sand-fly fever, he had a crop of shiny red boils on his face, his hair had not seen scissors for weeks. Montgomery took a long time looking at his new acquisitions from the First Army, which he always regarded as inferior to his own Eighth, and finally his critical gaze rested upon Secombe's red face. This young gunner, very conscious of the poor figure he cut, felt impelled to say something to explain his rather pathetic appearance, like 'I've been ill, sir' or 'I'll get me hair cut tomorrow, sir'. But no words came out until there was a lull in Montgomery's pep talk, and then Secombe heard himself calling out: 'We're with you, sir.'

Montgomery made no reply. He spoke a few more words about how easy it was going to be in Italy making one landing after another up the length of the long boot, cutting the German army's supply lines. And then he drove off, waving his fly whisk and leaving Harry Secombe wondering what kind of an impression he personally had made upon the great man. He was in little doubt though, he recalled, 'I must have reminded him of Wellington's words before the battle of Waterloo: "I don't know what effect these men will have upon the enemy, but by God, they terrify me." '

Now with the invasion of Sicily underway, all commanders were very conscious of the need for an improvement in morale. And suddenly, almost as if the commanders had received a directive from above, a spate of notices appeared in the Daily Routine Orders of all three Services, calling for anyone with theatrical experience to volunteer for concert party duties.

David Clark,[7] then serving with Number 500 County of Kent Squadron in North Africa recalled: 'My CO was only too pleased to put my name forward and I was interviewed by the Officer in Charge of Entertainments at RAF headquarters in Algiers and welcomed there with open arms.' Prior to joining the Air Force in 1938 he was involved in amateur dramatics with the Pantheon

Club in Glasgow and the Griffnock too.

Hubert Haines,[8] who had recently arrived in the Middle East with an RAF draft found he had a golden opportunity to pursue his own ambitions to go on the stage. As a young lad he had become stage-struck, hardly ever missing a show at the Manchester Palace theatre. So keen was he that he took elocution lessons, went to a dancing school and gave up a safe job to take his first stage job as a comedy acrobat in the Christmas pantomime *Jack and the Beanstalk* at the Manchester Palace. From there he progressed to music hall doing burlesque impressions. He had only just arrived in the RAF transit camp when the padre picked him out and asked him to do a turn on stage with another young lad called Alfred Marks. The future in the fly-infested Middle East looked decidedly more interesting for Hubert Haines than he had ever dared to imagine. Concert parties were definitely now *de rigeur*.

But not everyone had such a wealth of dramatic experience to call upon as Hubert Haines. James McGrath,[9] for example, had virtually none. But he still volunteered. Reflecting, with a wry smile, upon those days he said:

> I'd been long enough in the army to know that when volunteers were called for, then people were only too keen to accept any story you liked to spin about previous experience. There was no way of checking anyway. I saw this as my only chance of avoiding the 'meat grinder' of the assault landings we had heard so much about in the last few days. Frankly I don't mind admitting now that I had seen too many of my pals die horrible deaths, clutching their bellies, blood oozing through their fingers. I had tried once before to get into a support unit like the RASC but there were too many wanting to be drivers. So when this request for volunteers with theatrical experience appeared I was not going to let the chance go by for lack of experience. I put my name down right away with a string of rep companies I had been with and variety turns I had done, naming theatres I knew existed. The trouble was that I could not play an instrument and the only time that I had been on stage was in the first year at grammar school when I played Mabel in Gilbert and Sullivan's *Pirates of Penzance*.
>
>   My voice had not broken then and the teacher had me dressed in a frilly bonnet, ringlets and a flowery red dress. I can still sing 'Take a pair of sparkling eyes'. Nobody thought of making fun of me then, as they probably would a young lad today. And, to be honest, I'd quite enjoyed the excitement of being on stage. But I had not done anything since. Now, though, I could see that this was going to be my last chance of getting out of the Poor Bloody Infantry.

I knew from other concert parties which had visited the unit in the UK, that what went down best with troops, apart from community singing and dolly birds from ENSA, were the lads who came on as women, either as panto-type dames with saucepan lids as a bra, or as exaggerated versions of glamour girls.

The day after my application went in, I was told to report to the adjutant's office for an audition, later that afternoon. Well, I had to get a move on. I decided to do a Carmen Miranda take off. I remembered how the Brazilian Bombshell always sang and danced in her films with loads of fruit and flowers decking her headscarf and bra. A pal of mine produced a red silk scarf, which he had bought as a present for his girfriend before she had written to tell him that she was now going to marry an American pilot. We wrapped the scarf, Miranda style round my head to cover my 'short back and sides' and then bits and pieces of my outfit came from all parts of the unit – especially the cookhouse.

I had already seen Mickey Rooney's impersonation of Carmen Miranda in a film called something like, *Babes of Broadway* and I knew the act was good for a laugh. What seemed to bring the biggest laughs were the accidental revelations – like lifting the skirt and showing big army boots or something like ATS passion stoppers – their black pants. I also left my dog tags and AB 64 Pay Book dangling down my back on a bit of string. A sheet served as a sarong-like skirt, and another strip from it was tied tightly round my chest as a bra, padded with two halves of small melons, scooped out of course. By the time everyone had finished adding bits and pieces as bracelets, necklaces and earrings I looked like something straight out of Covent Garden fruit market. Someone used a black map-marking pencil to draw huge curved eyebrows and a concoction from the cookhouse gave me a ridiculous red-lipped look. The finishing touch was a piece of mosquito netting, as a half veil. Then I was ready. And just in time.

I knocked on the adjutant's door and then, not waiting for a voice to tell me to come in, I launched straight into a song, waving my arms above my head and my hips swaying: 'Ay Ay, Ay Ay, would you like to come to a party, For you're looking so fit and so hearty ...' I was just making up the words as I went along. There'd been no time for anything else and the last line rhymed with 'hearty' accompanied by a rude raspberry sounding noise.

For the first time I saw that snooty adjutant's face crack into a smile and then a guffaw as he slapped his thigh and shouted, 'Enough, enough! You'll do.'

I was in. Or rather, I was out. And that was what mattered most. I was out of the poor bloody infantry!

That afternoon I packed my kit, jumped into the back of a fifteen hundred weight truck, and set off for the Algiers Entertainments unit. I never went back to the infantry again, and for years I've told the tale, over a pint of beer, how Carmen Miranda saved my life.

It was about this time too that Lance Bombadier Harry Secombe got himself into an army concert party in North Africa, but only for a short time. It was, however, a beginning. In his autobiography, *Arias and Raspberries*[10] he tells how keen his unit was to put on a show for the bored troops. They took over the little George Metaxas theatre in Tunis and a few chaps who could give some sort of turn were gathered together. For the first part of his act, Harry did his impressions of popular radio comedians – Stainless Stephen, the Sheffield comedian whose speech was punctuated vocally as he went along, 'speaking from the B full-stop, B, ditto C, ditto, studios London, full-stop'; Sandy Powell, with his catchphrase of 'Can you hear me, Mother?'; Stanley Holloway reciting the story of 'Albert and the Lion' in that famous seaside place called Blackpool; and finishing his act with an impression of Deanna Durbin, singing her better known songs in a falsetto voice.

The highlight of the second part of his act was one of those songs soldiers always love, poking fun at the absurdities of the life they had been leading and joking about the SNAFUs – (Situation Normal All Fucked Up). His act finished with a song which really went home to his audience, a parody of the Australian song, 'Waltzing Matilda', and called 'Lost at Tebourba'. It was at Tebourba that a Royal Artillery Field battery of Secombe's brigade, had been surrounded by German tanks. They were dive-bombed by Stukas and shot at by the tanks from close range but the battery managed to knock out seventeen German tanks before losing seven of their eight guns. One of the tanks was only three yards from the gun that destroyed it. The surviving gunners managed to withdraw, but ever afterwards if an item of equipment was missing at a gunner's kit inspection, the soldier would answer, 'Lost at Tebourba, Sir.'

Secombe, who was in most of those desperate actions with 78 Division before the fall of Tunis, remembered later that the first verse of his parody went something like this:

> Lost at Tebourba, lost at Tebourba,
> Lost all my kit at Tebourba I did,
> And they moaned and they sighed
> As they went up to the quarter bloke,
> Lost all my kit at Tebourba, I did.

During that strange two-month interlude between the end of the North African battles and the assault on Sicily and Italy, a man who eventually was to make his name with Harry Secombe, was also clowning round Tunisia. Before the war he had been a semi-skilled fitter in Woolwich but when his call-up papers arrived he took with him into the army, something more than the prescribed toilet kit and pyjamas. He took his trumpet.

Soon he was the unofficial bugler for 56 Regiment, Royal Artillery, blowing reveille from his bed, pushing his trumpet out of the window and then snuggling back into the warmth of his blankets for those last few precious moments. After training had finished for the day, he played for his mates in the barrack room, sentimental ballads such as 'These foolish things' and 'You stepped out of a dream' and it was after one such impromptu session that he confessed to his listeners that he wished he could play the trumpet as well as Spike Hughes. From then on he was 'Spike' to his friends though still to the army, Gunner Terence Alan Milligan.[11]

As so often was the case in the Services, musicians were seldom alone for long; they attracted each other, like iron filings to a magnet, and 56 Regiment was no exception to this phenomenon. Soon Milligan had a band. They played at dances and birthday celebrations and always featured the favourite tune, 'Honey-suckle Rose'.

When orders for overseas came, troops were instructed to leave all non-essential equipment behind. Not surprisingly, the band managed to smuggle all their instruments on board ship and what a good job they did too, for on the very next evening after they had docked in Algiers, they were asked to play in the old French colonial Opera House there. Spike recalls that evening as a thrilling and stimulating occasion with every seat in the stalls, dress circle and upper circle filled.

But there the fun ended.

Orders came to move into action and Spike's battery was soon in the thick of the fighting through the crags and muddy ravines on the road to Tunis until the city was taken and the enemy destroyed.

Again, almost immediately hostilities had finished, Spike saw the notice in Routine Orders. It read: 'Anyone who has the ability to entertain will parade tomorrow at 10.00 hours.' The next day, 'The Jolly Rogers Concert Party' was formed and it presented its first show in a small theatre in Setif. More followed and it was during this period that Spike developed another aspect to his trumpet-playing repertoire – clowning.

It could well have been his personal reaction to the stress of battle, but whatever the reason, clowning came into his act and it worked far better than anyone expected. What happened was that when the band was not actually playing, Spike and the other musicians would dress up in weird outfits and walk across the stage in the middle of some other chap's serious act. The audience loved these interruptions. 'It was pure lunacy,' recalled Spike Milligan, 'No rhyme or reason in it. It was meant to be pointless. Just like the war.'

The fame of the 'Jolly Rogers' spread. Commanding officers asked for it for their own units. The show went on tour and Spike Milligan began to spend more of his time as a comedian than as a trumpeter. He suddenly discovered he had the power to move an audience, 'blitzing' officers, NCOs and the Army Council with his unique brand of inane military goonery. Then, as so often happened to concert parties, it all had to stop. Orders came for the regiment to embark for a much bigger show – the showdown on the beaches of Salerno.

All over North Africa then, however, other concert parties were in action. Unit commanders had cottoned on to the idea that drama and variety on stage had a noticeable and beneficial effect upon the morale of their men. Those of them who had already been in action were sensitively aware of their vulnerability, they knew all too well what to expect when they next went into action. One of Milligan's mates in the concert party put it succinctly: 'It's simple arithmetic, the longer you are alive in action, the nearer you are to getting your lot. I came ashore with B Company. At the end of three days, me, the Sergeant and one private were all that were left. If I go back to the mob I'll never see Blighty again.'

No wonder concert parties were given such enthusiastic support and they were often formed from men who had never been on a stage in their lives before, yet from the ranks of these amateurs, eventually emerged many of the stars of the future, on stage, television and cinema screen.

They appeared often under appalling conditions and with improvized equipment. Richard Roberts,[12] a fitter with 459 Squadron, RAF, has vivid memories of how the concert party was formed at Gambut, near Tobruk.

An airman called Hodgkinson made a complete drum kit from old oil drums cut down to size and covered with linen which was painted with aircraft dope and left to dry in the sun. A few musicians got together as a band and from this there came a concert party. Its star performer was a Hawaiian dancer. She received a tremendous ovation and encores galore from an audience who did not know that the girl waggling her alluring hips in front of their eyes was none other than the hirsute moustached unit MT driver who had shaved off all the hair from his face and body for the performance.

As soon as RAF wireless operator Arthur Clements[13] arrived in the Middle East at that time, he too became involved with concert parties. He was stationed at the Telecommunications Middle East unit at Heliopolis and he teamed up with a pal to present an act called 'The Eastern Brothers', modelled on the famous London 'Western Brothers'. Such a turn, with the drawling aristocratic accent, was an ideal medium for taking the mickey out of senior officers, especially the base wallahs. He recalled: 'We had a magnificent concrete stage made for us by Italian prisoners of war, a masterpiece really for they even managed to sculpt the RAF crest in concrete right on the front of the stage's base, facing the audience.'

The success of Clements' 'Eastern Brothers' act owed a lot to the advance party which went to each new location a day or two before the main party in order to set up the stage and props.

Whilst they were there, [recalled Clem] they would talk to the lads about the whims and idiosyncracies of their officers and senior NCOs. There was one Station Warrant Officer, for example, who prided himself on playing the violin and put everyone's teeth on edge whenever the opportunity arose for him to take out his fiddle. It was easy for us then to work a burlesque of such characters into our own programme.

Twins, Rey and Ellis Gill,[14] who had hit upon the same idea when stationed with the RAF in Malta, were asked to perform with the RAF Mirth Makers at the Globe Theatre, Alexandria. For their act, 'The Harrow Twins' they were smartly dressed like the 'Western Brothers', monocled and their suavely drawling songs satirized the absurdities of service life. One typical Western Brothers effort 'Keeping up the Old Traditions', was the perfect medium for poking fun at very senior officers and the War Office brass hats. Naturally, when there was some topical reference it went down very well and especially so when they performed for troops close to the forward areas.

The demand for these unit concert parties was tremendous and surprisingly there was no shortage of talent for performing or for technical assistance back stage in those critical months of 1943. Jim Whitehorn[15] recalls how he was base posted to Heliopolis after a long spell in hospital and as soon as he was discharged from medical care, his services as stage sparks were immediately taken up by the RAF Mirth Makers. 'Sometimes we would be performing in a real theatre, a cinema or dance hall and at others we would be outdoors using the headlights from trucks as our lighting.'

It was remarkable how theatrical ability emerged when it was needed. Even in remote parts of West Africa, concert parties came to the fore. Cyril Risbridger,[16] stationed at RAF Ikeja, Nigeria in 1943, got to work with colleagues, built a stage and put on several successful revues and serious plays. And in RAF Jum, a few airmen built a theatre for their own shows and the occasional visiting ENSA company, in an attempt to keep themselves and others sane. What it was like to be stationed in such a place can be gleaned from John Harris's description in his book, *A Funny Place to Hold a War*.[17] 'There wasn't even a decent war, and the incidence of going round the bend among men brought up in sophisticated cities and flung down in this God-forsaken spot close to the equator in Sierra Leone was surprisingly high. Life at RAF Jum consisted largely of foot rot, gut rot, and nut rot,' wrote Harris.

Harris writes about the usherette of that theatre, the eccentric Aircraftman First Class Anthony Derek Tristam, known to all as Trixie because of his slender figure and the fact that he liked to bleach his hair, pluck his eyebrows and tie his mosquito net with pink ribbon instead of the usual white tape. On the night of theatre shows this Trixie would put on his high heels and play the part of an usherette. Harris's book, based on his own RAF experiences there, presents situations found so often in Forces camps remote from all the amenities which those men regarded as civilization.

An airman who found Harris's book very true to life there in West Africa, was Thomas Booth.[18] He was an RAF nursing orderly at Takoradi, where the temperature averaged 114°F and where it hardly ever rained but was always hot and humid. He soon discovered how important the concert parties were in keeping up morale.

> Our evening off duty time was spent in our own hospital NAAFI where we would drink locally brewed beer, sing songs, for there was always someone who could tickle the ivories a little, but as the evening progressed the ballads would become more than a little bawdy and even boring, and so you can see that there was a real need for a proper concert party bringing in sketches and music of a different kind. One thing that surprised me however about those concerts was that although there was a large staff of Nursing Sisters on the unit, the women's parts in plays and revues were always taken by men. I've often wondered why.

David Clark,[19] another airman who served in Africa then and later in Italy, found that there were almost always some young men who would happily dress as women for the shows to entertain the others.

We had a grand chap in our outfit, there was nothing odd about him, he certainly wasn't what one might today call 'queer'. He was very keen and helpful. He found it was just one act that he could do well and he was so very keen to stay with the concert party that he never failed to be the first to arrive at the theatre or hangar where we were playing. He would be ironing his gowns and dressing his wigs but he was always willing to iron other people's kit. He often looked after mine whilst I was busy helping with the stage and props. He was a good lad, and after the war I saw him appearing in the chorus of a show which appeared in the Largs theatre. He'd made a lifetime profession out of his concert party days.

One young airman, Jack Blades,[20] who had never even dreamt of being on stage actually achieved a distinction which few of the top stars ever earn. It was in the early summer of 1943, when he was feeling bored with the inactivity and anti-climax following the end of hostilities there in the Western Desert, and whenever he could he would get down to Cairo or Alexandria to see whatever show ENSA had coming through. On one of these occasions he was in Cairo and noticed that there was a great deal of activity outside the Royal Opera House. It was a most impressive edifice that had in its recent past resounded to the varied strains of Italian arias. The foyer was a spacious affair of red, gold and white, with various ante-rooms leading off it. The auditorium was oval-shaped and lavishly decorated. Above it the roof was dotted with hundreds of electric light bulbs which gave a glittering effect to the general decor.

In that auditorium were two Royal boxes, because the King and Queen never appeared together in public. Adjoining His Majesty's box was another for the use of his harem. This grandiose theatre was surely not the venue for a complete beginner like Jack Blades to make his debut. But fate planned otherwise. He recently recalled how it all came to pass:

I was standing outside the Opera House with my pal and thinking what an impressive sight it was that night. Certainly as spectacular as any Hollywood First Night. And passing through the portals of the Opera House that evening was more gold braid than I had ever seen before. Making the most of his entry was the devious reigning monarch of Egypt then, King Farouk himself.

Organizing everything behind the scenes was the leader of the Gang Show, Ralph Reader. He was keeping things buzzing as people and material went in. My pal and I would have liked to have been going in too, but this was obviously a special show and we did not have a chance of a ticket. We pondered the situation

and both seemed to have the same idea simultaneously, for we
turned casually and began to walk down the side of the theatre
where, we had noticed, musicians were already walking in with
their instruments. Obviously there would be a side entrance. But
we also realized that, as with British theatres, there would be some
burly chap at the door to stop the likes of us gaining admittance.
Nevertheless, nothing ventured nothing gained, we walked
nonchalantly towards the doorway, chatting confidently and our
luck was in. No one was at that side door. We entered boldy as if
we had every right to be there. No one tried to stop us and we
found ourselves free to explore all the nooks and passageways
back stage and we even chatted to some of the performers
appearing that night. Suddenly we got a shock as a red-faced
senior officer appeared, stuck out his arm and ushered us
authoritatively behind a huge backdrop where we were alongside
other servicemen all clad in summer khaki drill like ourselves. We
seemed to be in some kind of formation, but before we could exit
stage left, the huge curtain opened up and brilliant footlights hit
us. The stage was alive with light. And suddenly all the chaps
alongside us opened their mouths singing, 'Where have you been
all the day, Billy Boy, Billy Boy? Where have you been all the day,
my Billy Boy?' We were part of a choir!

After one more song the curtain closed to a great roar of
applause. We stayed with the choir for the refreshments and
chatted with the stars appearing on the same programme.
Eventually we took our departure from Cairo's Royal Opera
House, both seasoned Royal Command Performers.

Amongst the enthusiastic amateurs treading the boards in North
Africa by this time, were the stars of showbusiness, for High
Command wanted no more threatened mutinies and were
determined to do everything possible to raise the morale of the
troops ready for the big show about to start in Europe.

Ironically enough, one of the first of the big showbiz names to
arrive in North Africa, was the German-born star, Marlene
Dietrich, the woman with the most highly insured legs in the
world. Her husky chanting of 'Lola' and 'Falling in Love Again'
was at the heart of her performances which always were
rapturously received. What was more, she soon learnt how to
deal with a serviceman's audience, how to answer if they
shouted, how to play up to them and how to make them laugh.
She took her work very seriously and later said: 'Once you have
caught the attention of front-line troops who might be about to
die tomorrow, and know it, then you can catch the attention of
anybody anywhere.'[21]

She put together an act which was little more than a projection of herself and it was the songs which really carried her through. Sentimental songs were what those lads lapped up. In her deep-throated mannish laments for lost loves, for lost youth, for lost ideals, she appealed to men in that strange post-battle mood in which relief at being alive was mingled with anxiety for what might be coming next.

Her songs knew no nationality, they were not about a single country or a single victory, but rather about survival, the survival of ordinary men and women who had to cope with terrible problems. Perhaps she was singing indeed for a world that had torn itself apart. Whatever it was, it went down well. She encouraged the wounded, brought comfort to the sick, and cheered those who were fearful.

After beginning her tour at the Algiers Opera House, she gave open-air shows to troops in muddy wadis and in swirling desert dust. They were exhausting, lightning tours with hours of driving, often in jolting three-ton trucks, during the heat of the day and yet she still managed to appear on rickety stages that same evening as fresh and alluring as ever.

Other stars followed similar arduous tours. Tommy Trinder, the lively cockney star, for example, gave fifty shows for Eighth Army troops in fewer than three weeks, as well as making radio programmes. 'We played Algiers, Cairo, Khartoum, and then travelled to Basra, Jordan, Lebanon, and Palestine. From Haifa we went to Cyprus,' he recalled. Those shows were rarely in established theatres. 'I dropped in on Algiers on the way home and did some one man shows where more than six people constituted an audience.'[22]

The Lancashire lass, Gracie Fields, who in her childhood had scrubbed out neighbours' backyard lavatories yet in her heyday received flowers from the Prime Minister when she was seriously ill, and a CBE from King George VI, flew out to Algiers and immediately roused her audience into a patriotic fervour. At the end of each show she would sing, what now seems a very corny, patriotic song of the war years yet one to which even the nationalistic Scottish, Welsh, Irish and Commonwealth troops responded:

> There'll always be an England
> While there's a country lane,
> Wherever there's a cottage small,
> Beside a field of grain …

By the time she got to the last verse, everyone – Scots, Irish and Welsh too – was singing with her,

And England will be free
If England means as much to you
As England means to me.

During those few months of rest, recuperation and retraining, scores of well-known performers under ENSA and USO auspices rushed out 'to do their bit' for the troops. Jack Benny, Wee Georgie Wood, George Formby, Elsie and Doris Waters, Judy Shirley and, of course, the Forces' sweetheart, Vera Lynn, appeared as if by magic, bolstering the efforts of those who had already arrived before hostilities ended. On one occasion, over one hundred of such ENSA artistes were among the passengers rescued from a small Dutch troopship holed and sunk by German dive-bombers in the Mediterranean.

London born Bob Hope,[24] who had tried to join the US Navy immediately after the Japanese attack on Pearl Harbour, arrived in Algiers in June 1943 to do exactly what his President, Franklin Roosevelt had urged when Hope had tried to enlist. Roosevelt, who clearly saw the real value of artistes of Hope's calibre, had said, 'We want 'em to do just what they are doing – entertaining the troops.'

Hope had left London in such a hurry that he was still in clothes suitable for a cool English summer and before he even got out of the aircraft at Maison Blanche, Algiers air base, he was soaked in sweat. A US colonel lent him a light-weight green suit for the next four weeks of his non-stop tour. For entertaining then for stars and concert party amateurs alike was simply, 'Go!Go!Go!'

The troops gave each one of those stars a great reception. Even tough guy, Humphrey Bogart, seen so often in gangster films, in trenchcoat and soft felt hat, but who had just won the war in the desert almost single-handedly as a tank sergeant capturing 500 Nazis in Columbia's film *Sahara* was forgiven and greeted tumultuously when he toured Africa with USO. He was not, however, altogether quite so *persona grata* with senior American officers. On one occasion after some horseplay which resulted in his being locked in his hotel bedroom, he systematically began to break the door – just like the Bogart of *The Maltese Falcon*. It was then that an irate US colonel appeared and shouted at Bogart, 'Stop that! And give me your name, rank and serial number.' Bogart, who was in USO uniform, had no love for chair-borne colonels – in fact he despised them – yelled back, 'Got no name, rank and serial number and you can go to hell!'[25]

Bogart, like so many of those stars on lightning tours of Africa then, had one objective in mind – to give the fighting troops all he could. If ever a group of stars put their backs into a job, they all did then. All of them working towards one end, getting the troops ready for the real-life show coming shortly, the assault on 'the soft under-belly of Europe', as Churchill euphemistically called the attack on Hitler's 'Festung Europa'.

The top brass had done their best to ensure that morale was high in North Africa. Showbiz amateur and professional, had worked flat out to support them in this. There would be breakdowns of morale, such as the minor mutiny of 1200 men on Salerno beachhead in the September of 1943 but, as King George VI signalled Basil Dean, Director of ENSA that month at his Headquarters in Drury Lane, it was, undeniably, 'Well done, ENSA!.'

Well done indeed. Those men who had been picked for the most exacting and critical operation of the whole war up to that date were as ready as any army could be for the invasion of Europe.

They were as ready as ever they could be for the chaos, mismanagement, and the sheer stupidity of some of their commanders. They were ready even for the storms that would buffet their assault craft, and the gale force winds which would drive airborne troops into the sea. Their morale was all right. 'The men were ninety-eight per cent unemotional about the whole operation,' wrote war correspondent, Christopher Buckley[26] who was to go ashore with the second wave of assault troops.

They were ready for the slaughter of Sicily.

5

The Best Medicine

Everything still seemed to be going wrong. The planning of the Allies' return to German-occupied Europe, which had begun in London in January 1943, had been fraught with problems and miscalculations but at last the armies for this, the largest amphibious assault in all history, bigger even than D-Day, had gathered. Four divisions of General Patton's US Seventh Army and four divisions of General Montgomery's Eighth Army were to assault the coast of Sicily simultaneously along a front of one hundred miles. From ports as far apart as Suez and Gibraltar the divisions would sail, all timed to reach their goal in the hours before dawn on Saturday, 10 July 1943. The first troops were to land at precisely 02.45 hours. But some three or four hours prior to that, parachutists and glider-borne troops would land in the rear of enemy positions with a view to spreading confusion in general and in particular seizing airfields and vital bridges.

Back in Algiers and Cairo showbiz groups waited with other support groups for the time when their own call forward, would come. Two days before the great armada had sailed, Will Fyfe, the greatest Scottish comedian, had put the finishing touches to the pre-invasion entertainment programme with an open air performance for the Seaforth Highlanders.[1] Now those ENSA groups destined for Sicily were also packed, prepared, and ready for whatever was in store for them, now that the assault troops had sailed.

One can imagine the spectacle of that invasion fleet at sea. Armies moving forward in full war panoply; 2,500 ships all heading for the enemy coastline. But then, when all the problems of logistics appeared to have been solved, the weather turned against the Allies. Gale force winds howled across from Africa. The sea, hitherto so calm, heaved ominously, buffeting the convoy, rolling and pitching the troopships so that soldiers below

Real-life combat pilot, James Stewart, as a captain in the US Army Air Corps, 1943, flew on many operational missions against the enemy during the two years he was stationed in Britain

Below Tommy Handley, beloved radio comedian star of *ITMA*, whose cheery 'Hello Folks' lightened the gloom in the darkest days of the war

Below Generals Montgomery, Eisenhower and Bradley, all of whom at various times during the war were said to have 'lookalikes'. Repertory actor, Clifton James, played his part in May 1944, impersonating General Montgomery, to create doubts in the minds of German Intelligence as to where the invasion forces would strike

The Fifteenth Scottish Division Concert Party formed in 1939, 'The Tam O'Shanters', distinguished itself with its 'front-line concerts' in Normandy and France. Note on the far right of the picture the young Kenneth Connor, star of many *Carry On* films and television shows

Chorus of the 27 Squadron RAF, Risalpur, India, 1943. When touring the North West frontier the chorus narrowly escaped 'a fate worse than death' when a band of Sikhs

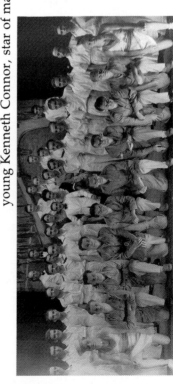

The entire company of RAF Risalpur, North West Frontier Provinces, concert party

Wilfred Pickles, who, during the period when Germany threatened to invade Britain, was given the job of BBC news reader because his Yorkshire voice was so well known and inimitable by German broadcasters, who might try to spread alarming false information during an invasion

Actor Nigel Patrick who arrived in Egypt as an infantry reinforcement officer but was told that at 29 he was too old for that duty. He was put in charge of providing all services entertainments in North Africa and southern Europe

Bradford playwright and novelist, J.B. Priestly giving one of his popular, morale-boosting talks after the BBC's nine o'clock radio news

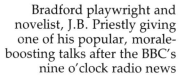

Film star Douglas Fairbanks junior who toured the United States drumming up support for Britain. Later, when America had entered the war, Fairbanks joined the US Navy

Lance Bombadier (now Sir Harry) Secombe of the Field Artillery, with 78 Battleaxe Division. In between the North African and Sicilian campaigns he made a name for himself as a concert party singer and comedian

Airmen Ron Rich, Steve Stevenson, Denis Norden and Gordon Dell, rehearsing the 83 Group musical revue, *Three Bags Full* at Eindhoven, Holland, 1944

Marlene Dietrich, the legendary European sex goddess and a great trouper who well deserved the awards for gallantry and distinguished service entertaining troops in the forward areas

Lili Palmer in *The Gentle Sex* made in 1943. The film was a tribute to the contribution made by women to the war effort

'The One and Only Phyllis Dixie' captioned this publicity picture of the stripper who took wartime London by storm

'We had a smashing war', wrote Sylvia Wade of the Air Ministry
concert party, Harrogate (pictured here)

Eric Sykes, Bob Errington and
Steve Stevenson as three
members of the WAAF

Carmen Miranda, in
the film *That Night in
Rio*, set the style for
many subsequent
impersonations by
professionals and
amateurs alike, such
as Able Seaman
Molloy shown here

These Gravesend gunners had to
man the guns in drag when a German
raider interrupted their concert
rehearsal

Marlene Dietrich had no need of the glamorous clothes shown in the publicity picture in order to captivate an audience as can be seen from the contrasting photograph of her with the US infantry in North West Europe

It was to men living in fox holes like this that showbiz folk such as Marlene Dietrich came. They brightened their lives temporarily and brought a few moments of forgetfulness

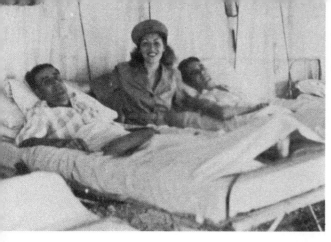

'Forces Sweetheart', Vera Lynn, visiting a casualty clearing station in Burma

Vera (now Dame Vera) Lynn in her ENSA uniform

The original George Mitchell choir formed from members of the Royal Army Pay Corps stationed at Finsbury Circus, London. George Mitchell is on the extreme right of the picture

decks lay prostrate in their own vomit, past caring.

On their airfields in Africa, commanders of the US 82nd and the British 1st Airborne Divisions were horrified at the prospect of mounting the operation with winds roaring from west to east at thirty-five miles an hour. In Britain and the United States, practice jumps were always cancelled when the wind reached between twelve and fifteen miles an hour!

To Eisenhower came a wire from his boss in Washington, General Marshall: 'Is the attack on or off?' There was no turning back now. The operation just had to go on. Any delay would imperil the whole of the mighty fleet from attacks by German aircraft and submarines. Eisenhower radioed Marshall, the attack was on. Later he was to write: 'There was nothing we could do but pray, desperately.'[2]

One disaster followed quickly upon the heels of another. The inexperienced American pilots who had never been in action before, and who were towing gliders of the 1st British Air Landing Brigade, started releasing their gliders without making allowances for the gale force headwinds. Once on their own, gliders just could not keep airborne; one after the other, sixty-eight gliders plummetted down into the rough sea. The Division Commander himself, General Hopkinson, had to swim ashore. Many of the surviving fifty-four gliders were coned by searchlights and had to face the terror of anti-aircraft fire with little scope for manoeuvering. Most of those that reached land, smashed into the high stone walls typical of that part of Sicily or up-ended on the rocky ground.

The final reckoning was that of the 2,000 British red-bereted soldiers of the gliderborne force which had set off from North Africa, a pathetically small handful ever reached their objective – the bridge at Ponte Grande.

Similar disasters befell the paratroopers. The fierce winds blew their aircraft off course and when sticks jumped into the dark sky they too were taken by the wind and scattered over a wide area. Of the 5,000 men of the 82nd US Airborne Division only 3,000 could be found. Not one of the airborne troops took their objectives, casualties were 27% in the first forty-eight hours and Eisenhower ordered an immediate cessation of all airborne operations. (Unfortunately this order was forgotten when, later, Arnhem was planned and thousands more airborne troops were lost.)

The seaborne landings fared somewhat better, although many landing craft were lost. For the next thirty-eight days, though, the German army retained the initiative and Allies paid dearly for their gains. It was a very hard slog northwards.

Doing a great job supporting the infantry of 11th Infantry

Brigade of 78 Division then were the twenty-five pounders of
Harry Secombe's regiment of the Royal Artillery, as this writer,
then leading a platoon of the 5th Northamptons under a barrage
through the night towards Bronte, has good reason to remember,
and was most interested to read, in Sir Harry's autobiography[3]
close on fifty years later, what the situation looked like from the
gunners' viewpoint;

> Bronte was a hard nut to crack because it was on the lower slopes
> of Etna's lava fields and there was only one single-way road into
> the town. We had to break down stone walls to get the guns into
> position, and in some cases fired from the road itself. However, on
> the afternoon of 8th August, the infantry of 11th Brigade took the
> town. Incidentally, I found out from Joe Cattermole that Nelson
> had been made the Duke of Bronte, and as far as I was concerned
> he was more than welcome to the place.

This writer felt exactly the same, as he had lost all interest in the
place at five minutes past eight that morning when a burst of
Spandau fire despatched him to the luxury of clean linen hospital
sheets and being entertained by what must have been the most
unusual of all singers to visit a hospital ward. He was about the
height of six pennyworth of coppers, perhaps nine years old and
had a voice like that of Connie Francis. He was, in fact, singing in
Italian, a song she made popular some years later, 'Mamma'.
Someone had brought him in from the street and his fee was paid
in cigarettes and cioccolato.

Eight days later, at six o'clock on the evening of 16 August,
thirty-eight days after the Allies had landed, the forward
companies of the US Third Division, entered Messina. The
Sicilian campaign was over.

By that time, however, the German army had succeeded in
evacuating most of its men and equipment, leaving behind no
more than 6,000 third line soldiers as prisoners and a few
thousand dead. The cost to the Allies of conquering Sicily, was
some thirty thousand men, dead, wounded and missing. That
'soft under-belly of Europe', Churchill had spoken of, had proved
to be 'a tough old gut'.

Two days after the Sicilian campaign finished, Harry Secombe
and other former concert party members, left their military duties
for those of the stage again. The lessons had been learnt,
entertainment kept morale and battle fitness high. Harry's party
were off to a flying start. They toured units in their three-ton
truck on the side of which was painted: 'The Sicily Billies – Lava
Come Back to Me'. The troops really appreciated the shows given

from the back of the truck and with headlights for spotlights. 'They laughed and applauded our efforts as if we had been a West End Revue company,' recalled Sir Harry. 'Sometimes the audience would contain local peasants who sat mystified throughout, and would only laugh when Lieutenant Bracken came on to do his serious monologue.'[4]

That short breather between battles for Harry Secombe's concert party came to an end on 16 September when his 78 Division and other Allied forces took up their arms again and began the long hard haul up the boot of Italy. It would seem to be an endless slog forward against desperate German resistance. Each river line or mountain ridge, captured at appalling cost. The young and the brave of more than a dozen Allied nations were to die in that campaign and the wounded filled casualty clearing stations and hospital beds from Catania in Sicily to Bologna in the north of Italy.

It was to those casualties that showbusiness folk had to perform. And that was not easy. Those who visited for a second time went with understandable trepidation. They had come to pain-racked men with shattered limbs, men with splintered jaws and formless faces, other young men with features newly moulded with fear, despair and uncertainty. These pitiful sights appalled even the most hardened of professional entertainers, men who had served in the First World War. What could they give to such men in their audiences?

Some entertainers just could not face it. Even a stalwart like Marlene Dietrich, eventually asked to be taken off hospital duties. She confessed:

I'm too tender hearted. It's only with difficulty that I can keep back my tears, and the wounded notice that immediately. I've too much respect for soldiers to tell them fairy tales such as 'The war will soon be over,' or 'You're not as seriously wounded as it seems.' I can't endure the pain in the eyes of the bedridden, the despair in their voices, their frail arms round my neck.[5]

It took a special kind of person to cope, people of the calibre of Bob Hope, for example. But even he had to find a special way of dealing with such unnerving situations in hospitals. He learnt that what those troops appreciated most was not sympathy but jokes that made fun of their plight and the dismal circumstances in which they found themselves. It was a technique which he varied by taking the trouble to find out something before each show, about the particular circumstances of the men in the hospitals and of the battles in which they had been wounded; preparation, as always, the mark of a true professional.

Fortified in this way and by his own natural ebullient personality, he went into hospitals and casualty clearing stations – anywhere in fact where there were wounded men needing cheering. Several times on his tours of forward units he came under shell and machine-gun fire. From fox-holes to burns wards, before audiences from two to two thousand, reports tell how he raised the hopes and morale of servicemen and women throughout the world. His cheerful, off-beat, self-deprecating technique with affectionate insults, earned him laughs and appreciation from those in hospital who had given and lost so much.

Another professional who coped so well with the difficulties of entertaining badly wounded men, was movie star Mickey Rooney,[6] remembered then mostly for his teenage roles in the Andy Hardy films. Rooney, an accomplished musician as well as actor, invented a new type of wartime entertainment – the jeep show. Instead of one large show touring the theatre of operations, the Special Services group was split into twenty jeep shows comprising three or four artistes in each jeep, one of which towed a trailer holding stage and amplification equipment. They would breeze into a hospital, do their show and breeze out again.

The amateurs of the unit concert parties had more difficulties with their hospital visits. Harry Finchley,[7] a former journalist who had taken comedy roles in local amateur dramatics before the war, recalled to the writer in graphic detail, what it was like for him when he visited the 65th British General Hospital in Naples.

You can imagine how I felt, walking down a hospital corridor behind a briskly stepping nurse, rehearsing in my mind the patter, and the jokes I was going to tell, and the cheery songs I was going to sing to a bunch of soldiers in bed. Then I walked into the ward and got the shock of my life. I shall never forget that moment; the sights I saw have lived with me ever since.

There were two rows of beds, about fifty on each side of the long ward which had windows looking out onto a picturesque Italian countryside, craggy hills with villages perched on top. Some of the men were propped up on pillows, some in plaster of Paris, their limbs strung up on pulleys, many of them had tubing strapped to their wrists and stretching up to a saline drip bottle hanging on a wall-hook above head height.

Some men had terrible facial burns. There was a tank crew lying in beds, side by side, their faces blotched by bluish fragments of metal and explosives blasted beneath their skin. Nurses padded softly from one man to the next, noting pulses and signs of post operative shock, reassuring men calling out in their dreams.

Before we even started our show, a surgeon came clumping into the ward in his wellingtons, flowing gown and tight skull cap. He sat down on the sister's table, looking worn out and drawn. He did not speak but just shook his head.

Further down the ward one man was crying quietly, partly propped up, whilst a visiting soldier, struggling with his own emotions, pressed gently on the man's arm, trying to bring comfort. Then I suddenly felt so completely out of place, and that I should not really be there. Here men were dying and I wondered what they must be thinking, knowing they were going to die a long way from home. I looked at the others, they were all such young lads really, barely out of their teens but yet somehow looking much older than their years, faces lined, mouths tight drawn. They had known horror, the bitter sorrow of losing pals they had joked with and drunk pints with back in the Blighty that now seemed so far away and long ago. Here were the lucky ones who had survived battles which had left so many of their unit dead. For them now, true, the war was over, they were at least safe lying in freshly laundered sheets, professionally mitred at the corners.

Men not in pain were waiting patiently for a show to begin. On some of their locker tops there was a bottle of NAAFI beer and a glass. All my confidence had left me and I did not know if I could do a turn or not.

Perhaps it was then I remembered a snatch of a conversation I had heard earlier that week. An old Scottish trouper was drinking at a table near to us in an Italian bar … 'You've just gotta clear your mind … yer there to do a job … be like a professional. You canna do anything but take a deep breath and begin.' Fortunately for me on that day, I wasn't the one who had to start. There was a rumble behind me, a piano was wheeled in and the first chords tinkled out, to lead in Judy Ray, singing 'South of the Border'. She brought to it all the nostalgia that troops liked with their songs, it was a tune from their teens. And then with hardly a pause, she switched to other ballads, 'The Rose of Tralee', 'We'll gather Lilacs', 'A Nightingale Sang in Berkley Square' and, of course, 'The White Cliffs of Dover'.

The patients clapped and whistled and then cried out for more. But with those calls there was another more insistent one, for a particular song which somehow meant more to them, a song which came over more movingly in German and Italian than in the trite English version – 'Lili Marlene'. When she had finished they clapped again and then called for Taffy to sing it.

Shyly, Taffy stood up from his bed. Both his short arms were heavily bandaged. He said something to the lad in the next bed who reached into a locker, pulled out Taffy's wallet, and withdrew from it a sheet of paper, folded many times. A young nurse stepped forward, spread the sheet of paper and propped it up on top of the drugs trolley. Taffy smiled, nodded to the pianist who ran his fingers expertly along the keyboard, finishing with an emphatic chord giving Taffy the starting note. Then the ward was filled with a marvellous tenor voice which took me by surprise. He was singing in Italian:

> Tutte le sere sotto quel fanal
> Presso la caserma tu stavo ad aspettar
> Anche stasera aspettero e tuto il mondo scordero
> A te Lili Marlen
> A te Lili Marlen

Not a sound came from the listeners as Taffy went through four verses and then, as he started the fifth, his eyes closed and tears welled from beneath the lids as he almost whispered the words of the last verse:

> Se chuido gli ochi il viso tuo m'appar
> Come quelle sera nel cerchio del fanal
> Forse domani piangerai ma dopo tu sorriderai
> A chi Lili Marlen
> A chi Lili Marlen

Taffy was no longer looking at the words, he was looking at his sweetheart in Sicily who had once taught them to him. And he was just wondering ...

When he'd finished I picked up the carefully typed paper and was about to pass it to him when I remembered he had no hands. 'You keep it,' he said. 'I can see all the words in my head.' I looked at the name written so immaculately under the song, 'Ti amo tanto, sei la cosa piu bella che io abbia, Rosetta.'

Once that song was behind us, the rest of the programme flowed smoothly and quietly towards its end. We bade everyone goodnight and God Bless and without talking amongst ourselves walked out of the hospital and into the truck taking us back to the Reinforcement depot on the hill above Naples. Before we got there, we stopped, as if by some unspoken agreement, at a bar we sometimes patronised. There I gulped down a drink that I had never touched before and never tasted since, a large Bols Cognac mixed with Martini Vermouth, straight ...

The emotional stress of performing in front of severely wounded soldiers, which had made such an impression upon Harry Finchley, that he could recall so vividly nearly half a century later, was definitely more than many artistes could take. They even preferred to be nearer the front, risking their own lives. Joyce Grenfell, for example, the lantern-jawed comedienne who had already made her mark in the London theatre world by 1939 and who was to devote most of the war years to entertaining the troops, sometimes wondered if ENSA performers were doing more harm than good when they visited wards with very sick and maimed men. She recalled[8] how, on one occasion, whilst she and others were playing and singing, the ward sister was doing the dressings, nurses feeding patients with tubes and calming those in distress. And at the same time as the medication and entertaining was in progress, orderlies were bringing men in from operating theatres, and others, bandaged and bleeding straight from the line.

> About half the ward was too ill to listen or care; the others lay back and took it in with their eyes. One patient, whose injuries forced him to lie on his stomach had difficulty in turning his head far enough to see her, so he called out and asked if she would be kind enough to move further back so that he could at least peer at her with the one eye that was free.

This sort of thing knocked the stuffing out of Joyce Grenfell who, after one harrowing visit wrote in her diary:

> Oh God, the sights I've seen today. We haven't touched the war till today. Bed after bed filled with mutilated men, heads, faces, bodies. It's the most inhuman, ghastly, bloody hellish thing in the world. I couldn't think or work or even feel in the end. It was quite numbing.

When she visited the burns unit and the ward for head injuries in the same 65th British General Hospital, she was terribly upset.

> We did three shows, three of the most extraordinary I ever hope to do. A blinded Scotch boy called Dan, still dazed by his wounds was in an awful mood of gaiety. I was asked by a baby soldier from Devon if I would sing a song about a mother and all I wanted to do was take the lad in my arms there and then and hand him over to his mother he was longing for.

Somehow though she found her voice and sang for him.

Film stars, Anna Neagle, famous then for her portrayal of Nurse Edith Cavell, Bebe Daniels and Ben Lyon were left with exactly the same feelings after their visit to the Queen Victoria Hospital, East Grinstead, where plastic surgeon, Archie McIndoe and his team, remade the faces, the eyelids, noses and ears; the fingers, feet and limbs of airmen and soldiers who had been 'fried' in blazing aircraft, tanks and gun positions. 'I know we all felt completely inadequate, giving a light-hearted performance for these mainly young men,' Anne Neagle wrote later.[9]

At the beginning of World War Two it was thought that the best thing to do with such badly burnt men was to tuck them away in some secluded country mansion where they would never be seen again and would be spared having to face the real world. It seemed kinder to protect these men from the public gaze, for it was believed too that the sight of such men would depress general morale of servicemen and women and civilians alike. But Sir Archibald Hector McIndoe and his team had other ideas. They took the mutilated casualties of the war into Ward Three, a small, brown, army wooden hut at the back of the main hospital building. There it was that McIndoe's operating theatre – his Maxillo Facial Unit – worked wonders.

Even though artistes were warned and prepared for unnerving sights, they still found such hospital visits an ordeal.

The blasé and versatile Noel Coward, 'playboy of the West End World' who was said to be the 'Jack of all trades and master of them all', was at a loss when it came to entertaining badly wounded men in hospitals. But, this man, who would one day leave behind him over fifty plays, twenty-five films, hundreds of songs, a ballet, two autobiographies, several volumes of short stories and countless poems, sketches and paintings, was determined not to be beaten by the emotions aroused by hospital visits.

Ironically, Coward, who played the stiff upper-lipped Royal Navy ship's captain in the film *In Which We Serve* found his own lower lip quivering like that of a schoolboy about to be caned, whenever he visited the critically injured. But he fought back his emotions and discovered the trick was to appear unaware of the grotesque sights and the dreadful smell of gangrenous wounds. Sometimes he sang but sometimes he would just walk round the ward talking to the men as they lay in their beds.[10]

There was, however, another difficulty that showbiz folk had to contend with sometimes when they visited hospitals – the uncooperative attitude, even antipathy, of some senior medical officers and matrons, and it takes little imagination to appreciate just how off-putting this problem could be, when, all in good faith, these performers arrived at a hospital or convalescent depot.

Noel Coward recalled how he was received discourteously by a bored medical corps colonel and a matron stifling a yawn, so he just set off touring the wards chatting to patients. He noted later in his diary:

The men of course were fine. I shook hands and talked to about five hundred of them. They were pleased to see me and I was pleased to see them. It is a moving and inspiring lesson to see the courage with which our countrymen face the suffering and indignities of being bed-ridden. I was profoundly glad I went.

Glad, perhaps, but very annoyed too. At the end of his handshaking marathon, he asked if he could wash his hands before tea. 'I was hot and sticky having shaken hands with all sorts and kinds of malarial cases, paratyphoids, dysenteries, diphtherias etcetera, as well as the wounded, whereupon I was shown into an outside lavatory where there was only cold water, a damp and filthy roller towel and no soap at all.'

All this, however, did not put him off and he continued to visit hospitals, though there were other problems too, hazards which others had encountered. For example, when he once stopped by the bedside of a cheerful little man who was sitting up in bed singing quietly to himself, he made the mistake of asking what had brought the man into hospital. The soldier cheerfully explained that a mine had exploded at his feet, and as a result, both his legs, right up to the top of his thighs, were just charred flesh. All the lower part of his body was under a sort of frame, like a tent, but suddenly, whilst they were talking, the soldier whipped the sheet back completely and said 'Look!'

Coward noted: 'He showed his legs with great pride. They had been painted with Gentian Violet which had coagulated in places and made the hanging fragments of flesh look like obscene purple grapes. The stink was awful but I have never seen a man more cheerful. He came from the North of England and said he was doing "right champion".'

In another bed, a soldier was about to have a blood tranfusion and was 'bright green at the thought of having it done' so Coward popped round to the other side of the bed and engaged the man in conversation until the incision was made and the contrivance worked properly.

There was more to hospital visits than anyone could imagine.

A typical piece of cockney humour was encountered by Coward at another bedside. A chipper little man who had been shot full of shrapnel and machine gun bullets was very chatty. 'I asked him,' said Coward, 'what he thought of Sicily and he said: "The Germans were all right and the Eyeties were all right too, but the mosquitoes were bloody awful!"'

Nearly all the entertainers, professional and amateur, were impressed with the behaviour and courage of servicemen and women. Strangely perhaps, those fit and healthy peformers were left with a feeling not so much of pity for these men but rather of admiration. As Coward wrote in his diary, 'One can privately, very privately, allow oneself a little personal compassion for their broken bodies, but their spirit is clear and high above pity. They transcend their sufferings and their surroundings and all the violence and horror they have endured, with indescribable dignity and grace.'

Dr Ray James,[11] now a veterinary surgeon in Victoria, Australia, had a similarly moving experience in Colombo.

> It made such an impression that I have never forgotten it. Our ship's concert party was asked to put on a show in a Military Hospital in Colombo which was full of former Japanese prisoners of war. They were all too weak to stand and were in a terribly emaciated condition and suffering from dehydration as well. These poor chaps were wheeled into the ward on beds which often had an intra-venous drip apparatus attached. They made an effort to be cheerful but it looked as though many of them would never live to reach home. What courage!

Naomi Jacob, who was the public relations officer for ENSA, was faced with a totally different situation, pathetic and yet amusing in an odd sort of way, when she visited one of those little known units for soldiers who needed to see, what they called, 'the trick cyclist'.[12] These were medical units for cases coming under the category of NYDN – Not Yet Diagnosed Neurosis. One of the best kept secrets of the Second World War was the establishment of psychiatric hospitals in remote parts of Britain for the treatment of men who showed signs of combat fatigue. By the end of the war there were eighteen special hospitals for the treatment of disturbed neurosis, five centres for mild neurosis, and four psychiatric centres and thirteen NYDN centres. Once a unit medical officer thought a man would respond to treatment and would fight again, he would refer him to a neuropsychiatric specialist. Some of these sailors, soldiers, and airmen were in a pitiful state. Many had a facial tic; they were nervous and hesitant when they talked even about ordinary matters. One minute they would be acting quite normally and the next they would be jumping about and starting an argument over nothing at all.

It was one of these psychiatric hospitals that the ENSA Public Relations Officer, Naomi Jacob visited to see if the right kind of entertainment was being provided. It was situated well away from all other units, south east of the ancient city of Perugia, where, legends have it, miracles had happened. St Francis apparently was once so tempted to sin that he stripped himself naked and flung himself into a prickly thorn bush to keep his flesh under control. The bush, so the legend has it, transformed itself into a thornless rose tree.

Naomi wondered what sort of miracles she might find there. Her notes of the visit make interesting reading:

> The patients looked fit and well to me. I asked one man, 'What's the matter with you?'
>
> He said, 'Me, Mam, me? I'm bomb 'appy.'
>
> 'What does it feel like to be bomb happy?' I said.
>
> 'Feel like? Well … feel like…? it feels like bein' bomb 'appy.'
>
> Another man said, 'I'm what they call a psy-clog-ical case, Ma'am.'
>
> 'I said. 'What does it feel like?'
>
> 'I dunno, carn't really say. Kind of overish, if you get what I mean. Times when yer don't know if yer comin' or goin'. Oh, it's a funny business. Still, this is a nice place to be ill in, if you have to be ill.'

It was indeed a nice place. And they got their fair share of entertainment eventually, to help them back to fitness so that they could perhaps go back to their units and get killed.

Entertainers never quite knew what to expect when they got requests for visits. Maxine Andrews, of the famous singing trio, 'The Andrews Sisters' has never forgotten one of those nerve shattering hospital visits, when the trio had to summon up all the courage they could muster. They were asked to visit Oak Knoll Hospital where the badly wounded from the Solomon Islands battles were brought. It was ghastly, she recalled:[13]

> They were known as basket cases. We were working at the Golden Gate theatre in San Francisco when a Red Cross nurse asked us if we would come out to the hospital to do a show. She kept us outside the ward for a while. She said it would be something different from whatever we'd seen. The most important thing was not to break down. The last thing the boys needed was tears.

At last, the nurse ushered them into the ward. It was very very quiet. The nursing sister announced that the Andrew Sisters had come to sing some of their favourite songs. There was not any applause at all. The nurse then gently pressed the girls forward into the centre of the ward, a long ward with beds in front of them and behind. Finally the girls looked at the patients lying there.

The sight was terrible. We saw boys with no arms or legs, with half faces. The three of us held on to each other, because we were afraid we were going to faint. The terrible thing was to try and hold back the tears.

It was pathetic to see those young boys listening to one of our well-known songs about a soldier leaving for overseas service, asking his girl to be faithful:

> Don't sit under the apple tree with anyone else but me,
> Anyone else but me, no,no,no.
> Don't sit under the apple tree with anyone else but me,
> Till I come marching home.

One thing was for sure; those men listening would never be marching home. For forty minutes, those girls sang the hit tunes of those days – 'The Boogie woogie bugle boy of Company C', 'Rum and Coca-Cola', 'I'll be with you in Apple Blossom Time' and 'Oh Johnny, Oh Johnny, how you can love'. All of these were difficult songs to be singing to men who knew they could never again cuddle a girl.

'One of the boys, all clothed in bandages, started to cry. He was crying throughout the numbers,' Maxine recalled. He cried until one of the lads nearby called out to Maxine, 'Don't pay any attention to him, he's only dreaming about his girlfriend.'

That afternoon, they went from ward to ward, singing in the way that had brought them fame and pretending the audience was no different from normal. Just as they were thinking the emotional ordeal was over, a male nurse came over to them, and hesitantly made a special request. He said he had a young patient who could not be with the others in the ward yet would love to hear them sing. Would they please sing something soft, nice and easy. The request seemed to be couched in such a way as to suggest that here was something really different. They were led down a long corridor and eventually stopped in front of a door that two male nurses were guarding. The male nurse ushered them inside, turned and walked away, closing the door firmly behind him. The girls were now alone. They were in a padded cell!

Crouched in one corner of the room was a figure, his face close to the wall. The girls looked at one another, quietly mouthed one word, 'apple' and started to sing 'I'll be with you in apple blossom time'. When they were about half-way through the song they heard a strange noise, a discordant one which got louder and louder. The hunched figure was humming. They got to the end of the song, took a couple of deep breaths and started again, right from the beginning. And they just went on and on, repeating the same song over and over again. At last the figure sat up and faced the Andrews Sisters. But it was an unnerving sight, said Maxine. 'His eyes were looking at us, but he wasn't seeing us. He was lost in another world. He was just humming and humming. He was so handsome and young.'

For a few precious moments, the Andrews Sisters had made a handful of young lads forget the awful limbless plight into which they had been plunged. But there was a strange and happier ending to Maxine's experience that afternoon.

It happened a few months later when the Andrews Sisters were again performing at the Golden Gate theatre in San Francisco. The uniformed attendant from the Stage Door came to their dressing room to say there was a visitor outside, and without waiting to see if the girls were ready to receive him, he ushered in a serviceman. On his back was another serviceman with no arms and legs. It was one of the patients who had heard the girls singing in Oak Knoll Hospital. On this day though, he had on his artificial arms. He said, 'I never asked you for your autograph on that day because I said that one day I was going to give you mine.' He leant over on the dressing table and carefully signed his name. It was Ted.

What a magnificent way of saying, 'Thank you.'

This though, was the real face, the real picture of war, which the public never saw at the cinema.

6

Hollywood Waves the Flag

The battle seemed endless. Shrieks of the wounded mingled with the hoarse shouts of the fighters – a pitifully small force of US marines holding their ground against wave after wave of Japanese assault troops attacking with fanatical intensity.

The ground rocked and quaked with explosions, black plumes of smoke leapt up all around into a cloudless blue sky as mortars searched the folds of the ground in which the leathernecks had hastily dug their shallow weapon pits. In one of the foremost of these a young lad, his face smeared with sweat, blood, and dirt, snuggled more closely to the butt of his light machine-gun and peered into the smoke screen covering the beach. He waited a second or two as the hordes of Japs came crowding into his sights. Gently he squeezed the trigger. Bodies littered the sandy scrub between the smoke and the fox holes. But on came another wave, stumbling forward, appearing from the fog of battle like images in a photographic developing tray. The marine again squeezed his trigger, and gusts of animal rage swept through his body.

Now, amidst the cracking bullets and exploding mortar shells, a young major, bronzed and fine-looking, ran from one fox hole to another, rallying and encouraging his men, deliberately exposing himself to enemy fire, bolstering morale.

There was no respite. On and on the battle raged.

In the US major's weapon-pit a thin marine sat with earphones on, by his wireless, listening to a constant crackle of voices from the ether. Suddenly he sat up and tugged at his officer's jacket. 'Sir,' he shouted hoarsely. 'Sir, the Jap colonel's calling for our surrender.'

The grim faced, marine major turned to him, his lip curling disdainfully and said: 'Tell him to come and get us!'

The meanest gangster in film history, James Cagney, the cornered psychotic killer in *Public Enemy*, could not have said it better.

Well, such a tough-guy cast as Brian Donlevy, Robert Preston, MacDonald Carey and William Bendix battling against the little yellow men on Wake Island would never surrender either. Would they?

When the film *Wake Island*[1] was shown at the Quantico Marine Base in 1942, two thousand marines stood and cheered it with thunderous applause.

Here was propaganda working so efficiently, so effectively, through a cultural phenomenon, motivating an audience conditioned from an early age to respond positively to emotive words and scenes on the silver screen. Service and civilian audiences throughout America thought *Wake Island* was a great film. *The New York Herald Tribune*[2] said in its review: 'Brian Donlevy is utterly right as the commanding major, Robert Preston and William Bendix contribute an undercurrent of captivating comedy as a couple of tough Marine pals. MacDonald Carey's portrait of a grief stricken, vengeful flyer is entirely convincing.'

But was it real? Or was it fantasy?

Newsweek, at that time, thought it was real enough, saying, 'Although the United States has been at war for nine months, *Wake Island* is Hollywood's first intelligent, honest, and completely successful attempt to dramatize the deeds of an American force on a fighting front.'[3]

A first attempt no doubt it was. But it was still little more than a flag-waver. And the press was prepared to go along with the deception. It was really just another in a spate of films made in those days glamourizing war and not showing the reality at all. Indeed, the reality then was far too shocking for the public to accept. For during that first year at war America had suffered one defeat after another. On 27 December 1941, Wake Island had fallen, in January '42 the Japanese had laid siege to Bataan and in February General MacArthur had fled from the Philippines to Australia. In March 1942, the Adaman Islands were lost and in April, Bataan surrendered. For the American public there seemed no end to disasters.

Now, more than at any other time in the year, American morale was at a very low ebb and the last thing the public needed were films showing what war was really like. And so films were produced which were more of fantasy than of fact. 'Flag-wavers', as they came to be called. Films to bring a surge of pride to a patriotic breast. The heroics were emphasized. Marines fought and died in the finest traditions of their indomitable corps. But the dead and the mutilated were never realistically shown.

Instead, the old formula, so successful in Wild West films, was used again. Everyone knew who the good guys were and who were the baddies. The issues were clear cut and the hopes and fears of the films' characters mirrored those of the nation as a whole.

The film makers, however, were not entirely altruistic in their tasks. The bottom line was still the same then as it is today – profit. And there is no getting away from the fact that those flag-waving films were highly profitable – no matter how corny they might appear today. Films like *Guadalcanal Diary*, laying stress upon how a cross section of US social types could act together as a team without losing their own individuality, made a lot of money, perverting the truth by showing a sanitized version of the war bereft of all its horrors. The public could quite happily swallow lines like those of Preston Foster as the dutiful, self-sacrificing chaplain there on Guadalcanal who, when told that he should not go in with the first wave, asked, 'Why not? That's when I'll be needed most.'

There was even more corn with *Flying Tigers* where John Wayne, the archetypal American hero, then in his late thirties and already rejected for military service on health grounds, is leading a gallant air squadron in China. Almost as bad, and certainly most unpopular with the British was the 1943 film *Sahara* where Humphrey Bogart (also rejected for military service) almost single-handedly defeats the German army in the western desert of Libya. No mention is made of the fact that almost all the fighting in that western desert was being done by British and Commonwealth troops.

In that same year of 1943, MGM released its morale-boosting film *Bataan*, a fictional version of a handful of brave men fighting to the death to delay the Japanese offensive in the Philippine peninsular so that the retreating American forces could make good their escape.

Once again this was a film full of ethnic stereotypes with whom the audience could readily identify. As producer Dore Schary pointed out:

> The stereotype always appears in war pictures. Every war picture we made had a Jew, an Italian, a Pole, a WASP. (White Anglo-Saxon protestant). But not always a Black man, because blacks weren't integrated in the Army at that time. I put one in *Bataan*, just put one in, that's all. I said 'To hell with it, we're going to have one Black.' We got a lot of letters from people complaining.[4]

Blatant flag-wavers though those films were, they certainly played a vital part in the total war effort for without doubt they did boost morale of civilian and servicemen alike. Those marines in Quantico Marine base who stood and cheered were not alone. They were cheering films like that from Cairo to Casablanca and Sierra Leone to Scarborough.

So important were such films seen to be that both the United States and Britain formed special units to show films. Indeed, when the American Air Force opened a new base Huckstep, at Heliopolis, on the outskirts of Cairo, where civilian cinemas were already operating, high priority was given in the planning of the base to the building of a cinema. Arthur Clements, then stationed at the RAF's Middle East Telecommunications Centre, recalled how amazed troops were when they saw what had been built:

> It was such a plush cinema that it compared most favourably with those in London such as the Empire in Leicester Square. It was carpeted and the decor was magnificent, the seats were of the best quality upholstery and it was equipped with the very latest in projection equipment. It lacked for nothing. They even had smart usherettes with torches to show patrons to their seats.[5]

It was at this time that a series of films made by US film director Frank Capra between 1942 and 1943 was released. They appeared under the generic title of *Why We Fight* and were made expressly for showing to troops and not for general release. The American public was not yet ready to accept the realism of war. Or so it was believed.

Consequently there was an abundance of films, the documentary, the training, and a mass of entertainment films available for boosting the morale of troops though not all units were so lavishly catered for with cinemas like that at Huckstep, Cairo.

Hugh Berry,[6] of 127 Squadron RAF, stationed at Alexandria, was given only a three-ton truck and two 35 mm projectors, when, in the summer of 1942, shortly before the battle of El Alamein, he was caught up in the drive to show films to troops in the forward areas. Apparently his documents had shown that in civil life he had been a cinema projectionist and he was hastily detached from his squadron and loaned to the cinema section of ENSA where his professional skills would be of much greater use to the war effort. Film shows now were seen to be important for sustaining the right attitudes within the fighting units.

He reported to ENSA headquarters at Cairo where he found a number of other former cinema projectionists had been gathered to man five mobile cinemas which were to go forward into the Western Desert to show films to both the Army and the RAF. He recalled how exciting and rewarding his new life was to be:

I was still getting my RAF pay which would be sent home to my parents and in addition I was given a weekly allowance of twenty-five shillings. This was more than enough to satisfy our immediate requirements in those days.

We had a few days instruction, were sent out to try out our skills on local units and then we were despatched in pairs to make our own way to units 'up the blue' in the desert. It was a great life, we thought, as a change from our days of squadron duty. What pleased us particularly was that we were entirely self-contained, had our own camp beds and drew rations from any unit at which we were playing.

By now the great El Alamein battle was raging and I often felt that we were near enough for Jerry to be watching the films through his own field glasses from the back of the screen!

Taffy Davies, the driver and also a former projectionist, and I would normally go out for two weeks with a programme playing 13 nights out of 14 to different units. On the 14th day we reported back to Rear Air Headquarters wherever they happened to be, took off the old programme, picked up the new, and had a day's rest.

The padre would then give us a routing for the next two weeks. Sometimes these units would be quite accessible near the coast road but at other times we had to put the truck into four-wheel drive and travel miles into the barren desert. It was not all beer and skittles but there we were like a couple of civilians, our own bosses and doing a job we knew.

And so we drove westwards following close behind the Eighth Army and Desert Airforce as they gradually pushed the Germans away from Egypt until we reached Benghazi, where we narrowly escaped disaster.

We had just finished showing a film to a whole wing of about two thousand airmen when German dive bombers arrived and bombed the area intensively. Fortunately the film show had just finished and troops had begun to disperse. If those bombers had arrived a few minutes earlier Jerry would have caught the whole two thousand gathered together in one place.

Being on our own and having to find units in the forward area, we were never quite sure just where exactly the enemy positions might be, especially when the front was so fluid. On one occasion we had been driving along and stopped to brew up tea and the water was just beginning to simmer when we were fired on by an unseen German or Italian sniper. We did not stop for the tea.

Driving a truck across the desert could be a hazardous business; there were unmarked minefields that sometimes caught the first truck in. Also there was always the possibility of having Stuka dive bombers screaming down out of the sun upon a lone truck or convoy. When this happened there was no time for talking, simply a drill to be followed immediately, as Driver Roberts recalled:

> As soon as we realised we were being attacked, we pushed the lorry out of gear, opened the door, punched the passenger so that he rolled out into the sand, grabbed one's rifle and ammunition and hurled oneself away from the still moving lorry. We became quite adept at leaving a lorry in the shortest possible time.
>
> Driving across the desert terrain was dangerous enough merely due to the natural hazards. Roads were treacherous, often being little more than rocky tracks winding their way up precipitous escarpments. Sand played the devil with working parts, and any attempts to repair a broken down truck usually ended with more sand being included in the reassembled parts. A truck would rarely stand up to more than three months' desert work. After that, most vehicles had to be overhauled and refitted.

Such were the day-to-day difficulties with which Hugh Berry, Taffy Davies and Jack Kay had to cope as they kept up with the Eighth Army's troops until they eventually arrived in Tunisia's Cape Bon area where Von Arnim's German Africa Korps was penned. 'This cape was illuminated at night by flares to stop the Germans escaping by sea under cover of darkness, and our cinema was in a direct line with this operation. I'm afraid I was more concerned with what was going on there than what was going on on the screen,' recalled Hugh.

Not all cinematographers were as well equipped as Hugh Berry though. David Clark,[7] then stationed with the RAF in Algiers, remembered one projectionist chatting to an American in a bar there one night and bemoaning the fact that his projectors were so poor. To his surprise he heard the American say: 'That's no problem. I'll hitch a lift to the States this week and bring you back a new outfit.' Bar talk? No, typical American generosity which was extended to so many British and Allied officers in wartime. Five days later the American returned with a completely new outfit, as promised.

Cinema shows were certainly given surprising priority.

It was not only in the actual theatres of operations though that the message about films was being received by unit commanders. Even the smallest units in remote parts of Britain were about to set up their own cinemas, one way or another, as Freddie Smith found. He was surprised one morning to be summoned to the commanding officer's office. What had he done wrong, he wondered. The CO came directly to the point as Freddie Smith now recalls:[8]

'Smith,' he said, 'I've been looking through your records and I see you've been in cinema work most of your life since leaving school.' Well, I had. I started when I was sixteen and some of the happiest years that I've spent were in the cinema, particularly at that place the 'Outwood Empire', superb manager, taught me so much, great friend.

The CO then said to me: 'Having seen this in your documents I wondered what you could do for us in the cinema line. Could you put on film shows for us? We need someone now.' So I told him that I had a full set of thirty-five millimetre cinema equipment back at home, which I had set up in the cellar of my mother's house. In the early days, this machine had been used only for silent films and I had converted it for sound, again due to the generosity of the cinema manager, and actually built arc lamps, for it as well. It used to knock hell out of my mother's electricity bills. Anyway, the CO said, 'Are you prepared to bring it up here and get it set up?' I said I would but it would take some time to get it cased and transported back to camp. He said he would give me three days. I agreed but I quizzed him again, saying that it was a bit dodgy bringing all the stuff up because I could be posted the next day. He didn't seem to think this was a problem for he said he would take it up with headquarters and let me know. It wasn't long before he told me to pack up and go for the equipment. Obviously, higher authority thought films for even this fifty-strong unit were important.

I dashed off home, made packing cases, dismantled the machinery, packed it and brought it back to camp all in the three days. We installed it in a small empty building which had previously housed a little-used billiards table. Two or three willing lads helped me to set up all the gear. We did one or two naughty things like breaking in to the 'Works and Bricks' compound and 'spiriting' away a hut in the hope that they would not notice it being missing and from the equipment section we got the loan of three sheets – airmen did not have sheets, only officers and WAAFs – we sewed them together and this became our screen. We 'found' a multitude of chairs from all over the place and we were almost ready. Films were no problem. They were ready and waiting for us from ENSA and the Army film unit.

We had only two shows a week, Thursday afternoon and Thursday evening so as to cover both watches. Shortly after we opened I was standing outside the make-shift cinema when I saw coming up the hill towards the camp, droves of civilians. What on earth was this I thought? What ae they coming for?

They were coming to our cinema.

This threw me into a panic. Fortunately the CO was there and he said that we were to let them in seeing as they had walked all the way up the hill from the town and the cinema was outside the barbed wire anyway.

Throughout that summer the civilians and soldiers had a great time at our little cinema. It was like 'Cinema Paradiso', so cosy and friendly but one night we had a violent thunderstorm and, as I've already said, we did have arc lamps on this old machine and they were run from a small transformer set above one of the cinema buildings in an alcove. You could see this thing glowing red at times when we changed over but then it settled down to a gentle slumber generating a steady heat but on this particular night I think it must have been struck by lightning or something for the thing took off and exploded. We had just got to the part of the thriller when all was to be revealed about who was the murderer. And so, by the light of hurricane lamps, which was our only standby lighting, I had to go out to the front, before all the crowd and explain what had happened, 'who done it'!⁹

Mixed amongst the 'who done it' films and the musicals being shown to troops and civilians then, were plenty of morale boosters portraying clean cut heroes fighting as one for a common cause. The best example of this genre is, without doubt, *In Which We Serve*. It was made in 1941, shortly after Lord Louis Mountbatten and his great friend, Noel Coward had talked long into the night about the possibility of making a film about Mountbatten's destroyer, HMS *Kelly* which had just been sunk in the Battle of Crete with the loss of nine officers and 121 men.

Mountbatten, who was never averse to publicity, persuaded the Royal Navy and the Ministry of Information to collaborate in the making of the film, based on the *Kelly* with its name changed to *Torrin*. Essentially the film was a biography of the ship from its building, launching and eventual sinking in the Mediterranean. It was yet another film which presented the Allied cause in a most convincing manner. The film opens with the voice of the ship's captain – Noel Coward – saying: 'This is the story of a ship.' But *The New York Times* saw it as more. Their film critic wrote: 'It is more than a story of a ship. It is the story of man's heroic soul and selfless indomitable spirit by which a whole nation endures. The devotion of men to their ship is a subtle symbolization of everything that they are. The ship represents themselves, their families. It is their nation. It is their world.'¹⁰

The reviewer concluded that the film 'is far more than a magnificent war film. It is a stirring testament to men of good will, in whatever age they may have loved, fought and endured'.

That was the way the film was seen then, in the mood of a world at war.

Today the stiff-upper lip ship's captain might be seen quite differently. It is a class-conscious drama told in flashbacks from the sinking of the *Torrin* and concentrates on the musings of three survivors: the ship's captain, (Coward), the chief petty officer (Bernard Miles), and an able seaman (John Mills). An unusual aspect of the film is the recognition of fear portrayed by the teenage coward below decks, the stoker (Richard Attenborough). The sentiments expressed by them now certainly seem dated but they were more than acceptable in wartime Britain and in America.

The public saw the film as one showing national pride shared by the whole country – the civilians and Forces alike – fighting as one in the common cause. The captain of the ship, the officers and the men of the destroyer were behaving as a happy efficient unit in peacetime and in war. Noel Coward played the captain in such an understated way that would be seen as almost laughable today. Nevertheless, the film had a tremendous impact upon morale. Having seen the film, sailors were said to go away more resolved than ever to live up to the example their shipmates had already set them.

The film was a great success commercially too in both Britain and America. The US National Board of Review chose it as the outstanding film of the year.

In retrospect, this 'flag-waver' of a film had its amusing moments, one of which John Mills, playing the able seaman, recalls in his autobiography.[11] When the *Torrin* sank, Mills had to swim to a 'Carley' float whilst the dastardly German dive bombers were coming down strafing the men struggling to keep afloat in the oily sea littered with debris of all kinds. The film effects man had great difficulty in achieving the right picture of bullets hitting the water in the studio tank and of Mills being hit in the arm. In the end he had a flash of inspiration and sent a man to the local chemist's for a few packets of condoms. These they inflated and tied to an air tube beneath the surface of the water. Mills then had to swim along the line which received the blasts of compressed air to explode the condoms, and finally an electric charge was sent down a wire into Mills's arm. This made him realistically jerk and shout in pain before being heaved aboard the float.

Mills later was to claim that he is the only actor ever to have been shot in the arm by a 'French letter'.[11]

One feature all these soul-stirring films had in common was a powerful, moving climax which carried a clear message to the audience. Nothing was left to the imagination. Feelings were carefully manipulated to inspire a patriotic response.

We have, for example, the emotion-charged farewell speech of *Torrin's* captain to the surviving members of his crew on the dockside of Alexandria; and in the even more moving film *Mrs Miniver* – it still stands as a four-kleenex-weepie – the local vicar stands in the ruins of his blitzed church and delivers a rousing sermon. He says: 'This is not only a war of soldiers in uniform. It is a war of the people and it must be fought ... in the heart of every man, woman and child who loves freedom.'

Mrs Miniver, played so well by Greer Garson, stands for every woman, and every mother, protecting her family during the Luftwaffe's blitz on London. The film is a tribute to the lasting traditions of an average British middle-class family and there is no doubt that in everybody's mind it came to symbolize just what the Allies were fighting for – the right to lead a free and civilized life within a tolerant and well-ordered state.

The film begins by showing what life was like before the war with the family concerned with their roses, with the village social events and latest county cricket scores. When war is declared the oldest son joins the RAF, Mr Miniver answers the call to go to Dunkirk to take soldiers of the British Expeditionary Force off beaches, and the intensive bombing of Britain begins. Mrs Miniver, also with stiff upper lip, sits in the air-raid shelter reading *Alice in Wonderland* to her children.

Contemporary audiences were enraptured by the film, and moved also by its subtle propaganda. The value of that alone, said Prime Minister Churchill, was worth a hundred battleships. And President Roosevelt found vicar Henry Wilcoxon's sermon at the end of the film so moving that he ordered thousands of copies to be dropped over occupied Europe.

Later critics have viewed the film as 'a load of absolutely wonderful hokum', but in 1942 it did not matter that the whole thing tended to be spurious for it projected an image of Britain at war which appealed to the American people and it was said that the struggles of the Minivers against all the horrors of war did more to capture the hearts and minds of men and women in the United States than any amount of direct propaganda could have done.

True, it was a 'weepie', but Hollywood saw that this was an ideal time for 'weepies', for as the war went on and more and more men were drafted away from home, the majority of the average cinema audience was inevitably women. It was therefore a time when films for women made economic sense. It became a boom time tor tinsel city. Hollywood film factories turned out films with special appeal for women such as *Rosie the Riveter*, *Swing Shift Maisie*, and a *Journey for Margaret*. Typical of these films directed towards the women in the audience was *The War against Mrs*

Hadley, which dealt with the way the civilian homefront in Washington adjusted to the war. The story featured a pampered society matron who saw no reason why the war should disrupt her lifestyle but found ultimately that what was more important was the defence of democracy itself. Aimed at a different level of society but still essentially a woman's film, was *Tender Comrades* where three women welders who have husbands away at the war, decided to set up home together. One of the trio is Ginger Rogers and it is her husband who is killed in action. The way that the three girls rally round and support each other, is a message which the audience can really take to heart.

But these films have another message for women in wartime. It is that there is no need for them to sit at home and mope whilst their husbands are away. Hard work, even in a factory, can be satisfying and provide opportunities for fun too. *Millions Like Us* showed how two girls working in an aircraft factory could overcome social barriers and find work of national importance to be rewarding in more ways than one.

Now, more than ever before, women were being valued for their potential in the work place and in the Forces too. They were needed and were wooed for their services with films of the mid-war years.

Just before his mysterious death on a flight from Lisbon to London in 1943, film star Leslie Howard made the point strongly in a film he directed himself called, *The Gentle Sex*. Seven girls from a wide range of social backgrounds join the Auxiliary Territorial Service and prove themselves quite capable of doing jobs previously considered for men only. It was a message which, in the interests of the total war effort needed ramming home to both Service chiefs and civilian bosses.

The cinema was now seen as a most effective way of influencing public attitudes.

It is interesting to note how the country could be roused to a common cause and yet at the same time fill the box office tills. By 1943 the film factories were doing this with a formula which had proved most successful with theatres in Britain and America during the First World War – the musical, packed with patriotic songs. One of the first of these manifestly jingoistic films, 'Yankee Doodle Dandy', was in fact set in World War One. This gigantic musical starred James Cagney in the title role of George M. Cohan, patriot, showman supreme and one of America's all-time flag-wavers. The film was full of heart-stirring musical nostalgia, high lighting such songs as 'Over There', and 'Yankee Doodle Dandy'.

So effective was this film that *Time* magazine said: 'The picture goes overboard with an elaborate presentation of the song 'You're a Grand Old Flag'. That, and the restaging of Cohan's presentation of his cocky war song 'Over There' was enough to send audiences straight off to battle.'[12]

These indeed, were the heydays of the musical, and for these spectacular extravaganzas America had no equal. By the end of 1943 forty per cent of all films produced in the US were musicals. Most of them were linked to some particular aspect of the war and engendered the right kind of attitude to the war whether at the front, in a factory or at home.

Another musical using a First World War setting to put a patriotic message over to the public was *For Me and My Gal*. Of the many films of this kind released at the time, this film is memorable because of the unusual plot. It is designed to point out the need for everyone to put the country before personal considerations. Early in the film there is a startling scene in which dancer Gene Kelly slams the lid of a steel trunk down hard upon his hand to break the bones so that he would be unfit for military service. Kelly does not want anything to interfere with his career as an entertainer. It is a difficult role for Gene Kelly, making his film debut with Judy Garland as the star. She, patriotically entertains the troops, singing 'After You're Gone', 'When you wore a Tulip' and 'For Me and My Gal'. As the film progresses there are some moving interludes showing the impact of war on individuals and the way that most people and the entertainment profession in particular, have risen to the occasion, putting the country before personal interests. Towards the end of the film Kelly redeems himself with a heroic act while on duty as a non-combatant.

The same theme of being called up for military service is used in *Private Buckaroo* which is also full of ultra-patriotic songs. But the two extravaganzas to beat them all must be *This is the Army* based on Irving Berlin's stage shows, and *Stage Door Canteen*, a superstar studded tribute to the American Theatre Wing which ran the canteen for servicemen in New York. Ninety per cent of the profits from the film went to the canteen fund. The stars gave their services free, again showing men and women of the armed forces just how much Hollywood admired what they were doing for the country and that they were not forgotten.

In all these musicals one name stands out above all others – that of Betty Grable. She was undoubtedly the most popular and sparkling musical star of the war years. She appeared in *Pin-up Girl*, *College Swing* and *Sweet Rosie O' Grady*. Whenever she was interviewed Grable would always say that she was 'strictly an enlisted man's girl'. And she was reputed to have 'the attraction of the pretty girl behind a Woolworth's counter', a nice girl a soldier could go home to and marry. Her contribution to the war effort was unique for she almost certainly now will hold the title of the most famous pin-up girl in history. Her photograph, in the 'back glancing' pose, was pinned on almost every bulkhead and behind barrack-room locker doors all over the world.

For the record, and equally deserving of mention for their contribution to the total war effort, were those musicals which deliberately ignored the war, such as *Night and Day* and *Rhapsody in Blue*. They served a very useful purpose in providing opportunities for people to escape for a short while the tedium of war. There was a real place in wartime for such escapist films.

It was not until late in the war that film makers stopped escaping from reality, however, and produced films which skipped the false heroics and concentrated on facts, sparing no detail of the real horrors of combat. The finest of these films was *The Story of GI Joe* directed by William Wellman. It depicted the front-line infantryman, how he lived and died miserably. The film was based on the writings of war correspondent, Ernie Pyle, who later lost his own life. It was far and away the least glamorous of all war pictures, and was an honest tribute to the foot-slogging soldier, fighting stubbornly without knowing much about what was happening around him.

Participating in the picture were many ordinary infantrymen of the US Fifth Army and when they saw the picture their verdict was: 'This is it.'

General Eisenhower called the film: 'The greatest war picture ever made.' And *The New York Times* was equally lavish in its endorsement saying: 'It is a tale of men who live and fight together, wanting nothing more than to be back home again.'[13]

Eventually some of those men did get back home. And what did they find? Problems. Difficulties and anxieties in converting to civilian life again. The situation facing returning veterans is vividly portrayed in William Wyler's film, *The Best Years of Our Lives*. The picture deals with three men coming home after fighting; each in his own way will never be the same again. The one with the biggest problem is the young sailor who has lost both his hands. His part is played by Harold Russell whose hands were in fact amputated as a result of injuries received. He played in this one picture only and for it won two Oscars. One for his fine performance and one for bringing 'courage and hope to his fellow veterans'. A decorated Air Corps captain comes home to a sluttish, unfaithful wife and a menial job as 'soda jerk'. The sergeant, who has seen so much violent action, has great difficulty in settling down to a safe humdrum existence.

The film does a good job in showing to relatives and friends of returning veterans that readjustment to peacetime civilian life is not easy. The great merit of the film is that it is tremendously entertaining yet at the same time carries a serious message, which leaves audiences with serious ideas to contemplate.

But this, after all, was what most of those wartime films did so well, wasn't it? In a wide variety of ways they moulded public opinion, marshalled the efforts of the Allied nations and sustained the spirit of men and women of all ranks and creeds in the fight aginst the evil brutality of Nazi Germany and Japan.

Now we can look back upon all those in the American and British film industries and say, unequivocally, that their inimitable contribution to the war effort was of immense value.

7

All Change

Wartime London was feverish, crowded and eager for entertainment. Of all kinds. The whole of the south of England was packed with troops preparing for the Allied invasion of Europe and the bloody battles that would end Hitler's insane gamble to dominate the world.

Assault troops swarmed into the city for one last frenzied fling before being sealed off in their final staging camps. The square mile of London bounded by the American Forces' 'Rainbow Corner', the British Forces' 'Nuffield Centre', the cinemas of Leicester Square and the meeting ground of Trafalgar Square, teemed with khaki and olive drab and all shades of blue. And, without doubt, for most of these fit young men what leave meant was beer, girls, and a good show.

Now new forms of entertainment came to London, and predominant amongst these was sexual titillation.

In those grim years before the autumn of 1942, when there was little good news, London audiences had witnessed a return to the romantic and melodious genre of shows; Offenbach's *Tales of Hoffman* was revived and the return of *The Dancing Years* accorded a tumultuous welcome. Then came more old favourites such as *The Maid of the Mountains* and *Blossom Time* to transport audiences away from the gloom of London. It was almost as if the settings and the haunting melodies of these shows brought back poignant memories of a world that seemed lost for ever. For a couple of hours the audience could relax in the ambience of happier times such as that of old Vienna a century earlier with Richard Tauber rendering some of Schubert's loveliest songs.

But by 1944 the mood of London theatre-goers had changed and so too had the fare being offered. The 'Whitehall Theatre' which had previously housed musical revues was now packing in service and civilian personnel to a completely new form of entertainment – sexual voyeurism. It was catering for those wanting to enjoy sex in a safer way than experiencing it practically with those women waiting on their own stretch of pavement in Soho and Piccadilly, jingling a bunch of keys and inviting lonely servicemen, or war-workers away from home, for a short time in some dingy hotel room.

In the spring and summer of 1944, the chances of a soldier walking down Piccadilly without being accosted by women, were as slim as trying to stroll through Berlin in a British uniform. Not only were there the hardened prostitutes on the game accosting but also the gin-primed teenage 'amateurs' attracted by the cash in the on-leave servicemen's wallets.

Complaints were numerous, and vociferous. US press correspondents cabled lurid stories back home to the States telling of the risks US troops were running. Alarmed, US medical offices issued to all units, posters depicting a skull in a frothy pink hat inviting the kiss of death. Beneath the picture was the warning: 'The easy girl spreads syphylis and gonorrhoea, which unless properly treated may result in blindness, insanity, paralysis and premature death. If you run the risk, get skilled treatment at once.'

For this, 'Blue Cross' prophylactic treatment centres were set up all over London, especially near the high risk areas around Piccadilly.

But more preventive action was demanded by worried US parents and the Allied High Command, anxious about the real risk of casualties from VD depleting their outfits, as they already had seen in Italy.

Somehow off-duty troops would have to be entertained in ways that kept them out of trouble. Two positive measures were put into operation. Firstly, strengthened British and American Military Police street patrols were drafted in to break up soldier-prostitute negotiations and secondly, the laws relating to nudity on stage were relaxed. Freer licence was given to those theatres offering safer-sex experiences through a completely new form of nude show. The most famous of these was at the Whitehall theatre.

The essential feature of the relaxed regulations for these nude shows was that nudity on stage was permissible if it took the form of a tableau representing perhaps a copy of some famous painting, or if it had 'some artistic merit' of its own. With such vague terminology to satisfy the more prudish elements of local government, it was not surprising that the conditions were not always strictly followed.

Even so the acts were still supposed to be 'tasteful' and inoffensive. Producers of such shows were obliged to submit photographs of their intended tableaux to the Lord Chamberlain's office. Newspaper reports suggested that officers regarded this as 'a perk for the job'.

Two regulations however were to be strictly observed on stage: all movement by the nude women was forbidden and there was to be no direct viewing of the pubis. Here again newspapers could not resist satisfying their readers' curiosity by going into the detail of how the area was covered by flesh coloured elastoplast and of the pain incurred in the cause of 'art'.

For some time the Windmill Theatre had been presenting nudity in a variety of ways and some small groups of their company had toured the provinces. But it was not until Phyllis Dixie, 'The Queen of Strippers' came to the Whitehall Theatre in 1944 that nudity became more daring and a tremendous attraction.[1]

The Watch Committee would probably have made more fuss had it not been for pressure from some high government source. As one member of the Lord Chamberlain's office put it so succinctly: 'Viewing is better than doing'.[2]

One now wonders how high would have been the VD casualties amongst the Allied Forces if these outlets had not been available. There is no doubt that they were very well supported. Queues of soldiers formed outside the Whitehall Theatre from two in the afternoon until nine at night in order to see Phyllis and her entourage baring all for their delectation and doing their bit for the war effort.

To give the show a more American appeal, Phyllis Dixie changed the name of her show from 'The Whitehall Graces' to 'The Varga Models'. Varga was the artist who painted the leggy voluptuous women with their ballooning breasts in the US magazine *Esquire*.

However there was one entertainment body which would not give the Phyllis Dixie show its accolade of acceptance and that was ENSA. No matter how popular with the troops her girls were, ENSA would not have them on its books.

Perhaps the point which ENSA, and many others in the entertainment industry then, missed was that so many of the young men in the audience were different from those in the same age group pre-war. Today it is not easy to understand what war had done to them. They were no longer 'ordinary'. A lot of them were home on leave in civilized surroundings after months in action, years in some cases, and they had experienced a whole gamut of emotions that can come to mankind. At some times they had been heroes galloping into an attack, at others, panting cowards cringing in fox holes making a private pact with God for safe deliverance. They had seen mutilation and death at close quarters and were used to it as part of their normal daily lives. Not one of them would ever be quite the same again.

Another point about these men, made later by Phyllis Dixie herself was: 'We forget how young the armies were in World War Two. For many of the children who stamped their feet and shouted for more it was the first time they had seen a naked woman. Sadly for so many too, it was to be the last.'[3]

Not one of them knew just how much time was left to him, and each of them wanted to make the most of the present. Not surprisingly they got drunk, they whored. They fought in the pubs and on the pavements. They had lived off their nerves for long periods, hiding their secret fears and nightmares. Some of them had come to the conclusion that the brave and the willing, were just as likely to be rewarded with death and degradation as with honour and profit.

Their experiences affected their tastes in entertainment, if only temporarily. Similarly the entertainment tastes of civilians had changed too. To meet the change in the audiences' mood, the romantic and melodious shows were abandoned in favour of a new menu altogether. Strip shows, many of them dubious 'clip joints', mushroomed. But one of the most remarkable developments was the appearance of more revues featuring the female impersonator in a completely different role.

It had long been a tradition of the British theatre for men to play the 'dame' in pantomime, with comedians such as Douglas Byng, Sandy Powell, and Arthur Askey appearing as old ladies in curlers, but mainly acting as themselves in dame costume and letting the audience see that inside the skirt was really a man. By 1944, however, the female impersonator began to play more glamorous and teasing roles as, for example, Henry Kendall in May 1944, dressed in long blond wig, tights and high heels, playing Alexis in *Services Rendered* at the Ambassadors.

A convincing reason for this new form of female impersonation was later given by actor Donald Sinden,[4] who was himself busy entertaining troops just before D-day. His simple explanation is that:

During the war of 1939-45 thousands of men were thrown together, often in battle situations but sometimes in long periods of boredom with no entertainment save for an occasional visit by an

ENSA troupe. They therefore created their own. A large number of today's finest comedians were to start in this way, but who was to provide the glamour of the opposite sex? Many a serviceman found himself donning a home-made wig and a skirt.

Perhaps it is true to say that the drag artiste grew out of necessity. But the movement in any case was ready to emerge out of popular demand. It was a trend in entertainment which had been developing, tentatively but surely, in the cinema for many years. Cross-dressing and other sex exchanges, once a strange and rare phenomenon, was becoming a recurring motif in many films, as Rebecca Bell-Mettereau discovered in her research for her book, *Hollywood Androgyny*.[5] In her study of 250 films she showed how some form of role exchange or transvestism was a major point of interest often violating the unwritten dress and behaviour codes previously taken for granted in the majority of Hollywood products.

The reason for this development was, as always, money. Directors and producers recognized the popular appeal of cross-dressing routines; Bob Hope makes brief appearances in a sarong in the 1940 film, *The Road to Singapore*, a harem girl's outfit in *The Road to Zanzibar* (1941), a lady's bathing suit in *They got me covered* (1942) and a look-alike Carmen Miranda outfit in *The Road to Rio*. Carmen was a popular choice for impersonation and Mickey Rooney does a relatively authentic imitation of her in Busby Berkeley's *Babes on Broadway*. And the 'happiest pick up in box office history' was Cary Grant's *I was a Male War Bride* which grossed $4,100,000.[6]

In her research into this phenomenon, Rebecca Bell-Metereau concluded that cross-dressing in films often suggested a rebellion against the military order but there can be no doubt that it was an audience puller, whether it were to be of the male as female, or female as male such as portrayed by Merle Oberon in *A Song to Remember*, Jean Arthur in *The Plainsman* or Marlene Dietrich who often chose to wear male attire in her personal life as well as for her film, stage, or cabaret persona.

German cabaret traditions which had launched Marlene on her career, had already proved the attraction cross-dressing had for audiences and in his autobiography, Joseph von Sternberg, the German film maker, described the sexual ambiguity common in wartime Berlin cabarets:

At night, when I went out to dine, it was not unusual for something that sat next to me, dressed as a woman, to powder its nose with a large puff that a moment ago had seemed like a breast.

To differentiate between the sexes, was, to make an under-statement, confusing. Not only did men masquerade as females, wearing false eyelashes, beauty spots, rouge and veil, but the woods were full of females who looked and functioned like men.[7]

In the United States, Marlene Dietrich performed in cabaret dressed as a man, singing in French and circulating among the audience seated at tables and occasionally favouring another woman with a kiss. Sternberg, commenting on the way he presented her said: 'The formal male finery fitted her with much charm, and I not only wished to touch lightly on a Lesbian accent … but also to demonstrate that her sensual appeal was not entirely due to the classic formation of her legs.'[8]

In various ways, von Sternberg devoted himself to enhancing Dietrich's mystery and eroticism so that her films were suffused with an erotic aura that almost shimmered from the screen. Sex, he realized, was a real money spinner. Film critic, Jeremy Pascall recently made an interesting comment upon the sexual presentation of Dietrich. He said:

> The image of her seated on a barrel, a top hat on her head and her amazing legs sheathed in silk stockings drawn taut across her thighs by black suspenders is the stuff of masturbatory dreams. Couple this near-fetishism to Dietrich's mystery and to that crooning, seductive voice husking out *Falling In Love Again* and it is not difficult to see why she was a sensation.

Sexual sensationalism was certainly in vogue in 1944. In films, on the stage and in cabarets, sexual boundaries were explored in ways that had the audience enjoying pleasurable fantasies. The unusual situations of wartime made such presentations even more acceptable, especially where on all-male units, the producers of sketches and revues had to persuade men to take female roles. Rarely, though, was there a shortage of volunteers.

Alf Lewis,[9] formerly a leading signalman on the Royal Navy's HMS *Cumberland* from 1941 to 1946, joined the ship's concert party which became so successful that by the end of the war it was ready to put on a show at London's Stoll Theatre. In that show was a high kicking 'chorus line' of able seamen so glamorous that they sometimes were the cause of amusing arguments amongst the audience, as Alf Lewis recalled:

> Once, after a show in Fremantle, Australia, a woman councillor refused to believe one of the beautiful 'chorus girls' was a matelot and we had to take her back stage to prove he was. It cost her £5 – a donation to the Crippled Children's Seaside Homes – for whom we

had put on the show. After three nights' performances we raised just over £2,000 for the charity – a sum which in today's values would equate with the cost of two family houses.

On another occasion when they put on a show for the RAF at Kormaksa, they were invited to the RAF Sergeants' Mess afterwards. 'It was a sight to behold,' recalled Lewis, 'RAF Sergeants dancing with our 'chorus girls' who were still in their costumes.'

Peter Selby,[10] then a young airman serving on a wartime seaplane base called China Bay, in Ceylon, recalled some strange sights he witnessed when he joined the unit concert party.

The producer of those excellent shows was a chap called Tony Cundell. Apart from the quality and variety of the shows that he presented, his speciality was the ballroom scene. He transformed the dull stage of the airmen's canteen into glittering life and light. He bullied and cajoled airmen to dance and waltz together and to ignore the whistles and catcalls of their mates until he had them almost to Astaire and Rogers elegance. He borrowed lavish constumes from ENSA, appearing 90 miles away in the comfort of Colombo, and the result was a lavish and glamorous revue.

Regina May,[11] stationed at RAF Coltishall, remembers the tremendous reception the audience gave to Len, who played the double bass in the concert party band there. 'He had a short act miming a woman undressing and getting into a bath. It was absolutely hilarious, people rolling about in their seats convulsed with laughter and not a word was spoken from beginning to end of his performance.'

A point made by former RAF Sergeant Baker,[12] then stationed in the Middle East and by many other concert party members, was that none of the men taking the woman's role on stage was the least bit effeminate. 'It was just that someone had to play the part as there were no women available and it always went down well with the troops.'

So well in fact were they received that at the end of one show presented by Ronnie Taylor, then an RAF Corporal Radio Telephone operator and later to become Director of BBC Northern Variety, the audience of Naval personnel could hardly be restrained. W.A Lovett[13] who was there said: 'I well recall the show on board one of HM ships at Bizerta in Tunisia when our female impersonators were showered with boxes of chocolates and packets of cigarettes at the end of the performance by a crew of wolf-whistling, frustrated matelots.'

Navy concert parties have produced many famous female impersonators. Perhaps the most famous of these was Britain's King Edward VIII, who, pre-war, starred in a play on board HMS *Repulse*, called *The Bathroom Door*. It was a farce which in act one had him attractively bewigged and prancing round in a frock. It was a frock that would make the news fifty years later when the auctioneers, Christie's, offered for sale a photograph of the Prince in it. Holding the old photograph up for all in the auction room to see, auctioneer, Edmund Pollinger said, 'He looks extremely effeminate but it's a very jolly picture.'[14]

Famous though he was, for other reasons, Edward must give pride of place in the world of drag to another former matelot, a World War Two crew member of HMS *Alaunia*, Daniel Patrick Carroll. In a career spanning four decades his success has been amazing. Modestly this former sailor describes his act simply as himself 'playing a woman knowing that everyone knows it's a fella'.[15]

That former sailor is, of course, Danny La Rue.

Once an altar boy of St Patrick's church Soho, he joined the Royal Navy as a 17-year-old and did his basic training on the concrete ship, 'HMS *Royal Arthur*', located in what was Billy Butlin's Skegness holiday camp. After this training he was posted as a steward to a Royal Naval depot and repair ship, HMS *Alaunia*, part of Lord Louis Mountbatten's Task Force destined to help finish off the Japanese war.

Life on the ship was particularly boring once work finished in the evenings and so Daniel Carroll volunteered for the ship's concert party. He found, as did many other concert party members in the army and airforce, that rehearsing was far more fun than being on call for the more routine tedious duties of the day.

The first part given to this young steward, we now know as Danny La Rue, was that of a native girl in Leon Gordon's play, *White Cargo*. Set in Borneo, the play's pretty native girl is loved by two tea planters. Recalling just how it was for him he wrote: 'I'd seen Hedy Lamarr in the film role in 1942 and was a great fan. I played the native girl, Tondelayo. I looked stunning. I was a very good looking young man with jet black hair, and the sun had turned my skin dark … I looked like a native.'[16]

All he wore for the part was a white sheet 'borrowed' from the officers' quarters – the cheapest costume he's ever had. What is interesting is that whilst he was playing the part, he was not at all conscious of wanting to be a female impersonator. He was just putting on an outfit to play a part like any other actor.

However, the foundations of his future career were now laid. The laughter and applause from his shipmates were stimulating. The rest is history. Danny La Rue rose right to the top of his profession: he starred in seven major West End shows and was invited to appear in three Royal Command performances, yet he remains a kind, unassuming man well deserving the tributes so frequently paid to him by other professionals such as that by the great star Anna Neagle who said of Danny La Rue; 'He is one of the kindest and most generous men in showbusiness.'

Although no other drag artiste achieved the same fame and success, there still were many of those who began their career in unit concert parties dressed as a woman who did go on to make a good living on the stage in the last year of the war and afterwards. The most famous of these shows was *Soldiers in Skirts* which toured Britain from its formation in 1945 until it was finally disbanded in 1952.

These were the heydays for those men who in the gloomy days of the war took to dressing up in women's clothes for a role in a unit concert party sketch. They seem to have begun a trend which has brought a situation in London today where three thousand drag enthusiasts, men and women in fantastic outfits and hairstyles, flock to the Empire Ballroom, Leicester Square for the monthly Kinky Gerlinky club meeting, one of the liveliest events in London's nocturnal calender. And even more surprisingly, a situation in which top fashion designers Thierry Mugler, Jean Paul Gaultier, and Pam Hogg have put transvestites – the very last image one would expect to serve as a retail 'come-on' to women, on their catwalks![17]

One never knows now what fashion will dictate next.

Certainly in the entertainment world of 1944 the fare offered for audiences – and their reaction to it – was unpredictable. Who would have thought that the way to fill the theatres to capacity would be to put on murder plays? It was a surprising situation which caused the critic of *Theatre World* magazine[18] to write:

At this present juncture a casual visitor from Mars would, I am sure, be somewhat surprised at our preference for homicide. In a world given over to mass slaughter and torture he might be forgiven for wondering why the mental processes of this or that murderer should be so absorbing. But like the lightest of musical shows, I believe the murder play is a form of escape. If we were asked to consider on the stage that world wide slaughter of the nations we should feel ourselves implicated, as indeed we are. Murder on the other hand is a thing that touches our consciences not at all since few, if any of us, are likely to harbour even the barest shadow of a homicidal thought. Thus we are able to sit back comfortably in our seats and watch the author dissect his characters like specimens in a museum.

The plays he was referring to were: *Ten Little Niggers, A Murder for a Valentine, This was a Woman, Uncle Harry, Guilty,* and *The Rest is Silence.* In addition to these and in a class of its own was the ever popular play of mass murder, *Arsenic and Old Lace.*

There is no doubt that in that last full year of the Second World War such plays, occasionally descending into melodrama of the most lurid kind, had an undeniable attraction for civilians and servicemen and women alike. People who had good reason for wanting to escape from the reality of the war. And it was good for them.

Another offering from the entertainment world which became startlingly popular, was ballet. It's appeal surprised performers, critics, and impressarios who were at a loss to explain why it had suddenly gained such an enthusiastic following. Some thought the appeal stemmed from the way ballet transcended the harsh realities of wartime – an appeal of romanticism to the emotions. The more cynical observers thought audiences with no real love for or knowledge of ballet, regarded it merely as a pretty spectacle.

Whatever the reason, there was an overnight growth of numerous companies which toured the country, and later the continent, presenting the major classical ballets such as *The Wanderer, Hamlet* and *Swan Lake.*

Credit must be given to Sadler's Wells for carrying the responsibility for keeping ballet, and opera, not just alive but thriving, in wartime. Their theatre, bombed during the first Blitz in 1940, had to close and the company had to work from makeshift bases until their New Theatre was taken over in 1943. It was during this period that the leading figures of the ballet world, Ninette de Valois, Margot Fonteyn, and Robert Helpmann, gave so much impetus to the tremendous growth of ballet's popularity.[19]

It was the Australian-born Helpmann, who received such enthusiastic receptions all over North West Europe when he appeared in ENSA concerts for the troops on leave from the front. Lynn Booth Hilliard,[20] an ATS gunner stationed on an anti-aircraft gunsite near Brussels, witnessed such a reception and the scene has stuck vividly in her mind ever since.

I remember the night Sadler's Wells ballet came to Brussels so well for the audience comprised only service men and women. I shall never forget the beauty of *Swan Lake* and seeing Robert Helpmann dance. He had us all entranced. We stood and cheered and clapped until our hands were sore. There were so many curtain calls. Many of us didn't understand ballet for that was one of the arts reserved for the upper classes. It is nice to know that having been given the chance to go and see ballet in wartime, made many more people understand what they had been missing.

Lynn Booth Hilliard's reaction was just what the far-sighted impressarios and the Council for the Encouragement of Music and the Arts were specifically wanting to achieve.

They realized that with the Forces they had a captive audience of men and women who had been torn from their homes and their old ways of life. It was an audience that could be influenced. Often too, it was an audience which craved for good, classical entertainment as an antidote to the boredom and mental paralysis so often engendered by barrack-room life. Here indeed was an opportunity for impressarios looking to the future, to give these men and women the chance of tasting the joys of the theatre.

In 1939, showbusiness had gone to war with a will, giving the Forces plenty of light-hearted entertainment, but towards the end of the war many of the more enterprising members of the profession saw that they could recruit from these large audiences of Forces personnel, the playgoers of the future, if their appetites were given the right sort of fare. Hopefully they set about their task of developing an interest in the more serious aspects of the theatre that would swell the theatre-going public to three or four times its size in 1939.

Already, the Council for the Encouragement of Music and the Arts had done a good deal to promote opera, ballet and concerts of classical music, and audiences in all these fields grew steadily as the war went on. In July 1943, for example, Eve Kisch, a 'music traveller' for CEMA wrote:[21]

> Call it escapism if you like; but the present general urge to listen to Beethoven symphonies is very different from the ostrich mentality which sets night clubs and music halls booming all over a wartime world. Rather it is as if the ordinary person finds some sort of spiritual anchorage in witnessing drama that bears no relation to the spatial world, but is played out between characters existing only in the dimension of time and tune.

Because of this growth in the public following for the more serious arts, government grants to CEMA rose from £100,000 in 1942 to £235,000 in 1945 when CEMA changed its name to 'The

Arts Council of Great Britain.'[22] Of course, there were those who criticized the way that CEMA was pushing drama and music. One violinist complained in *Our Time* magazine that 'music was being ladled out, like soup in the canteen and was regarded with no more interest'.

Right wingers complained of waste of public money. But the lie to all these criticisms was given by the people who flocked to good plays and concerts. The most famous of these, and deserving of the highest praise, were the lunchtime piano recitals given by Dame Myra Hess in the basement shelter of the National Gallery.

On one occasion she continued to play and the audience sat attentively, whilst an unexploded bomb was being dug out of the Gallery's Inner Court. Those concerts continued throughout the whole of the war. They have been satirized since as a symbol of Britain's cultural resistance to the barbarism of war. But there is nevertheless something emotionally moving about Stephen Spender's description of the way the audience in the National Gallery behaved at one lunchtime violin concert when a delayed action bomb exploded in nearby Trafalgar Square: 'In the trio of the minuet which they were playing, the musicians did not lift their bows from their strings. A few of the audience, who had been listening with heads bowed, straightened themselves for an instant and then resumed their posture.'[23]

What should not be overlooked either was the good work done by ENSA. Most people are inclined to consider ENSA's work as being mainly confined to light entertainment but it did also put on nearly four hundred full-scale symphony concerts between 1943 and 1946, and also commissioned work from contemporary composers.[24]

Giving troops the opportunity to experience serious music and plays was not without its hazards however, as actor and man of many parts in the fullest sense of the word, Sir Anthony Quayle discovered one night.[25] He was then a British Army officer stationed on the rock of Gibraltar and as he had already produced several light-hearted shows and pantomimes for the troops there he was tempted to give the garrison something more serious, something for them to think about once they had left the theatre after the evening's performance.

Courageously he chose Andre Obey's play *Noah*. He believed the play had just the right blend of humour and serious drama as well as ending with a message for the audience to ponder later. Furthermore, interest would be aroused by having girls in the cast drawn from the detachment of Women's Royal Navy Service serving on the Rock. He set about recruiting the prettiest. Additional interest would be aroused, he thought, from having animals in the cast. Here again this was no problem for with his contacts in London he could track down the animal costumes used in the last production of *Noah* there.

All went smoothly. Everyone rehearsed with enthusiasm. The back stage crew worked wonders with scenery and at last all was ready for the first night. How would it go down with the rank and file of the troops?

Their reaction was magnificent. It was a great show. For a week every seat in the theatre was taken. Then, just as the company were about to dismantle the set, the garrison commander came along with a special request. Could the cast manage just one more performance, please? The cast were only too pleased to oblige.

That next day, however, a badly battered Naval Force F which had been escorting a Malta convoy, entered the harbour. Shore leave was granted to those sailors at once. They made a beeline for the bars and within two hours, Naval pickets were rounding up the drunks. 'The streets were awash with blood and "red biddy" ' recalled Sir Anthony. 'By the evening the square in front of the theatre was solid with sailors, gloriously drunk but so tightly packed that they could not fall down. They swayed, they sang, they ranted and roared and all with the best of good nature.'

One can imagine what happened next. As soon as the theatre doors opened they swarmed in filling the seats with navy white. Only a few khaki uniforms managed to squeeze in at the back.

The cast acted the first half of *Noah* to a background of catcalls and whistles but gallantly they pressed on until the last speech of the play. It was here that Anthony Quayle, playing the lead, had to get his final message over to the audience. But long before he reached that moment he feared the worst. All his instincts told him not to tackle the speech. He wanted to stop and end the play before that part. But he knew that he would just have to say those last few words. Otherwise the electrician would not know when to flash the rainbow onto the backcloth and the curtain crew would not know when to let it fall.

In this last scene Noah is seated on the top of Mount Ararat. He is calling to a God who no longer hears him. His wife has gone mad, his children are fighting each other for possession of the earth. The bear has tried to kill him. Noah is in despair.

'Forgive me, Lord,' he says, 'I know I should not complain. But if I could only hear Your voice, have some sign – just to know You are satisfied. Are you satisfied?'

At this point God's answer usually came – a rainbow flashing in the sky. Now Quayle had reached those last few words. He lifted his head and called to heaven: 'Lord, I am satisfied. Are you satisfied?'

For a moment there was absolute silence as the rainbow appeared. Then before the curtain could fall, a stentorian voice from the gallery – a voice that could only have come from a leading stoker – shouted out, 'Am I fuck.'

So it was that Quayle recalled that terrible night. A night when he learnt that there is a time and a place for the presentation of serious drama. It was not his night.

Nevertheless in 1944 the efforts to attract young people to the theatre, concert halls and even the art galleries, was bearing fruit, proving so wrong the cynics who said, 'There is no such thing as culture in wartime.' Young people were getting their first taste of culture in many ways apart from concerts for the Forces. In the Royal Ordnance factory hostels, for example, munition workers were provided with their own, specially built theatres, and Eric White's history of the Arts Council tells us

It is a startling fact, that, at the beginning of those shows, only about two per cent of the hostels' audiences had ever seen a stage play before. In the early days many of them did not know how to behave before live players. But gradually they acquired a theatre etiquette and ceased to talk, walk about, and drink tea during the performances.[26]

During the factory lunchtime break music recitals were given and were well received. Once this pleasing kind of audience reaction was generally realized, then theatre groups and musicians took their talents to small mining villages, fishing harbours, to parish halls and remote anti-aircraft gun-sites and isolated airfields on the east coast. Audiences who had never seen a play by Shakespeare before found themselves gripped with curiosity, wanting to know what happened and how it ended, just as those jostling members in Shakespeare's Globe had been.

It was all so tremendously encouraging. And what a sad reflection upon our present day situation when the Arts Council is deprived of money to foster similar cultural activities on the same scale. If it was good for a country at war, is it not equally good for a country trying to cope with the problems of modern living? The answer is obvious to anyone who can see a little further than those awful words; 'market economy'.

The need for a cultural renaissance is greater now than ever before. In those grim wartime years entertainment, in so many forms, was seen to be essential for the morale of a nation, a state of mind which made both troops and civilian war-workers stick determinedly to the tasks prescribed for them despite all the attendant dangers and discomforts. Do we not need a little of that spirit now?

8

A Moment or Two of Forgetfulness

'Ten minutes of distraction, that's all girlie. That's all they want of you. Can you give it to them? Do you think you can do it?'

The tough, pistol-packing General George S. Patton – 'Ol' Blood and Guts' – commanding the US Third Army, looked hard at the wan-faced woman now slouching in the front seat of the mud and snow-spattered jeep. The 59-year-old general never did like women at his headquarters despite his cultivated image of a womanizer or, in his own parlance, a great 'swordsman'. Now, as he gave instructions to this woman he wondered it it was worth all the hassle. Would this slender blond with the finely pencilled eyebrows, Maria Magdalene, daughter of Berliner Frau von Losch, really live up to her reputation and do something about the morale of those men now on the German frontier.

If any soldiers were down in the mouth and needing their spirits lifting, they were. Things were not working out as they had been led to believe. Earlier that autumn of 1944 they were told that victory was just around the corner, that the Germans were now using horse transport because they had no gasoline, that their Luftwaffe airfields had been battered into nothing by Allied bombers, their factories a mass of rubble no longer producing tanks … Yet here the mighty Allied armies were bogged down, dug in for the winter making no progress at all. Despite the terrible casualties they had incurred in November and December, 1944, nothing of significance had been achieved.

From the Allied Supreme Commander Eisenhower downwards, the generals were worried. The US Army was losing three thousand men a day, ninety thousand a month, and front-line divisions were down to seventy-eight per cent of their normal strength despite the transfer of manpower from support troops in the rear. 'Morale now,' said Eisenhower, 'is a problem of first importance.'[1]

What could a slip of a woman do about that? Patton had already pondered this question and that of what soldiers might see in this woman who, he remembered from pre-war appearances, had set a new style, in both America and Britain, of women dressing in masculine jackets, trousers and trilby hat bought from male outfitters. How would rough soldiers, hungry for the sight of a glamorous woman, react to one who openly declared that she was not particularly feminine in her attitudes? Hardly the stuff to give the troops?

On the other hand, Patton had been told that this woman, Marlene Dietrich, had already made a name for herself with her tours of front-line troops. A real tonic for them she had been. And something just had to be done about the way those troops of his, stuck in the snow bound forests of the Saar, were feeling. Squatting in fox holes and gutted houses in sub zero weather, they were in no fit condition for the kind of hard fighting Patton had in mind for them. Within a few days he hoped to launch yet another assault on the Saar. But would they fight?

In that bitterly cold winter of 1944 the Allied soldier of every nation had had just about all he could take of the war.[2] To the public back home nothing seemed to be happening; the newspapers called it the 'quiet front' but for the veterans of General Patton's Fourth division it was far from quiet. Daily they were subjected to the harassment of shell and mortar fire and then the need to send out fighting patrols by night. All this, plus the long wearisome battle against the elements, day after day squelching about in the freezing water at the bottom of slit trenches, took its toll on their physical and mental fitness to fight. Many men found their feet were turning grey and puffy, wrinkled skin peeled off in long smelly layers once they took off their socks, and to some indeed this was a pleasing sight, such were their feelings of discontent and disaffection. Trench foot, as the condition was called, meant being sent back to a hospital in the rear where entire wards were filled with infantrymen, lying in clean beds with their feet painted Gentian Violet, their swollen toes separated by tufts of cotton wool.[3] And where there was no one shooting at them. Not yet, any way. That was to begin later with the execution of Private Eddie Slovik who found himself unable to face a return to duty up front. But then, that execution was as nothing compared with the nine thousand men the German army shot for similar offences that bleak December.

Such was the situation facing commanders that winter of 1944 and it was therefore not surprising that even to a doubter such as General Patton, anything that might help to keep his soldiers in the line, was worth trying. Even if it meant sending women up to the front as entertainers.

He looked searchingly into the face of the now rather bored-looking former German fraulein the United Services Organization had sent forward, as he delivered his final words of advice: 'If you lose your nerve then it will make matters worse, but if you can swing it ...' he paused and slapped his thigh, 'then Bravo! It'll do the soldiers good to know you are at the front. They'll tell themselves the situation can't be so bad. after all, if we were all going to be mown down, the old man certainly would not send up Marlene Dietrich.'

Marlene spoke quietly. 'I'm not afraid of dying, General, but I am afraid of being taken prisoner. They'll shave off my hair, stone me and have horses drag me through the streets. If they force me to talk on the radio, General, under no circumstances believe anything I say.'[4]

General Patton smiled, put his hand inside his windbreaker and pulled out a revolver. 'Here,' he said, 'Shoot rather than surrender! It's small, but it's effective.'

Marlene looked languidly back at Patton's earnest face and turned to the driver. The afternoon was drawing on and she had heard all that stuff before. Soon it would be dark. 'Let's go,' she said.

The four wheels of the jeep spun round on the packed snow and the open jeep slowly moved forward, gathering speed every second over the narrow track towards the smooth, white snow-covered hills. The debris of battle, half tracks and tanks literally wrenched apart, lay to each side, farm houses, with only four walls standing and around them empty ammunition boxes, the odd boot and bodies half covered in snow, sped by as they rushed along. Suddenly, perhaps attracted by the revving of the jeep engine, machine guns firing on fixed lines, opened up and bullets cracked overhead as they passed. The driver, crouching behind the wheel and driving like a man possessed, muttered curses. Marlene later remembered how the freezing wind dried beads of perspiration on their foreheads. Then, just as they entered a narrow track in a small wood, the jeep skewed and slithered to a halt. A dark figure emerged from the shadows and a harsh voice told them to get out and identify themselves.

Before leaving for the front, Marlene and her driver had been warned that enemy infiltrators, German paratroops wearing US Army uniform and speaking perfect American, were operating behind the Allied lines.

'Give me the password,' ordered the sentry.

They did not have one. 'We are in showbusiness,' said the driver.

'Showbusiness people, huh? Then tell me which song was number one on the Hit Parade in the summer and fall of 1941, just before Pearl Harbour,' demanded the GI rifleman, still unconvinced.

Eventually they were allowed to pass forward. Marlene's orders were brief: 'Begin the moment you get there. Make it short. The shed where you'll sing is under sustained fire.'

Inside the shed were groups of weary, lonely soldiers, a few gaunt-looking, unshaven men who really did not know what was going on in the war except for that small section of their own front and even of that very little. Shells were dropping around the area, some in front, some behind, bracketing. Men were talking in whispers. Then there was a lull, a note came from an accordion and hesitantly Marlene began to sing. It was a saucy song, heads turned around, she hooked them with her low purring voice. They liked the slow sad songs, 'There I go again' and 'Miss Otis regrets' and 'Taking a chance on Love'. Predictably, when she paused in between songs, they asked her for the song which every allied soldier had been singing since those days in North Africa, 'Lili Marlene' – and she sang it in both English and German, lifting up her chin knowing she was amongst soldiers who did not care it was in the language of the enemy – they were just soldiers too.

Here, anyone could see, was a true professional at work, matching her act to the mood of the audience. The cynics had said she was going to the front 'to lift morale by lifting her skirts', but time and again she had proved them wrong. She captivated her audiences, whether they were two thousand strong or twenty. She had flown in unpressurized aircraft at way beyond the recommended height, been jolted along by jeep, lorry and landing craft, never complaining. She frequently performed in forward positions subject to shell and machine-gun fire, sharing for a short time the hazards soldiers of her adopted country were enduring. She made them forget for a few moments that death was just around the corner.

Her efforts were all the more commendable in view of a secret few people then knew. She was working under a Nazi death threat.

Just before America entered the war, Nazi agents had urged her to return to her family in Berlin. They bribed her with honours, promised she would be queen of the German film industry, offered her a fabulous salary and a triumphant home-coming through Berlin's famous Brandenburg Gate. Tactfully, but firmly, Marlene had declined the invitation. Hell had no fury to match the wrath of those Nazis scorned. Shortly after the war broke out between Germany and America the Nazis asked her yet again to return, and when, once more she refused they promised to have her executed as a traitor if she were ever captured. They arrested her sister and imprisoned her in the horrific concentration camp at Belsen. There, on a deliberate starvation diet of thin turnip soup and small crusts of dry bread, thousands of living skeletons were suffering brutal punishment meted out by SS Guards and were dying of typhus and dysentery. It was all part of the Nazi instrument of domination through which the totalitarian state could control a nation with fear. Not fear of death, but a living death.

For Marlene Dietrich to perform so close to a front was to run a high risk of capture. That took courage indeed.

Added to the resentment the Nazis already felt because of her refusal to return to her native Germany, was their fury at Marlene for agreeing to a peculiar request she had received from the US Office of Political Warfare.[5] They had asked her to record a number of her best known songs in German which were then given a political twist and broadcast to Germany. She had done this with the same enthusiasm with which she approached all her performances for the troops. Later she was to say of these recordings: 'I've often been dissatisfied with my work but by recording these adapted songs, I believe I have done something worthwhile.'

No wonder the Germans would have loved to get their hands on her. They would soon have carried out the same death threat which the British had promised their *bête noire*, William Joyce, Lord Haw Haw, then making treasonous broadcasts to Britain prefaced by those words so familiar to British listeners: 'Jairmany calling, Jairmany calling'. On 25 May 1945 he was to make his last call, be captured, tried and executed in the Tower of London.

Marlene herself was very nearly captured two nights after the visit to Patton's front-line troops. At precisely 0530 hours on 16 December 1944 the whole front erupted in fire and flame as six hundred thousand German infantry and hundreds of tanks hurled themselves against the lightly held line in the Ardennes. Startled, awed and bewildered, the American infantry regiments were mauled and pushed right back.

'*Wacht am Rhein*' – as the Germans code-named their offensive – was on. Field Marshal von Runstedt's all-out attack with three armies hitting the Allies so hard that the impact threatened to decimate their divisions by nightfall.

Caught up in an enormous traffic jam that morning was Marlene

Dietrich. At any moment the whole mêlée of trucks and half tracks could have been cut off by pincer movements of Panzer units. Fortunately for Marlene, an American parachute colonel spotted her predicament. He grabbed her out of the snarl of traffic, pushed her into his own jeep and forced a pathway off the road and raced across country back to Army Headquarters. Narrowly she had escaped with her life. Others were not so fortunate. American losses in those first few days were very high and Eisenhower later recalled: 'Altogether we calculated our losses at a total of 77,000 men of whom 8,000 were killed, 48,000 wounded and 21,000 captured or missing.'[6] Put another way, it was a battle that left nine times more American casualties than the bloody fighting of D-Day itself. A battle that nearly turned the whole tide of the war.

It had been a close run thing for Marlene Dietrich and many other showbiz performers too, so that when General Eisenhower later recounted those events in his memoirs *Crusade in Europe*, he paid tribute to those entertainers who risked their lives along with the forward troops, as follows:

> They succeeded in giving the soldier an occasional hour or two of entertainment which he never failed to appreciate. I have seen entertainers carrying on their work in forward and exposed positions, sometimes under actual bombing attack. In rest areas, in camps, in bases and in every type of hospital they brought to soldiers a moment of forgetfulness, which, in war is a boon.

Most of those troupers, like Marlene Dietrich, were quite prepared to perform for the smallest section of soldiers. It became a legend indeed that wherever she appeared in the forward areas, every soldier she met wanted to kiss her. She rationed kisses to those about to take part in a battle. Later, she was to recall whimsically, 'The war gave me the opportunity of kissing more soldiers than any other woman of the world.'

By the time 40-year-old Marlene, looking barely thirty, went forward to visit Patton's troops, she was already a veteran performer. She had volunteered for USO – the American equivalent of ENSA early in 1943, landed in North Africa, went on to Sicily, up into Italy and then into North West Europe and once when she was with Patton when he made one of his surprisingly rapid advances, she went with him as interpreter. Undoubtedly, when she took her showbiz team to war there were no half measures, she took it all the way, and for her efforts she was awarded the Medal of Freedom, the highest decoration the

American War Department can give to a civilian. Her citation reads:[7]

> Miss Marlene Dietrich, civilian volunteer with the United States Service Organization Camp Shows, performed meritorious service in support of military operations in North Africa, Sicily and Italy and in the North Atlantic bases in Europe, meeting a gruelling schedule of performances under battle conditions, during which adverse weather prevailed and despite risk to herself. Although her health was failing, Miss Dietrich continued to bring pleasure and cheer to more than five hundred thousand American soldiers. With commendable energy and sincerity she contributed immeasurably to the welfare of the troops in these theatres.

General Patton and General Bradley also paid tribute to her efforts. Bradley, Commander of US Twelfth Army wrote: 'Many of us came to admire Marlene's spirit and to appreciate her contribution because she was so much interested in entertaining our soldiers over a long period of time, and because she quite often visited very close to the front.'

The final tribute however, came from France. At a private ceremony, the French Ambassador to the United States, presented her with the medal of the Legion of Honour.

Clearly the experiences of Marlene Dietrich, serve to illustrate what conditions were like for so many other showbiz people who demonstrated so convincingly that entertaining troops was so worthwhile and not at all a soft option.

The necessity for keeping up morale was not, of course, confined to US troops alone, front-line soldiers of every nation suffered the same anxieties. Sergeant Woodford[8] of the British 11th Infantry Brigade recalls just how crucial were the morale boosting visits of showbusiness personalities. Men of his platoon never underestimated the beneficial lift to their spirits of these 'moments of forgetfulness'. Woodford recalled:

> Entertainers made us forget for a short while, at least, what was in store for us at dawn the next day. Under training we had all been to 'battle schools' where we scrambled over assault courses with live rounds fired over our heads, we had all become familiar with the bangs and crashes of thunder flashes exploding as we sweated over climbing nets and twelve foot walls. But all the time we knew, deep down, that no-one was actually trying to kill us.
>
> When we went into our first attack some of that feeling of invulnerability of the battle school went with us, that belief too that bullets and shrapnel only hit other people. Then came the first

bursts of Spandau fire, and that brought reality. War was cruel. It killed you.

Entertainers helped us to forget all that whilst they performed.

Historically, soldiers are always supposed to be brave, to appear tough, itching to get into battle, feeling brave at all times. Some may be. But by the time the Second World War was into its second and third year, the Medical Corps of Allied Armies began to admit that battle wounds were not always physical. In a departure from military practice they recognized too that long periods in action, costly in lives, inevitably brought a large proportion of psychiatric casualties among those evacuated from the front.

When morale cracked, men cracked.

The same problem had been encountered in the First World War but then medical men decided to hide these battle casualties under the diagnosis of 'shell shock' a convenient label suggesting that the noise and blasts of the shells, a kind of concussion, had traumatized the soldiers nervous system. It was a label with which the Medical Corps and senior officers at base could live.

In World War Two, however, the reality was admitted in varying degrees by the medical services of the Navy, Army and Air Force. Dr Roland Winfield, DFC, AFC, who completed three tours of operations over enemy occupied Europe as pilot or air gunner whilst at the same time acting as a specialist in aviation medicine, was very much concerned with the problem of battle fatigue, which the RAF often cruelly labelled, 'Lack of Moral Fibre'. He found that, 'On the whole, the greater a man's intelligence and the more lively his imagination, the earlier in his operational tour did he become aware of the hard, inescapable fact that to continue operating against the enemy meant that he had to live his life in the continuous immediate prospect of violent death.[9]' Bomber Command aircrew fought an unending battle with fear for most of their tours. Many of them lost that battle, estimates put the figure at around fifteen per cent[10] though the Judge-Advocate General of the Forces is implacably unhelpful on inquiries relating to the problems of battle fatigue and disciplinary courts martial cases of aircrew 'lacking moral fibre'. Aircrew who felt they could no longer carry on, were treated by the RAF with considerable harshness. Exemplary prison sentences were awarded in order to dissuade aircrew from reporting sick with obvious symptoms of combat fatigue – insomnia, nightmares, headaches and bed-wetting.

The British Army instructed the medical services to adopt a

more humane approach to battle fatigue and to men who had broken down after being faced far too often with the horrific prospect of becoming just another brownish clump covered with dust and flies. Consequently doctors put men who got the shakes into the NYD(N) category – Not Yet Diagnosed Nervous – and usually evacuated them to a rear area for rest and recuperation before being returned to the line. In these rest areas, showbiz artistes played a vital role which can be seen in the government's adherence to the decision to keep actors and actresses 'at their posts', rather than having them called up for a less valuable job in the Armed Forces.

John Keegan, military historian and Defence Editor of *The Daily Telegraph*, recently wrote[11] that

> The incidence of psychiatric casualties evacuated from some of the big attrition battles in Normandy may have reached thirty per cent. The psychiatrists got it established with the High Command that battle was an intensely stressful and wholly unnatural experience for all but the most exceptional human being, and that a proportion of psychiatric casualties would increase with the intensity and duration of combat and would have to be accepted.

Hence, unit concert party members were withdrawn from normal military duties and employed in touring front-line areas, alongside showbiz professionals, giving some mental relief and relaxation to fighting troops brought back for a brief respite.

Bebe Daniels flew to Omaha beach to comfort the wounded and make recordings to show others just how quickly the wounded could be flown safely back to service hospitals in Britain. To the background of exploding shells and machine gunfire she recorded her talks with wounded men so that they could later be relayed to relatives showing how efficient was the medical evacuation service. The operation was a tricky one because before the programmes could be transmitted, the medical condition of each of the wounded soldiers interviewed had to be checked in order to make sure that he was still alive. For her gallantry and contribution to the war effort, Bebe Daniels was later decorated by President Roosevelt with the Medal of Freedom.

Within days of the landing two hundred and seven ENSA artistes were sent over to Normandy as the first wave of performers to cover the entertainment needs of the troops. The first to volunteer was Britain's top box office draw then, George Formby, the ukulele playing comedian with the toothy grin. He had been one of the first to go to France in 1940 in the desperate days before Dunkirk and was one of the last to leave Brest before the final evacuation of troops from the beaches.[12]

Meanwhile in the UK he had raised thousands of pounds for charity and even joined the Home Guard. During the height of the London blitz he performed in the London Underground, sometimes appearing on a makeshift stage and at others sitting on the track.

Incidentally, an interesting reflection on these shelter shows was that legally it was all right for George Formby to entertain men and women seeking refuge from the bombs but it was quite illegal for unknown entertainers. A 19-year-old youth was fined at Yarmouth for singing in a public air-raid shelter. The court heard he was surrounded by youths, girls and sailors, giving an impersonation of George Formby, 'to the annoyance' of other people.[13]

George gave Sunday concerts to raise money for the Air Raid Distress Fund, free of any fee for himself, whilst at the same time foregoing lucrative contracts and engagements elsewhere. The public loved him.

By June 1944 he headed the list of 'top money making stars' in British films. Behind him in order were Robert Donat, Gracie Fields, Arthur Askey, Charles Laughton, Will Hay, Gordon Harker and Anna Neagle. And in the International list George followed Mickey Rooney, Deanna Durbin, Spencer Tracy and Jeanette MacDonald. George was in fact, way ahead of Errol Flynn, Gary Cooper and, perhaps surprisingly, Bing Crosby.

When he arrived at a secluded Normandy orchard sitting alongside the driver of an ENSA truck, thousands of troops rose to their feet and cheered. There, in a rest centre to which soldiers were sent for a few days' recuperation after a long time in the line, George and his party set about erecting a stage, in a hollow which served as a natural amphitheatre. Soon the whole area was packed; the more fortunate of the troops sat on benches, others sat on the grass and stood on the rising ground.

One customary feature of the audience however was missing. And this was at George's insistence. There were no brass hats occupying the best seats at the front. Now they all knew better. On so many previous occasions when visiting units in the UK, George had some harsh words to say to the whole audience when he saw officers filling the front rows. 'Here, 'ahve come to entertain t'lads not the likes of you. Make room for them. Come forward lads.'

George had a way with audiences, a special relationship so that he could say things to them without giving offence. He had come up the hard way. Like Gracie Fields, and Will Hay, he had started his career as a variety comedian and progressed to being a comic actor in films, and so he took to these stage shows for the troops like a duck to water. He was the master of the saucy song, and the knowing wink; they were songs too that had an irresistible foot-tapping beat. In his films he usually played the northern 'gowk' who had no idea how to deal with women. Never were there any romantic scenes culminating in a passionate kiss. He was the shy, helpless type, so awkward when it came to wooing his sweetheart. Soldiers could relate to him easily. His formula for fun was to be the naïve type of comic with smutty songs full of lines which could be taken in a naughty sexy way. And service audiences would never let him leave until he had sung the song which the BBC had banned from his radio shows[14] – 'When I'm cleaning windows', because they objected to the last verse:

> Pyjamas lying side by side
> Ladies nighties I have spied,
> I've often seen what goes inside
> When I'm cleaning windows.

That last line always evoked a full throated roar from men who had heard it so many times before but found relief in laughing yet again. In that Normandy orchard and in smaller concerts in forward areas George put all he had into entertaining those men and he would sing all the songs they knew from 'Leaning on a Lamp-post at the corner of the street until a certain little lady comes by ...' to 'It serves you right, you joined', and a new one written specially for his tours in North West Europe, 'Rolling into France'.

It was a great effort and George Formby richly deserved the recognition the government gave to his work with the award of the Order of the British Empire. He gave so generously of his time and his energy when he was at the top of his profession. Sadly, when the war was over, he never again reached the same heights. Nevertheless he is still remembered today with great affection, especially by those servicemen and women whose lives were brightened by the northern 'gowk' he played so well.

To be able to make men laugh and forget their peril for a brief period, was a test of talent indeed. Those professionals with ENSA and the amateurs in unit concert parties and with RAF Gang shows and the Army's 'Stars in Battledress', were all hard at work in all theatres of operations wherever morale needed a boost.

The RAF Gang show and the Army's 'Stars in Battledress'

became something absolutely unique in the realms of military history for they represented a positive recognition by High Command and the government of the fact that entertainment was an essential element of a healthy service life contributing greatly to fighting fitness.

These Service shows drew their performers not from civilian entertainers but from amateurs and occasionally from professionals in the services themselves. They fulfilled an urgent need for entertainment taking their revues from one unit to the next. The audiences would vary from five men on an RAF 'Q' site to some 2,500 on a big camp. This again was no soft option. One RAF Gang show travelled 16,000 miles in one year – mostly in open trucks and in all weathers. After a long tiring journey they could never be sure what kind of a welcome awaited them. Nice warm billets, perhaps, but quite often a night on the guard-room floor.

The standard of these shows was often variable but generally they did a very good service not only in taking entertainment to service units but also in showing them how to make their own entertainment. The shows also gave performing experience to a new breed of entertainer who developed a taste for performing and who were to form an important sector of the Variety profession in the post-war years – Sir Harry Secombe, Spike Milligan, Tony Hancock, Dick Emery, Peter Sellers, Cardew Robinson, to name but a few who flew under Ralph Reader's RAF Gang Show banner.

Cardew Robinson and his group were in Normandy two-and-a-half weeks after the landings and in those days the front was by no means clearly defined. It was all too easy to take a wrong turning and finish up behind the lines. On one occasion Cardew Robinson was motoring along with a civilian driver when an army corporal jumped out of a ditch and shouted 'Hey, where the mucking hell do you think you're going?' Cardew informed the NCO that they were going to do a show. To this the corporal said with his most effective sneer, 'Oh yeh? Who too? The mucking Germans? They're just round the mucking corner.' By this time the civilian driver already had the truck in reverse gear.[15]

Wherever light relief was needed concert parties burgeoned. Nowhere was this better exemplified than in Malta. The ordeal of service personnel and civilians there in 1941 and 1942 was difficult for the public back home to imagine, but suffice it here to say that the whole might of the German/Italian Air forces and Navies attempted to reduce it to rubble.

Malta, with enemies on all sides occupied a vital strategic

position in the Mediterranean war theatre. Rommel had pleaded with Hitler to bomb it out of existence so that the RAF and Royal Navy could no longer operate from there and sink his Afrika Korps supply ships. For months on end Malta suffered heavy losses with raids every day. But the fortress of Malta, the most bombed part of the whole British Empire, though terribly scarred, remained defiant. In recognition of the island's ordeal, King George VI awarded the island the George Cross – the civilian VC – in April 1942. The courage and morale of everyone there had remained steady.

Everyone had played some part in this and once again the entertainers were in the forefront in providing those precious moments when service personnel and civilian could escape from the stress of almost continuous air attacks. Roger Key,[16] who was Air Ministry Clerk of Works during those years of intensive air bombardment remembered well how they formed the 'RAF-FIANS' concert party.

The governor of the island, General Sir William Dobbie – who had the reputation of fighting with a sword in one hand and a bible in the other – and the air officer commanding RAF Malta were very keen to see a concert party formed and it fell to the lot of Roger Keys, who had a job which took him round the island, to get one together. He soon found willing helpers.

I was very lucky in having a professional song and dance act couple to give me advice and much support, Cecil and Barbara Roche. Then, once the decision was made to get a concert party together, I was absolutely amazed at the quality of talent available. Most of it came from the RAF, some were professionals in civvy street who had been called up and others were just keen musicians or wanting to have a go on the stage. We started in a small way putting on shows for outlying units and as we went round we attracted more talent still. It was not long before we were able to put on much bigger shows in the theatres in Valetta and Slima. What amazes me now as I look back, is how we managed in the midst of all those air raids. Our biggest show was the pantomime, *Babes in the Wood*. The first performance was given to seven hundred poor children of Valetta. A show could not have had a better send off. The children roared with laughter at all we did, especially the pantomime horse. During the interval we gave them chocolate and at the end of the performance an orange to take home.

There were many amusing times for us too. I remember one time when the Fang Farrier, our unit dentist, got a call to return to the surgery as a matter of urgency. He was at the time playing the part in a play, of a German Luftwaffe pilot in full regalia. He left the cinema with two military policemen to keep him company but once the local civilians saw him, they gave chase and it was by the skin of his teeth that he just managed to make it back to the air base before the hostile Maltese caught up with him. On another occasion we managed to do what all amateur dramatic companies would like to do – bring the house down. But we did it literally. In the middle of one act something got caught in the rigging and the whole of the heavy front curtain came plunging down. I, as the Clerk of Works, had to solve the problem by turning the cinema screen into a temporary front curtain.

We had a good laugh too when one of our senior RAF officers blackened his face with burnt cork for his part as a Nubian slave in a sketch we were giving in a makeshift theatre, and then found to his dismay, there were no washing facilities and he had to walk back through the town and the RAF camp in that condition.

Frequently we had to perform to the accompaniment of anti-aircraft fire and the explosion of bombs but we found if we ushered onto the stage the chorus girl line, nobody bothered to leave for the shelters. Those girls were real beauties.

It was all great fun, and we were indeed 'Good Companions' all working together. And we came through with memories that have lasted through the years.

They had done a good job too. And they had been given the full support of all senior officers from the governor downwards. All now realized that everything that could be done to keep troops psychologically fit to fight had to be done, and that it was no longer enough merely to provide fighting men with good food and reasonable living conditions when under fire. These men had to have periods of mental relief too, a few moments of forgetfulness.

As Field Marshal Montgomery was later to write:[17] 'A soldier leads a most unpleasant life. He will put up with this as long as he knows you really care for him and will look after his interests, and that you will give him all the pleasures you can in the midst of his discomforts.'

One way of providing part of that essential pleasure, a way which armies have relied upon since times immemorial, was to bring on the bands with music which set feet a-tapping to a happy tune.

9

Strike up the Band

It was Friday morning on 15 December 1944 and Winter had its admamantine grip on the whole of Europe.

In the remote border country of the Belgian Ardennes, the stark, black tree boughs were heavy with new snow. American soldiers, each of them wrapped in a blanket, huddled down in their fox holes and amongst the ruins of half-wrecked hamlets, peacefully unaware that already German commanders were bent over maps of the area, adding final touches to their plans for an attack which on the morrow, would send the whole world reeling.

It was an offensive designed to break through the weak Allied lines and push on right to the Channel coast. For this, Hitler had scraped up more reserves than his commanders or the Allies believed possible. Now all was ready. At dawn the next day a barrage of 2,000 guns would herald an assault of quarter of a million infantry and Panzer troops moving forward under the cover of snow and dense fog. The Battle of the Bulge was about to begin.

Back at his Army headquarters in Luxembourg, General Bradley was revising his plans too.[1] He was going to a party in Paris but as all planes were grounded, through the thick fog and freezing conditions, he decided to set off early in his sedan.

In this way he could arrive at the French capital in time for lunch at the Ritz, where champagne flowed freely. There would be much more wining and dining for him that day for he intended visiting Supreme Commander, General Eisenhower who was throwing a champagne reception for two of his staff, who were getting married in the Louis XIV Chapel at Versailles, and then later the same evening throwing another party to celebrate his promotion to Five Star General. An admirer had presented him with a bushel of oysters, which he loved. They were to be served first on the shell, then as oyster stew, and then fried. For the generals it was to be a really festive party (except for Bradley who hated oysters and would have an omelette). And so, whilst the GIs were freezing in their fox holes the select few of the top brass were looking forward to a really good orgy – provided, of course they could get through the fog-bound roads to Paris.

In London on that fateful morning, apart from ambulances and vehicles engaged in rescuing the latest victims of the V2 rocket attacks, transport was hardly moving. The few red double-decker buses that were crawling along the city's roads, belching black exhaust into the yellow smog, often had the conductor walking ahead waving a white handkerchief to show the driver the way. Thick freezing fog had wreaked havoc with train timetables, points were frozen, connections missed, and in the packed, badly heated carriages, bleary-eyed servicemen and civilians cursed the weather, the railway companies and talked of writing a letter to *The Times*. Travel by air was completely out of the question.

One man however was determined to fly if at all possible. He was a 40-year-old bespectacled major, looking more like a schoolmaster than a military man, a man who imposed a strict discipline upon the forty men under his command. If he lifted his hand they would instantly be silent; when he entered the room they stood in respect. He was a man who held a unique position in the hearts of millions of US and Allied servicemen. His name was Alton Glenn Miller.[2]

As the leader of the famous United States Army Air Forces Band comprising forty hand-picked musicians, he felt it was high time that he got over to the North West Europe theatre of operations and gave those men at the front 'a hunk of home,' through his music. Once he was over there he wanted to take small groups of musicians as close up to the front as he could get. 'He wanted to play for the guys that were getting killed, as he put it,' recalled one of his band then, Bob Ripley.

Having made up his mind, Major Miller wanted to get started on the arrangements. Towards this end, the band had just spent a hectic eighteen days recording thirty hours of programmes, the schedule for the coming six weeks, which would be broadcast over the Allied Expeditionary Forces programme of the BBC, whilst the band was giving live concerts to troops in France and Belgium. After such intensive and sustained sessions of recording, it was frustrating for Miller to be kicking his heels waiting for the weather to improve so that he could get over to Paris and draw up the programme for the tour of Service units.

Early on that morning of 15 December, Miller received a

telephone call from a Colonel Baesell, who made frequent trips between London and Paris in his small Norseman aeroplane, and he had offered Miller a lift. Although the weather was too bad for him to get clearance for take off that morning, he thought there could be some improvement after midday and if Miller would like to take a chance on this, then they could meet at the RAF airfield at Twinwoods Farm, near Bedford. With any luck at all they could be airborne shortly after lunch. Miller was eager to take this chance of getting away and agreed to meet Baesell for lunch.

Afterwards they drove out together to the control tower at Twinwoods. The weather was still very bad. Visibility was awful, fog hung over the airfield and, to make matters worse, there was a very light drizzle falling, more like ice than water. A white frost coated every blade of grass. When the two men walked over it from the car, they left deep footmarks behind them. The bushes around the control tower were heavy with frost that had not moved for a week.

In that sub-zero temperature Miller and Baesell stared upwards into the gloomy, grey fog, which seemed to be getting darker rather than lighter. Baesell however was still fairly confident. He had telephoned for his aircraft and been told that it was on the way, with Flight Officer Morgan at the controls.

The two men paced about, crunching the pools of ice fringing the runway and occasionally peering hopefully upwards. At last they heard the engine of a light plane passing over the airfield. Could the pilot see the airfield? they asked each other. A few moments later the aircraft turned and came down smoothly, taxiing towards the control tower.

Rubbing fingers that felt like clumsy sausages, Miller picked up his bag and got into the plane. 'They say the weather is better over the Continent,' shouted the pilot above the noise of the aircraft's engine.

And so it was that at precisely quarter to two on the afternoon of 15 December, 1944, whilst Supreme Commander Eisenhower was offering champagne and schnapps to his guests, and whilst his GIs in the Ardennes forests were rubbing each other's frost bitten feet (as ordered to do so by their generals), the man who was coming to bring them a 'hunk of home' took off into the freezing fog hanging over Twinwoods airfield and the rest of Europe. He was never seen again.

That morning, 18-year-old Mollie Urquhart[3] of the WAAF Special Duties section was on duty in the group filter plotting room at RAF Stanmore. She was in high spirits because she was the envy of all the girls on the station. The previous evening she and her father were driving home through the dark lanes when they stopped to give a lift to an American Airforce officer. He was handsome, modest and friendly. He was the rugged romantic hero of the 1939 film *Gone with the Wind*, Clark Gable, and he had just telephoned to ask Mollie to meet him for coffee after her watch was finished. Now, though, she was concentrating on the image which had appeared on her monitor screen. Suddenly it disappeared. Later she heard it was Miller's plane that had gone.

Miller's disappearance is a mystery that has intrigued people for almost half a century, and what makes Miller's fate seem even stranger is that for some time before that fateful flight he was troubled with premonitions that he would never see his wife and adopted son again. Yet, shortly before leaving on that last flight he had spoken to the electrician in charge of stage lighting for the band's most recent performance, that he was not looking forward to returning to the States.[4] He looked worried and he had lost so much weight that the expensively tailored uniform he had bought from the fashionable firm of Saks on Fifth Avenue, hung awkwardly over his thin figure.

Lieutenant Don Haynes, Miller's close friend and executive officer of the US Army Air Forces Band, who had also been Miller's band manager in those successful two years before America went to war, noted how jumpy Miller had become. Once, when they were driving back to their base in the officers' club at Milton Ernest Hall, Miller dropped into a very sombre mood and confided to Haynes that he had a strong feeling that his name was on one of those bombs then falling on London. And he had also written in similar terms to his brother.

Could it be that his premonitions proved well founded, that his life was indeed ended by falling bombs?

That is the nature of one horrifying theory put forward to explain Miller's disappearance and the fact that over the last forty years not one of the many efforts made to find his Norseman plane has ever succeeded in locating even the smallest trace. That theory is that bombs did in fact kill him. Not enemy bombs either but those from RAF Bomber Command!

Navigator Fred Shaw[5] is said to have reported that when he was on an RAF bombing mission carrying sensitive bombs the whole operation was aborted due to bad weather and the entire force was ordered to jettison their bomb loads in the Channel before attempting to land back in their fog-bound UK bases. Shaw was reported as saying that as he looked out of his own aircraft he saw jettisoned bombs falling from another aircraft on Miller's Norseman.

Many years later when the Reverend Frank Wappat of BBC North was talking to Herb Miller,[6] then touring Britain with the band, he said, 'I suppose you are tired of being asked this question: What do you think happened to Glenn Miller? Do you think the British disposed of him?' Herb replied: 'That's probably the answer.'

The Court of Inquiry,[7] however, held at Bedford on 20 January 1945 came to the conclusion that Miller's Norseman aircraft, which was not fitted with de-icing equipment, iced up, got into difficulties over the Channel and nose-dived into the sea. No one could countenance the idea that Britain had killed America's most popular bandleader. But many questions were still left unanswered. Files have been closed. Ronald Reagan, a Hollywood film star and a great fan of Miller's music when Miller's death was announced, tried to find some of the answers to those questions during his term as US President but the ultimate conclusion we must accept is the one which his brother Herb made, as his last wish before he died on 20 September 1987, that his remains be with Glenn's in the Channel. Perhaps Herb was hoping that this was a way of ending all further speculation about his brother's death.

But that still goes on. The film critic of the London *Times* wrote on 4 January 1992: 'If Hollywood was making a biopic of Glen Miller today it would no doubt probe into all sorts of dark corners of the bandleader and present death as a form of suicide.'

And so speculation continues. A more positive form of speculation, though, would be upon the question of how it was that a bandleader who had only just achieved success in the States in 1939 and had been in Britain with the US Airforce band a mere six months, could attract thousands of fans and become a legend in his own lifetime on the strength of his many BBC broadcasts and hundred of appearances at military and civilian locations. Now, nearly fifty years after his death, the mystique that surrounds his name and his particular style of music remains as powerful as ever. It has stood the test of time. The magic of his music draws capacity audiences wherever it is played. No wonder he is acclaimed as the most popular bandleader who ever lived.

Yet his career lasted only about five years.

Fortunately his music not only made him the idol of millions of servicemen and civilians who listened entranced to the wartime Army Air Force band but that same music has beguiled their children and grandchildren.

How can we explain this phenomenon?

His music grew out of a combination of factors. First and foremost perhaps was the war itself. The forty strong all-soldier band which Miller brought to Britain in June 1944 was hand-picked. In peacetime no leader could have afforded to engage such a galaxy of musical stars. As soon as he was commissioned and promoted to captain in November 1943 at Technical Training Command based at Knollwood, Carolina, he was able to take his pick from all musicians entering the US Forces and of those already serving. All these were eager to serve with Miller, who in the last two years had become the most admired bandleader in the United States.

He was a hard task master but his music was new. He was not afraid either to buck the top brass who objected sometimes to his new fangled ways with military music. One classic story told of such clashes with senior officers and is reported by Chris Way: 'Many old-style bandmasters started to question Glenn's ideas. This resulted in Glenn and the Major of the cadets at Yale meeting face to face. The major said, "Tell me, Captain, we did pretty good with Sousa in the last war." To which Glenn snapped, 'Tell me Major, are we still flying the same planes we flew then?" '

Miller received official backing for his new ideas and his newly created marching music. Now he was able to build a band with no expense spared. He had authority to requisition musicians wherever they were stationed. They were posted to his outfit.

With such an array of musicians at his disposal Miller produced, in a matter of three years, a string of hit records which are still earning as much in royalties today as they brought at the time the records were first pressed. Hits such as 'Moonlight Serenade', 'Little Brown Jug', 'In the Mood', 'Tuxedo Junction', 'Pennsylvania 6-5000', 'Perfida', 'Chattanooga Choo Choo', 'A String of Pearls', 'I've Got a Girl in Kalamazoo', 'Serenade in Blue' and many more.[8]

He was giving his audiences just what they wanted – a touch of sentimentality, 'a hunk of home', and his audiences warmed to him. An idea of this rapport can be appreciated from a report of what happened in the Queensberry All Services Club on the night his plane's failure to arrive was announced. Geoffrey Butcher reported the words of the Club manager John Harding, as follows;

When the dramatic message was received at the Club that Major Glenn Miller was reported missing on a flight to Paris, I witnessed the most spontaneous tribute in my forty years experience. Unrehearsed and unasked, three thousand uniformed men and women in the audience stood up together in silent sympathy for the loss of one who did so much to provide entertainment when and where it was so badly needed.[9]

Despite the loss of its leader, the Glenn Miller band went on playing to Allied Forces and civilian audiences for the rest of the war. No band could have worked harder. It was estimated by Miller's biographer, Geoffrey Butcher, that during its thirteen months in the European Theatre of Operations, the band played to one and a quarter million Allied servicemen and women in Britain, France and occupied Germany. The effort involved is reflected in the figures – 956 separate performances, an average of three a day!

There never was any doubt that the band did so much to raise the spirit of all servicemen and women and it fully justified the now famous remark made by General Doolittle to Glenn Miller after the show at Bentley Priory in August 1944: 'Next to a letter from home, your music is the best morale booster in the ETO [European Theatre of Operations].' This was the show featured in the film *The Glen Miller Story* with a scene so well remembered where the motor of a flying bomb is heard approaching as Miller is swinging 'In the Mood'. The motor grows louder and louder but the band defies it and plays on.

There was, however, another way that Miller and his band went to war, apart from helping to lift Allied morale. He made special propaganda broadcasts to German troops so as to undermine morale and weaken their resolution to continue fighting.

Towards the end of October 1944 the band began a series of broadcasts aimed specifically at the military. It was called, 'Music for the Wehrmacht.'[10] Miller introduced each number himself in almost comical phonetic German. But interspersed in the programme were messages delivered by German-speaking presenters plugging the Allied cause. Guest artistes on these programmes included well-known stars Bing Crosby, Dinah Shore and many others.

Miller's contribution was part of a British government's programme which began in 1941 when they decided to use dance music as a propaganda weapon. Wednesdays were reserved for the Luftwaffe who were not infrequently regaled with bands comprising RAF players. A neutral journalist returning to Britain in May 1941 reported that the programmes were well received in the officers' mess at many a German Air Force airfield.[11]

Reports coming back to the US Psychological Warfare Division suggested that the programmes had achieved success far beyond expectations. Indeed, German propaganda Minister, Dr Joseph Goebbels had to make drastic alterations to the German radio programme to attract listeners away from the American and British dance music programmes.

Explaining these changes to the German public which had been brought up on a diet of stodgy classical music, Goebbels said:

> The vast majority of people both at the front and at home are so much strained by war that they no longer have the concentration in the evening to absorb more than two hours of an exacting programme. Good temper is important for the war effort. A soldier does not want talks from early morning until late at night, he wants some dance music! Dance music is necessary because it is liked by workers and soldiers. Music changes and we cannot live in the past with tunes of our grandparents. Those prudes who have objected to coarseness cannot be considered because that is how soldiers like to live and soldiers must come first![12]

Dance music was definitely in vogue. The dance halls were packed with young men and women, often far from home and searching for companionship. There were never enough dance halls. Town halls took over the role of the Ritz and the Mecca. Such was the demand for dance halls that the management of the Covent Garden had a dance floor built over the stalls in the historic theatre in Drury Lane.

The swinging and sentimental dance music of the Miller style was the most popular prescription for removing anxiety and depression. New dances were devised to get everyone on the floor holding hands, laughing and chatting together. These 'chain dances' to the tunes of 'Lambeth Walk' and 'Hokey Cokey' brought a jovial and informal party spirit into dance halls, whether they were elegant Locarnos or small village halls.

It was not long before the well-known British bands were imitating the Miller formula, reproducing the dreamy sentiments of hits like 'Moonlight Serenade'. And it was boom time for all the big bands. And that boom was not confined to London. Typical of reports of dance hall attractions was that for Joe Loss in Glasgow's Playhouse Ballroom. In his one week's residency there he attracted over ten thousand patrons. And when Lew Stone began a three weeks engagement in the same hall the opening night's patrons totalled 2,183![13]

The new service bands soon began to be much better than the well-known, pre-war civilian ones which had lost many of their younger musicians through being called up for military service.

Gay Mills, ATS, (now Gay Clark) with 'The Bombshell's' Army concert party and two rabbits who starred with Gay in the show. It happened that Lieutenant Donald Stuart (seated front right) who was in charge of the show, was also a magician and his act was to put Gay and the two rabbits in a box and make them disappear

'The Incendiaries' mobile theatre which toured even the smallest sites. 'We were told to go to units as small as ten men and we put on the same show as for a large audience,' said Gay Mills

Inside 'The Bombshell's' mobile theatre fifteen to twenty men could be entertained on gunsites and other very small isolated units

When Sister Winifred Beaumont of Queen Alexandra's Imperial Nursing Service was posted to Burma she was not surprised to find herself in hospitals close to the front line, but she never expected to be put in charge of organizing concerts without any facilities whatsoever. It was a challenge, however, which she accepted and found most enjoyable

Pauline Smith of Bailden, Bradford, began entertaining the troops in London as soon as war broke out. Seen here holding a photograph of herself in the uniform of the United States Entertainments Section

Douglas Marshall, who in 1940 after three weeks in the army volunteered to play the organ at his sergeant's wedding. As a result of this he was released from his unit and became a member of the newly formed 15th Scottish Division concert party

Lieutenant (now Sir Dirk)
Bogarde landed in
Normandy and went right
through the campaign in
North West Europe, as far
as Luneburg Heath

Gracie Fields, former mill girl from
Rochdale and Commander of the British
Empire who became a legend in her own
lifetime, entertaining troops in the Pacific
just before the end of the war

Anthony Quayle and
Noel Coward in Gibraltar,
1941

Echoing the feelings of
men and women who
came back to civilian life
after World War Two, the
film *The Best Years of Our
Lives* proved to be one
of the best movies of
the year

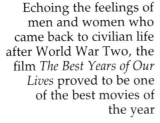

A dozen cheery members of the WAAF Gang show formed by
Squadron Leader Ralph Reader landed in Normandy in August 1944
and entertained troops in an old French château

Forty years on, Dame Vera Lynn with Marshal of the Royal Air
Force, Sir Arthur Harris, at a reunion dinner for members of RAF
Bomber Command

For these younger musicians there were opportunities for a very fine war indeed. Nevertheless there were still those who tried to evade the call up. The *Evening Standard* for example carried a hard hitting report under the emotive headline: SWINGSTERS WANT EXEMPTION FROM MILITARY SERVICE and the *Daily Express* carried a similar tirade headed DANCE BAND BOYS DODGE THE ARMY but there was in fact little evidence to suggest that dance band musicians were more inclined to dodge the column than any other group of young men.[14] In fact there is more evidence to support the opposite point of view, that musicians often volunteered well before their call up date.

Dame Vera Lynn recalled the amusing situation that arose when her fiancé, Harry Lewis, a dark and handsome clarinettist with the Ambrose band volunteered.[15] By 1940 it was pretty obvious that every able-bodied man was going to be drafted into one branch or other of the armed forces and that rather than be picked off individually it would be better if a group of them volunteered together so that they would have more chance of sticking together and what was more important, of playing together. So it was then that on one Monday morning when the band was appearing in Kilburn, Harry along with seven other member of the Ambrose band, still in their evening dress, took the tube train to Uxbridge and walked through the main gate of the RAF Recruit Training Depot to volunteer their services for King and country.

Soon each of them was stripped, medically examined and told to take the oath, swearing that he would bear true allegiance to His Majesty King George the Sixth, His Heirs and Successors ... and His Generals and officers set over him. Each of them received the King's shilling and when the last one had been through the routine they all turned to walk home.

'Where do you think you're going?' the astonished Sergeant asked. One of the band explained that they were working that night in the Kilburn Empire and soon the curtain would be going up.

'Oh no you're not,' replied the Sergeant in almost pantomime style. 'You're in the Airforce now. You've taken the King's shilling.' Fortunately for the eight band members, and for Ambrose, then pacing the backstage of the Empire wondering where half his band had gone, the RAF Station Commander gave them all leave for the rest of the week to complete the commitment at the Empire. They returned to Uxbridge on the following Monday and became the nucleus of the RAF Dance Orchestra – the Squadronaires. Soon they were joined by other top class musicians from the Lew Stone band and were led by the pianist and singer, Jimmy Miller.[16]

Ambrose was then left with the problem of finding replacements for his musicians and his lead singer, Vera Lynn had it seemed, like so many other women at that time, lost her fiancé for the duration of the war.

The idea behind the formation of the Squadronaires and other service dance orchestras was that they would complement the brass bands and play at dances and also accompany artistes at concerts and entertainments generally. They, like Glen Miller, were soon taking the cream of the pre-war dance bands which had been playing late-night dance music from the prestigious hotel ballrooms.

For those first few weeks of the phoney war the band was billeted in Mons Block of RAF Uxbridge and spent most of its time completing basic military training and in settling down to its own style of dance music. This, at first, was the same as its members had been following pre-war but then with the new freedom and change of environment alterations were made. Here was an ideal opportunity for a band to develop a style of its own.

The band leader, Sergeant Jimmy Miller (no relation to Glenn) and many of the musicians had already been influenced by recordings of the big American swing bands which were already gaining popularity with young people in Britain. Jimmy Miller decided this would be the style most likely to appeal to service audiences too.

At first there was some opposition from the orthodox school of military music which had to be overcome but Jimmy Miller was lucky enough to win support from the RAF's Director of Music Wing Commander R.P. O'Donnell, M.V.O.

So it was that by the time the Battle of Britain began, the RAF Squadronaires was ready to undertake a very full programme of tours. The band travelled to Fighter Command Stations at the height of the blitz, to military camps, to factories in blitzed provinical cities and those in the London area, and to dance halls large and small.

Air raids never deterred them. Once, when playing at Bristol, bombs fell on the hall in which they were playing and on to the terraced houses nearby. Instruments were laid carefully to one side and then the band spent the remainder of the night digging out victims from shattered houses.

From Bristol they went to play in the Manchester Gaumont cinema in Oxford Street, a part of the town which had already been heavily blitzed. Whether it was the adrenalin flowing more freely or just that the enthusiasm for the new style was in full flow too, it would be difficult to say, but the result was electrifying.

Music critics from the *Manchester Guardian* and the *Manchester Evening News* could not lavish enough praise on the night's performance. 'It is the best band this country has ever produced,' reported journalists.[17] And that night the tired fire watchers, the off-duty firemen and hundreds of airmen from Heaton Park aircrew centre went home with a much lighter step and memorable songs in their heads.[18]

It was a hectic tour programme from 1940 onwards which took the band from Land's End to John O'Groats and then across to the Continent. They played at every major military camp, Navy, Army, and Airforce; they broadcast regularly once a week, they played in hospitals and factories, for their fame brought demands from fans in all kinds of formations.

Long journeys in cold RAF trucks were often almost immediately followed by concerts given in bitterly cold hangars or draughty drill halls. This was no easy stint at all. Women guest vocalists such as Anne Shelton, Vera Lynn, Dorothy Carless and that dazzling blonde bombshell Evelyn Dall, often had to endure the same hardships as the men. It was no fun either driving back late at night after the concerts; cars and trucks had headlamps masked so that the smallest glimmer coming out did not contravene the black-out regulations. In towns driving was not too difficult but traversing country lanes leading from outlandish arifields in foggy weather was hazardous.

One of the most memorable of the Squadronaires' experiences was the opening of the stage door canteen in Piccadilly at the height of the flying bomb raids in the autumn of 1944. As those doodle-bug bombs were flying overhead the old groaner himself, Bing Crosby, without his toupé and surprisingly bald, was crooning with the band to an audience packed with celebrities – Foreign Secretary Anthony Eden, Fred and Adele Astaire, Jack Buchanan, generals, admirals and air marshals galore.

That summer of 1944 were trying times for the Squadronaires. They were awaiting a landing ship tank to take them across to France when a V2 rocket fell on their camp causing many casualties so that they missed the craft on which they should have embarked. The next day when they arrived in Ostend they saw the wreck of that same vessel in the entrance to the harbour. The bodies of four hundred airmen on that LST were later washed ashore.

For six weeks they performed in Brussels, Paris, advanced Fighter Command airfields and quite close to the front line army positions. They had just finished one performance in December 1944 when the commanding officer of the unit dashed over the band and told them to pack up right away. 'The Germans are coming through the Ardennes. If I were you I'd get back to Ostend.' They packed in such a hurry that the drummer had no time to pack his drums. 'Leave the bloody drums,' he shouted, 'I can always get another kit at Boosey and Hawkes.'

When they got back to Britain they heard the news that Glenn Miller was missing.

The chief rivals to the Squadronaires were the bands of the RAF Number One Balloon Centre – 'The Sky Rockets', the Navy's 'Blue Mariners', that of the Royal Marines – 'The Mariners' and the famous 'Blue Rockets' of the 'Royal Army Ordnance Corps'.

All these bands seemed to spring up quite spontaneously. For example, a few airmen were under training at Blackpool as balloon rigger fabric workers and, as they had brought their musical instruments with them, a handful of them got together and began playing. Once the news of the small band circulated, other musicians came forward and joined the band. It seemed a pity for such a successful group of musicians to be broken up and so when their training as balloon riggers was completed they were all posted together to the Barrage Balloon Centre at Kidbrooke. There they stayed for the greater part of the band's existence. Its leader was Corporal Paul Fenhoulet, formerly a trombonist and arranger with the pre-war Carroll Gibbons band of the Savoy Hotel.[19]

The demand for the services of the band grew to such an extent that the news of its popularity reached the ears of the Ministry of Information who, in conjunction with the Air Ministry booked the band to play for a two-year series of propaganda broadcasts to the German Air Force on the European Service of the BBC.[20] The 'Sky Rockets' went from strength to strength; it played in such popular BBC programmes as 'Ack Ack, Beer Beer' and 'Music While You Work'.

In addition to all these commitments, these hard-working musicians – for they were still employed during duty hours in servicing the silver barrage balloons, made long journeys to play for dances at Army and Airforce camps. At times it seemed that life was all 'Go, Go, Go', and that could sometimes bring haste that spelt disaster. Once, for example, when they were booked to play at Bristol they travelled by train, via Birmingham and Worcester. When they eventually arrived at the Bristol venue, eight hours after leaving Birmingham – they discovered that the guard's van, in which their instruments were packed, had been uncoupled at Worcester. They went on to the hall, packed with military and civilian personnel wondering how to cope with the situation.

Jack Parnell began the show by singing a few songs whilst one member of the band took a taxi to the nearest musical instrument shop and borrowed trumpets, clarinets, saxophones and a double bass. He got back to the stage just in time for the band to go on with borrowed instruments before an audience which was beginning to get restive.[20]

Travelling round the country giving concerts at short notice was not without certain hardships though the musicians would be the first to admit that rarely did they have to rough it in any way comparable to the life of those men and women who really were 'On Active Service'. Nevertheless, their itineraries did occasionally call for a certain amount of physical endurance. Pat Dodd of the 'Sky Rockets' never forgot a week's engagements at six ice rinks in Scotland for example, 'We played with our greatcoats on – boy, was it cold!'

Not quite so much in the limelight at dance halls and service camps were the Navy's 'Blue Mariners' and the 'Mariners' of the Royal Marines. They appeared several times at London's Stage Door Canteen and some of the better known provincial dance halls such as the Ritz and Locarno in Manchester. It was the drummer of the 'Mariners', however, who was eventually to have his name in lights and to find his fortune in films whilst employing a totally different kind of talent – comedian Norman Wisdom.

The Army's best known contribution to the dance band galaxy in those days was the band of the Royal Army Ordnance Corps – 'The Blue Rockets'. It was formed initially by Eric Robinson who would later be well known as a radio and television personality. At first, Robinson's band tended to favour swing versions of the better known light classics but gradually the leader realized that what the troops really wanted was music in the Glenn Miller style. And it was made clear to him that what the troops wanted they had to have. The leadership of the band was then taken over by Eric Tann, who developed the popular swing music, and Eric Robinson became concert master for the British band of the Allied Expeditionary Force.

This band, led by Regimental Sergeant Major George Melachrino, was formed from the Army Radio Orchestra and musicians drawn from many regimental bands. Its first live performance was given from the Queensbury All Services Club in

Soho at the height of the flying bomb raids on London in July 1944. The compere was Captain Franklyn Englemann with guest singer Corporal Denny Dennis of the 'Sky Rockets' band who sang 'Long Ago and Far Away'.

Thereafter, guest stars were a regular feature of the British Band shows. Later in the summer of 1944 the Queensbury Club was packed for the appearance with the band of Bing Crosby. He began with that popular sentimental song so often requested of Vera Lynn, 'I'll Be Seeing You'. But only a few in the audience then knew the poignancy of that song for the band's leader, George Melachrino. On the evening before the concert he had lost both his wife and younger son when a flying bomb plummetted straight into his house and blew it to smithereens.[21]

His orchestra knew of his loss and wondered how he had the courage to carry on with the concert that night. But that was the way people were then – a 'business-as-usual' spirit prevailed and the band played on.

Surprisingly the hard work put in by these service bands was not always given the credit it deserved. In fact the national press periodically affected to be outraged at 'these toy soldiers and airmen' having a 'soft war', and getting paid extra into the bargain.

But who was not having a 'soft war' then? In those middle years of the conflict, millions of servicemen, apart from those at the 'sharp end', were never in any more hazard than civilians in London and the provincial cities who had to endure the Luftwaffe's bombing. As cynical American infantrymen used to say: 'One man at the front and six others to bring up the Coca Cola.' Certainly there was no justification for the press to pick on the hard-working musicians. And frequently these bands did indeed entertain combat troops close to the front line.

However, such is the power of the press that this unjustifiable criticism caused the 'Blue Rockets' to be disbanded in 1942 but they were sadly missed and were reformed in 1943 to feature in a Ministry of Information film *Swinging into the Attack*.

The demand for dance bands seemed insatiable during those mid wartime years. It was boom time for dancing. Even throughout the height of the London blitz, dance halls stayed open. If you were rich you could dance in comparative safety in the prestigious hotels which had air-raid shelter facilities in their basements. The *Melody Maker* magazine published the venues of such 'safe' dances but ironically it was the venue which boasted the safest sanctuary for dancers which suffered more severely than all the others, the Café de Paris. Originally its site was a bearpit sunk below ground level, and subsequently it had been remodelled as a replica of the 'Titanic' liner. Because of its construction below ground it was advertised as London's safest restaurant, and it attracted celebrities and young officers on leave for a last fling before going overseas. Hollywood film star David Niven, then a lieutenant in the British Army Phantom Reconnaissance Regiment met his future wife, Primmie, whilst dancing there just a few days before a fifty kilo Luftwaffe bomb landed right in front of the band, killing its leader, Ken 'Snakehips' Johnson, the tenor saxophonist Dave Williams, and thirty two dancers.[22]

Grotesque and horrifying scenes followed. Whilst the debris was still falling and even whilst the dust from shattered masonry was still settling, men and women from the street clambered down into the wreckage, plundering and looting. They tore rings off the hands of badly wounded and dead women and made off whilst rescue workers were desperately trying to extricate the moaning victims.

The tragedy did nothing to dampen the dancing boom however and bands could almost command their own terms for appearing at the weekly local hops in the NAAFI canteen or local Town Hall. Musicians who had joined the Forces without ever dreaming of playing in a band were almost literally roped in.

Peter Bedford[23] today is amused to look back upon his own army days in the RAOC and the way he was employed to recruit muscians. His experience is so typical of many other musicians who found a profitable and comfortable niche in the army. A hard working one, but for six years he did little else than play his trumpet and organize the programme and transport for his unit bands.

In September 1939 I left the serenity of a London solicitor's office and proceeded to the Didcot, Berkshire, depot of the Royal Army Ordnance Corps, carrying under one arm a parcel of pyjamas and shaving kit. On the train I met another chap with a similar parcel and we began to talk. He was a pianist and that was the beginning of my playing and concert party days in the Army.

A few days after arriving at Didcot I went home for my trumpet and we formed a small band which rapidly grew into a complete concert party. We had played at several dances and given a few shows to different units when the professional musicians began to arrive and formed the 'Blue Rockets' band and I was then lucky enough to sit in with them too when we were accompanying ENSA shows on the station and at dances.

Once I had finished my training as a storeman, I was posted to

Hinckley on the staff and as soon as my playing experience became known I was given a table at the head of the documentation queue for new entrants. My job was to ask each new entrant if he played a musical instrument. Those who did were told to report for an audition and from that selection we formed the 'Toucans' dance band. We were so good that I then managed to acquire the ballroom of the George Hotel in Hinckley which accommodated fifteen hundred dancers. We played four nights a week and also for Saturday afternoon tea dances.

Those engagements brought a nice income for the unit PRI funds [extra comforts for soldiers] and also a nice bonus for me too. Unfortunately the unit was disbanded and I was then posted to a Leicester unit which had no job for me. Consequently I drew my army pay each week and I played with various local bands. Obviously, even the army could not let that go on for too long and so after a few months I was posted to Tel el Kebir in Egypt and sailed out on the troopship, 'Capetown Castle'. On board I met a tenor saxophone player who talked of forming a dance band in Tel el Kebir. He too had already experienced the advantages of being in a unit band, and within two days of our arrival we had got together a fifteen piece dance band called the 'Sand Stormers' and it was with them that I played out the remainder of my six years army service. Six years playing the trumpet.

Looking back now it all seems so hard to believe that it really happened, but wherever I was posted, a band just appeared, as if by magic.

Well, there was something quite magical about all those wartime bands, the professional and the amateur alike, something that has never been quite the same since the end of that war. Today, as the survivors of those turbulent years look back upon the times when they were young, they know that the music of those great bands lives on in their hearts. It comes out at odd moments when least expected, a line or two of the lyrics sung softly, absent-mindedly, bridging the long intervening years and lifting the spirit in just the same old way.

10

ENSA Revives a Battered Army

Ice in the cratered road was too thick to crackle under the wheels of the Bedford fifteen-hundred-weight truck bringing ENSA artistes, Madge and Cyril Ritchard, ageing and gallant stars of the real West End, and fellow performers, into the battered Dutch town of Eindhoven. It was the winter of 1944. All through the night they had inched their way up the jam-packed road passing scores of burnt out supply trucks in the ditches; everywhere wreckage was piled up on the road sides.

As they entered the devastated city centre one of the first things that caught the eyes of that ENSA party and lifted their spirits enormously, was a poster right in the middle of a shop window. They breathed sighs of relief. For once they were expected. Their show was heralded in bright colours and they were to perform, this time it seemed, in a real theatre, the Phillips.

But what kind of an audience would they have for what might be considered a rather unusual show for troops? Cyril Ritchard and his wife Madge knew how difficult it could be performing in front of an audience not accustomed to watching a serious play. For many years, in the twenties and thirties, they had played in front of pretty rough audiences in all kinds of Australian theatres when they were stars of musical comedy shows. Since then they had moved to London's West End to take leading roles in more serious plays. Now, having arrived at this forward base at Eindhoven they were more than a little anxious about their reception. What sort of an audience would there be in a place serving as a rest centre for weary soldiers coming out of one of the most terrible battles of all time – the battle for the bridge at Arnhem? How would these men react to the show ENSA was about to present – *The Merry Widow*?

What would these troops be like? Their numbers in that disastrous 'Operation Market Garden', designed to take the Allies over the Rhine, had been decimated. Far more of them had been killed and wounded than in the mammoth invasion of Normandy. In nine days Allied losses had amounted to more than 17,000. And for what? The Germans still held the vital bridge across the Rhine at Arnhem and the British Army were now being forced to sit in the mud and ice on the river bank watching for any move the enemy might make. What sort of mood would these men be in when they were relieved for a few days? How had they been living these weeks after their mauling and defeat?

A young officer there with an infantry division then, now Sir Dirk Bogarde, still vividly remembers just how it was there in the ruined village of Elst on the frozen banks of the Rhine, that November of 1944.[1]

> It was the darkest, coldest winter of the war, we were just across the river, watching the hideous death of a dream, a city and much of its population in helpless frustration. Uselessly one wept, or dragged muddied, soaking bodies up the slithering river banks, or watched as our youth (I was 23) drained away into the swirling waters of the Rhine.

The troops were sickened and exhausted by attempts at river crossings in which men seemed driven to fever pitch by rage and fear, by awe inspiring sights as they sat helpless in small boats as friends died all around them. They had fought through fields, orchards and houses and behind embankments amidst the marshy battlefield, under the fire of machine guns and artillery batteries. And it had all been for nothing. Or so it seemed to the dazed paratroopers and sad-faced infantrymen now in those freezing slit trenches on the Rhine, trying to keep warm, that November of 1944.

The hope that kept them going was the prospect of a few days leave in Eindhoven. For they had heard of the Dutch town, a few miles to the rear with the lights on in the streets where men and women walked without fear; smart, friendly women one could take to a bar, dance or even a show.

When young Dirk Bogarde got back to Eindhoven he jumped at the chance of seeing a show – *The Merry Widow*. He recalled:

> I was almost first in line. After the darkness and sadness across the river, the dead swinging silently in the current of the Rhine, *The Merry Widow* could not be missed. I sat enraptured in my plush seat, no heating, but snuggish in a greatcoat: the orchestra crashed into the overture and sheer glory, magic beauty, life and fun were there before us.

After the first night it was obvious to Cyril and Madge Ritchard that their anxiety had been unfounded; the weary soldiers were entranced. Here was something of the real world, something so wonderful they felt like tapping their feet, dancing with joy and relief. Here was laughter and cheer and there were glamorous women with long, shiny, legs encased in fishnet tights!

The answer to anyone who had ever criticized ENSA shows was there in no uncertain terms. They gave those deprived young men just what was needed, as Sir Dirk Bogarde recalled: 'They gave us back our youth which we were in severe danger of losing.' He felt that their laughter, their songs and their vitality brought those dispirited soldiers back towards a belief that maybe, just maybe, they could make it to the end, that they might just survive after all.

Young Dirk Bogarde went to every performance and he learnt that night in the Phillips Theatre, Eindhoven, what theatre could really mean to people and especially to those previously dispirited soldiers. It was a lesson which we could all take to heart, an experience which testified to the wisdom of organizing concert parties for the troops.

Close on fifty years later Sir Dirk Bogarde wrote of that night: 'It was glorious, glowing, colour, laughter, light and life with the added glory of music. Because of Cyril and Madge Ritchard and *The Merry Widow* which they and their company brought to us in that bitter, cruel winter, I swear that hundreds of us survived.'[2]

And what is remarkable about those white-haired men and women who now look back on those wartime years and the rare concert they attended is the indelible impression such experiences had upon them. Many of them feel exactly the same as Sir Dirk Bogarde does today and have, in a variety of ways echoed his words:

> The instant I hear the first notes of 'Vilja' or 'We are going to Maxim's' I am instantly, for a second or so, back in Elst, with the crumping mortars, the blazing train on the polder, and the brilliance, the bravery of Madge and Cyril Ritchard whose laughter, delight and energy revived a battered, almost defeated group of wretched soldiers for ever; in my case anyway.

What finer testimonial could ENSA be given?

ENSA did a fine job and today so many ex-servicemen who wrote to the writer, echo the words of Sir Dirk Bogarde and praise that much maligned organization. Doug Kneale,[3] for example, has a similar story to tell about ENSA. He was then a warrant officer, aircrew with 228 Squadron, on Sunderland flying boats

with Coastal Command when he was sent on detachment to the
Faroe Isles, to help give cover to the convoys en route to Russia.

I have to admit it was the most Godforsaken hole I have ever been
to in my life. We were stationed on Vaaga, the largest of the islands
in the group. It was the depths of winter, gale force winds, snow
and torrential rain. Everything was a sea of mud, alternating with
ice. Our flying boat was the only one up there. In fact we had the
only airplane in the area, and our base was an island lake, shaped
like a banana. On three sides were craggy mountains and at the far
end of the lake's landing area there was a hundred foot waterfall
drop into the sea.

To say the least, it was dodgy. We could only operate in daylight
– and there wasn't much of that, about four hours a day. On 24th
December we had been out on patrol over the convoy of merchant
ships bound for the north Russian port of Murmansk. There were
heavy squalls of sleet and snow, the seas were mountainous and
we couldn't help feeling that all those sailors down there deserved
medals as big as frying pans. We were spotted by a Junkers 88 and
after a running battle with him I just managed to get a better angle
on him and let fly with all four guns in my rear turret. Bits and
pieces flew off his port engine and we made off safely for base.

When we landed we discovered sixty bullet holes and one
cannon shell hit. But the more important discovery we soon made
was that an ENSA concert party had arrived in that 'Godforsaken'
hole. They were the 'Globe Trotters', one of the first shows put
together after the outbreak of war. And that night they put on a
really tremendous show, and with five lovely women in it!
Afterwards we entertained them in the Sergeants' Mess.

Everything was going well until some silly twit decided to
organize an 'excuse me' dance with the aid of an old wind up
gramophone. Well, what a business! Fifty men and five girls. One
would just get his arms round a girl, manage no more than three or
four steps, there'd be a tap on the shoulder and that was the end of
that. But the girls took it all in good part and after a late night we all
staggered off to our own beds.

What we had not realized was those tired girls and the rest of the
'Globe Trotters' concert party were flying off the next day, in our
aircraft, to Reykjavik in Iceland. We took off in weather that was
awful and for the next four and a half hours we were buffeted
about as never before. I felt heartily sorry for our guests. We at least
had our warm flying gear on but they had no extra protection. One
of the party, an elderly gentleman was propped up along the
fuselage catwalk, his hands under the armpits of his thin overcoat,
a scarf wrapped round his head and his trilby hat jammed over the
lot, being violently sick. Never have I seen anyone look quite so ill.

That night though, when the curtain went up in the Reykjavik
garrison theatre, who should be holding centre stage but the

gentleman himself, singing his heart out – 'Old Father Thames Keeps Rolling Along'. It was difficult to see how they had all made such a dramatic recovery – real troupers each and everyone of them.

Little did they know, on that flight to Iceland how vulnerable they were. It was an operational flight for us, we were fully armed, carrying a full depth charge load, and if we had spotted a German U-boat then we were committed to attack it. That might have brought a JU 88 on to us, as had happened earlier that week. But those troupers seemed game for anything and they brought delight to us on that lonely, base in the north Atlantic. I take my hat off to them.

Naturally, there were ENSA parties that did not come up to that standard. Often they were the butt for a poor comedian's joke and apparently fair game for the cartoonist's pen. Often too they arrived at units only to receive an inhospitable reception or one such as Naomi Jacob relates in her book,[4] *Me, Over There*:

Once, a small company was sent forward and on arriving at their destination the colonel sent for the artiste in charge, a rather shy little comedian. He eyed him up and down, then said:
    'Ha! Come to entertain the troops, eh?'
    'Yes, sir.'
    'ENSA, eh?'
    'Yes, sir.'
    'Good! Got Tommy Trinder and George Formby with you?'
    'No, sir.'
    'Why not? They work for ENSA, don't they?'
    Later when the show was about to begin, the colonel came round to speak to the comedian in question for a moment, to tell him what a good audience he had, what a number of distinguished officers and so on. The comedian listened, then asked:
    'General Alexander in front, sir?'
    'General Alexander? No!'
    'General Montgomery, then, sir?'
    'Good heavens, no!'
    'Brigadier Matthews in front?'
    'No, of course not!'
    'Why "of course"? They're working for the Army, aren't they?'

Tit for tat!
What has to be remembered is that the artistes worked for a pittance or gave their services free – as George Formby, Gracie Fields, Gertrude Lawrence and many other well-known stars did. At the same time they were foregoing the money they could have earned from the many lucrative contracts then available to them.

At one time whilst on a tour of army units in Shropshire, Gertrude Lawrence ran out of money completely. She did not even have enough to pay the train fare back to London to hunt for a new job.[5]

Then she had an inspiration.

The next morning she went to see the proprietor of the Red Lion inn, where she was staying and confessed that she had no money to pay her bill but that she would be willing to work off the debt if he would allow her. That market-day lunchtime a new barmaid with a mass of curly hair was polishing glasses and giving the locals as much backchat as they could give to her. Within a few days, the Red Lion was one of the most popular pubs in Shrewsbury and before long Gertrude Lawrence had paid off her debt and had more than enough money for her rail ticket back to London as well as still having some spare for a rainy day. And for Gertrude Lawrence the rain fell frequently.

Back in London, she began rehearsing her show – *The Gertrude Lawrence Unit* – in the underground cellars of Drury Lane, working late into the night and eating suppers cooked on a small gas ring. Soon they were ready for a tour giving three shows a day.

'Every noon we put on a show at a plane factory and at night we gave two concerts in military camps. At the Civic Theatre in Southampton we played to some four thousand men and women, representing all the Allied nations and all branches of the service.'

By this time, May 1944, the whole of southern England had become a vast military encampment. As far as the eye could see the countryside was packed with weaponry, stores and troops. Under trees, at the roadside, in fields, there was stack after stack of artillery ammunition, mines, engineers' stores, planks and barbed wire, bridging materials, all covered with corrugated iron or tarpaulin sheets.

Gertrude Lawrence's ENSA party was awed at what they saw, and so too were the soldiers. Tanks and vehicles were parked in rows reaching to the horizon. Most awe-inspiring of all though, were the troops: twenty American divisions, fourteen British, three Canadian, one French and one Polish, and hundreds of thousands of special forces, of corps troops, headquarters units and lines of communications personnel. They were crowded into Nissen huts, tents and country houses from Cornwall to Kent. And they were now not being allowed out.

Now, more than ever before, concert parties came into their own. Gay Clark and her husband in the 'Stars in Battledress' show, *The Bombshells* rushed from one encampment to the next performing before small groups of twenty and audiences of hundreds, now all cooped up, bored and anxious. 'It was a unique experience making "a raid on the blues", we called it. Unforgettable,' Gay recalled.[6]

By 25 May 1944 all camps in the invasion assembly area had been sealed with barbed wire fencing. Patrols of armed military police guarding every exit were primarily concerned with keeping troops in rather than with the problem of enemy agents infiltrating from the outside. There was nowhere for the bored troops to go except the big NAAFI tents in each compound. There they would sit night after night drinking weak NAAFI beer in an atmosphere thick with tobacco smoke.

Their behaviour matched the findings of John Keegan's later study of the psychiatric casualties of war and of how waiting to go into battle affected soldiers. He was to write that:[7]

> The prospect of battle, excepting perhaps the first battle of a war or a green unit's first blooding, seems always to alarm men's anxieties, however young and vigorous they be, rather than excite their anticipation. Hence the drinking which seems an inseparable part both of preparation for battle and of combat itself. Alcohol, as we know, depresses the self-protective reflexes and so induces the appearance and feeling of courage.

And so the days and nights of waiting dragged by. Training had virutally been abandoned and the hours were filled with fatigues, lectures and the odd football match about the result of which no one cared.

Tension among all ranks was expressed in different ways. Men who had been under fire in Africa and Sicily and knew what lay ahead for them, were quieter and more reflective than the younger recruits who had seen and heard nothing more frightening than the simulated war of the battle schools.

Every day and night huge fleets of bombers passed overhead on their way to smash enemy defensive positions and dislocate road and rail transport systems in France and the low countries. Sometimes, during the day, the whole sky would darken and throb with American low flying fortresses and above them squadron after squadron of RAF Lancasters. Clearly to all those waiting troops, D-Day was imminent.

Many of these young lads were not only anxious but homesick too, they were wondering just what they had let themselves in for. They thought about their pals back in civvy street earning big money, and they wondered if their own days were now numbered. All of them were excited, some appeared eager to get on with the great adventure which lay ahead. Many of them were wishing they could escape. Most of them were probably now, at least, glad to be escaping from the years of training.

Carefully, commanders had mixed the veterans of units who had seen action in Africa and elsewhere, with the raw green troops who had been languishing in Britain for so long.

Nevertheless, they all had one thing in common. They all needed diverting. ENSA was there to do just that. They did it well, especially during those critical days in the first week in June.

The Gertrude Lawrence party went to Camp 22 to give a show for 2,000 American and British Commandos – under canvas and in the pouring rain – and to an audience that was now feeling the suspense of the approaching assault. No one, of course, could or would say when that would be. But everyone knew the bases were now being sealed. And it was in the middle of that concert in Camp 22 when secret orders came for Gertrude Lawrence and her party to stop the performance and get back to London immediately. Nelson's blind eye prevailed as Gertrude recalled:[8]

> We carried on to the finale and afterwards went into the officers' mess – a tent with a trestle table – for supper. They put on a substantial meal and the refreshment was good old bathtub gin with a kick of a bronco. As we laughed and joked, I wondered whether the men knew that I knew this was to be their last party for a long, long time. And as we drove away in the darkness back to London I had a horrid feeling I was deserting them.

As the invasion started so too did the days of the pilotless planes, the 'Doodlebugs' as the Amercians christened them, which were proving more deadly than their euphemistic name suggested. It would have been unnerving for anyone but it was not the danger to themselves that upset those entertainers with Gertrude Lawrence then, as the sadness of it all. Young children being dug out of craters, wrapped in a blanket and carried off by weeping parents, young lads looking so brave and fit, so happy and laughing one evening and being sent off to the slaughter the next.

'We did shows in tents, hangars, garrison theatres, and under trees. Each time men would be gone the next morning. It gave one a sinking feeling to realize that these men were actually going into battle with the song in their hearts they had heard you sing only a few hours before.'[9]

Now this was one of the tensest periods of the war for both civilians and those in the Forces. Everyone was edgy, nervous, overtired, and yet desperately determined to keep up a front at all cost. And so entertainment flourished everywhere – from the splendid London theatres to makeshift stages in tented camps where unit concert parties often joined with professionals of ENSA to put on a show.

Pianist Doug Marshall and comedian/compere Bert Woodfield of the 15th (Scottish) Division Concert party – 'The Tam O'Shanters', recall how pleased they were to be with Gertrude Lawrence. 'She "adopted" our concert party just before we went over to Normandy with the invasion and presented us with a brand new song written specially for her which we used in our Field Show,' said Doug. 'She also gave us permission to call our mascot, a stage property horse, "Gertrude".'

For the invasion, the 'Tam O'Shanters' rejoined their respective units; Private Kenneth Connor now known more for his performances in the *Carry On* films and the current TV series of *Allo Allo*, went back to the Middlesex Regiment, Bert Woodfield, returned to his parent unit of the Royal Artillery, and most of them were in action right away. Bert recalled: 'We landed on D 7 at 1030 hours and at 1145 we were firing our twenty-five pounders.'

This was in one of the most brutal and hard fought battles of the war, the battle for Caen. After the success of D-Day, it was essential for the Allies quickly to seize the port of Caen ready for their breakout from Normandy. Every available man was needed for the fierce fighting which by August 1944 had accounted for 200,000 Allied casualties and 450,000 German.

Despite the desperate nature of the war sitution then, it might seem remarkable to some students of military history that the general officer commanding 15th Scottish Division decided to regroup the 'Tam O'Shanters' concert party as soon as the tactical situation permitted. Almost immediately then he sent them as far forward as possible to entertain fighting troops pulled out of the line for short breaks. The reason for this was that the Army Medical Corps and particularly the psychiatrists had already got the fact established with High Command that battle was too intensely stressful, a wholly unnatural experience for the majority of soldiers to cope with satisfactorily for long periods and that psychiatric casualties would increase rapidly according to the intensity and duration of combat. Short breaks were essential.

For men of the Allied armies in June and July 1944 those breaks proved to be needed not just for raising morale but, more importantly, for maintaining the mental fitness of the soldier. In the horrific battles of attrition that followed the landings in Normandy, psychiatric casualties counted for almost thirty per cent of all men evacuated from the front to hospitals. That figure could well have been much higher but for the diversions provided by concert parties giving shows near to the forward areas.

There had been the same problem of psychiatric casualties in World War One, but then the Army took a different view of them. The lucky ones were categorized as 'shell-shocked' – a term implying that the soldier's nervous system had been affected by the explosion of shells or mortars close to him.

But, sadly, far too many of the soldiers who suffered from psychiatric trauma caused by physical horror and the over-whelming sadness produced by the death of friends, were not diagnosed as 'shell-shocked'. They were categorized as cowards. Those who could no longer take the trauma and walked away, were shot. The grim statistics speak for themselves.

Britain declared war on Germany on 4 August 1914 and seventeen days later the British Army killed its first British soldier, a 19-year-old private condemned for desertion. Thereafter it continued to condemn them to death at the rate of sixty per month and execute them at the rate of six per month. Some months were better than others.

Fortunately by 1944, the medical services could no longer deny that all wounds in battle are not physical and that preventive action in the form of concert parties and rest was far better than the fear of a firing squad for keeping men in the line.

So it was that the 'Tam O'Shanters' concert party of 15th Scottish Division was soon making a vital contribution to the total war effort, as Bert Woodfield now recalls:[10]

> We gave three shows a day, each of two hours duration and at different locations ten or fifteen miles apart. It became a test of skill in performing, packing up, driving as fast as we could along roads choked with traffic and pitted with shell-holes, finding the new location and then getting our props in position for the show. It really was a case of accurate timing for troops could not be withdrawn for too long.

Doug Marshall, pianist and Jack of all trades with the party from its foundation recalled:

> Almost all the shows were in the open air. We had two 3-ton trucks which we parked about thirty feet apart with a tarpaulin sretched over the top of both, facing the audience. This protected the band and the performers from any sudden changes in the weather but fortunately we had a very dry period then. The rear portions of the trucks were used as dressing rooms.

On many occasions we were performing in areas which had been in enemy hands the day before – a mile from the front line was not uncommon and sometimes even we were under shell-fire.

Sometimes too they had to drop their props and costumes and pick up their weapons for fighting patrol work. Bert Woodfield remembers:

We were told to clear up a village which had been bypassed by the infantry. We went in and took eight prisoners, two of them were of a crack SS Regiment. Almost straight away from that little skirmish we were off in our trucks giving shows to the lads from the front. It was all go, sometimes we managed five shows a day. It did not matter to us whether the audience was 20 or 200, they always got the full two hour show. We just kept going as long as we could because the expressions on the lads' faces when they saw us arrive was thanks enough for us.

It was at this time too that their 'patron' Gertrude Lawrence got her orders to embark for Normandy. She was delighted. 'It was just what I had hoped for,' she wrote, 'the opportunity to entertain the fighting men at the front.'

So it was that on Thursday 19 August, 1944 she was in a convoy of fifty trucks, a hundred and ten artistes, the largest ENSA outfit ever assembled, sailing for Normandy. Included in that party were such stars as Diana Wynyard, Jessie Matthews, Bobbie Andrews, Margaret Rutherford, Ivor Novello and many others who had topped the bill in theatres all over Europe and the United States.

They were all issued with 'Geneva Cards' on which they were rated as lieutenants of the British Army, just in case they were taken prisoner.

As soon as they arrived across the Channel they drove to St Aubin, where, in a theatre that was once the 'Casino-sur-Mer', they began giving two concerts every day. The building was full of holes, no windows, no doors, no roof, and yet somehow they managed to put on a good show. 'The men come in hundreds,' wrote Gertrude in her diary, 'We are the first entertainers they've seen since D-Day.'

Now ENSA too was in action giving those troops something to laugh about, something to cheer, giving them in fact 'a few precious moments of forgetfulness' as Eisenhower once put it.

It was to St Aubin too that 'The Tam O'Shanters' came to give their shows which were now arousing interest in the press back in Britain. *The Scotsman*[11] carried a report under the headline: SCOTS ENTERTAIN IN FRONT LINE –

The Tam O'Shanters concert party who some months ago were packing theatres in Glasgow, Edinburgh and Aberdeen, and the principal towns in Scotland and England, are scoring even bigger success playing to the troops of the division right up in the front line in France. Already they have been shelled, bombed and machine-gunned while the show was in progress, but this does not daunt them.

Bert Woodfield can recall those days with 15th Scottish Division's concert party forty odd years later as vividly as if they were only yesterday:

The division always seemed to be in the forefront of everything; they were the first troops in Eindhoven – we gave a show in the Phillips Theatre there and were each given a present of an electric razor – we were in the vanguard right up to the end in Lubeck.
    We weren't always the most popular people in the division though, some people took a delight in putting one over us. There was, for example, a camp commandant in the Falaise Gap area who once caught us with our shirts off on a very hot day. After he'd raved and told us who and what our ancestors were, he sent us off with the punishment of burying three putrifying dead horses, killed by artillery fire, which were lying close to the camp (8,000 horses had been killed in the Falaise gap). The stench was stomach turning. An hour or so later when we came back he looked surprised to see us queueing up for dinner. The truth was we never went near enough to the horses to lose our appetites. A few packets of cigarettes and bars of chocolate changed hands and the locals were quite happy to do the job for us with the help of a tractor driver.

What with the dead from the battle, men and animals lying about and also the insanitary latrines infested by flies, it was not surprising that food was contaminated and *L'estomac de Normandie*, or simply diarrhoea, was rife. Consequently the primitive latrines were never without occupants, as Gertrude Lawrence found, when she was touring front-line units and was taken short.
'I discovered a row of three evil-smelling, ramshackle outhouses, all open at the top, behind the theatre where we were doing our show. They were used by troops and civilians. The arrangement was decidedly primitive. No seat, just a hole in the ground and two places for your feet. You simply crouched and let nature take its course.'
She, like the other stars coped one way or another. As long as she had her make up bag she could manage. 'I could always do a show as long as I had my false eyelashes,' she once confessed.

'And there was always the great satisfaction that came from doing something I did well for the troops.'

One can imagine the scene as soldiers arrived for an ENSA show: 'They came in direct from the line, some all bound up and dirty, tired but all in great spirits, and they sang as though their lungs must burst. It was great to be with them. And all our own grouses disappeared once the show was on. We felt that if they could take it then so could we.'[12]

This was the spirit of all the concert parties then and they came over to Normandy from an amazing variety of units. In August 1944, for instance eleven lively members of the Women's Auxiliary Air Force stepped onto a plane bound for Normandy carrying a comprehensive selection of theatrical gear with them. They were the WAAF Gang Show off to invade the Continent!

Their base was a lovely old French chateau which for the last four years had been the headquarters of the Nazi Normandy Command. By the time the WAAF lovelies arrived it had been converted into one of the famous RAF Malcolm clubs. Into this club everyday came truck and coach loads of RAF personnel serving on outlying units in North West Europe to see shows presented in the open-air theatre which had been built in the grounds of the chateau.

The WAAF Gang Show was the first of those formed by Squadron Leader Ralph Reader. As one can well imagine from looking at the photographs of the cast of this show, it was a huge success. After entertaining over 7,000 troops the girls flew back to Britain to go on a nationwide tour.

Better known to RAF personnel serving across the Channel then was the concert party formed by Flight Lieutenant Bill Fraser, who had been a manager and actor in pre-war London, appearing in the 1939 West End revue, *New Faces*. He became the Entertainments Officer of Second Tactical Air Force, 83 Group and quickly set about recruiting talent for revues. One of the first to volunteer was a low-ranking leading aircraftsman by the name of Denis Norden, and he was followed by another airman now equally well known, Eric Sykes.

How it all took shape was explained to the writer by Peter Fawcett,[13] another airman then in 2nd TAF:

Perhaps it was the ''Goonish'' sense of humour that prevailed among the Wireless Operating fraternity that spurred me into volunteering for the 83 group concert party then but I certainly never regretted the move and enjoyed every minute of my time with the concert party. Bill Fraser took charge of the auditioning and producing, Denis Norden wrote the scripts along with Bill

Fraser. Our pianist was Reginald Forsythe and Corporal Dickie Rouse was our solo baritone singer.

Gradually more and more men responded to the invitation in Daily Routine Orders for those with theatrical experience to report for auditions. Amongst these new volunteers was Ronald Rich who, with encouragement from Denis Nordon, was taken on with the particular role of providing original musical material.

What happened next was perhaps typical of what has been called the Concert Party Phenomenon of World War Two. It is that no matter how small or how far flung a unit might be, once an appeal went out for volunteers – musicians, actors, entertainers of any kind – there was never a shortage. Men and women came forward to perform on stage whilst others volunteered for technical work back stage. There always appeared to be a wealth of talent upon which to draw. And it was not always confined to stage work, as Tom Taylor,[14] once of Bomber Command aircrew, recalled with an amusing story:

Talent in wartime for various things came about because of the wide range of recruits. There was always plenty for concert parties or for anything else really. On my first station, for example, the officer commanding said he had forgotten the key for the small attache case he was carrying. An airman went up to the stage and in two seconds had the case open. 'What were you in civvy street?' asked the CO. The airman replied, 'A burglar.'

Be that an apochryphal tale or not, it illustrated the point and goes a long way to explain how it was that the response to Bill Fraser's appeal produced such a wealth of talent that three shows were written and produced within a very short time. Ron Rich recalls:

The first was *Bags of Panic* the second *It's in the Bag* and the third, of course, *Three Bags Full*. There were about twenty men in the cast, plus two pianists, a drummer, an electrician, and a stage manager (Flt. Lt. Leo Pappe). We did our own scene shifting and drove the Bedford trucks that took us to our locations all over Holland and Germany. Sometimes we performed in mess halls, on several occasions we used the tailboards of two trucks but for most of our shows the local theatre was available. In Lubeck and Hamburg the magnificent opera houses were the venues. In the Phillips theatre in Eindhoven, the show was recorded and broadcast over the Netherlands Radio. Among the songs, Denis and I wrote were: 'What's the second thing you'll do when you get home on leave?' and 'After I've liberated Europe, who's going to liberate me?'

Denis Norden's brilliant scripts made the maximum use of the mixed talents of the all-male cast, one of whom, then calling himself Rick Allen, was Eric Sykes. Even in those early days everyone recognized his excellent mimicry skills and fine timing, which marked him out as a performer with a future.

Another point of interest with these concert party shows was the appeal to patriotism in their rousing opening, which, when we look at it today might seem to be somewhat 'corny'. Peter Fawcett reflecting on the opening for the revue, *Bags of Panic* – shown below – said, 'This might sound "old hat" these days, full of "get up and go" messages but I suppose it's how we felt then and I guess we needed such propaganda to give us "heart" ... whether it would ever be the same again is hard to say.'

> Let's get on with the war,
> That's the job we're here for,
> Make a night of it –
> By all means,
> Don't make light of it,
> We've a fight for it.
>
> Let's get on with the war,
> There's no time for encore,
> It's an interlude,
> Let it be understood
> There'll be 'Bags of Panic',
> When we settle the score –
> Let's get on with the war.

Such was the experience of so many professional and amateur performers during those last months of the war. Bert Woodfield with the 'Tams' found his time on and off stage so rewarding.

It was good to know too, that Corps and Army commanders felt that our job had been worthwhile too. I remember for instance the time when we had given our last performance – Cinderella – on the stage of a Lubeck theatre and the general officer commanding our division climbed on to the stage. He turned to the audience and told them all what a marvellous job we had done since the invasion began. He said he was full of admiration for the way that we had been able, no matter what the weather or facilities, to lift everyone's spirit when it might well have sunk lower. It was nice to know we were appreciated.

There can be no doubt in the minds of military historians now that relaxation and entertainment made a great contribution to the mental fitness of the Allied armies. As General Montgomery said before the battle of El Alamein: 'Morale is the big thing in war. Therefore we must take no chances. We must raise the morale of our army to the highest pitch. They must enter this battle with their tails high in the air.' He had preached this gospel too before the new Eighth Army invaded Sicily and began its long haul across the rivers and mountains of Italy where weary troops were now struggling to keep their tails in the air at all.

11

Yes, They're Still Fighting in Italy

'I have never seen troops so angry anywhere as when a soldier sent to a Service newspaper here, a letter from his mother saying: 'Thank God they sent you to Italy and not to France where there is such dreadful fighting.'[1]

Such were the opening lines of a cable sent by News Review's correspondent to his editor, in December, 1944. He went on to say, 'The truth is that there is no harder fighting front in the whole world. I meet war correspondents continually coming and going between different fronts, the Russian and the Pacific included, and they are definite about this.'

Another representative[2] of an American magazine said he never saw a country so wrecked and torn from end to end; he never saw troops enduring such acute discomfort with such good heart. When he flew away to America with a permanently disfigured nose, a mountain road having crumbled away beneath his jeep as those water soaked roads tacked to the sides of the Appenines so often do, he was quite satisfied that the Italian front was the worst for the infantrymen.

Yet somehow they managed to relax with the occasional concert party organized under the most bizarre conditions.

What we have to remember about the war in Italy then is that on that front were the biggest proportion of the war's veterans, British and American alike. Consequently the German Commander in Chief, General Kesselring, was given the élite of the German army to hold them. A quarter of the twenty-nine German divisions being pinned down in Italy were the Reich's handpicked best. And all that led to fierce fighting with no quarter asked or given.

Another point to remember is that the prime task given to the Allied troops in Italy was to kill Germans, and during the winter of 1944-45 they were killing more per thousand men engaged than any troops anywhere. The campaign was one continuous offensive, held up occasionally, as offensives are bound to be, only by intolerably bad weather.

It was in such rare breaks that a few performers of ENSA, and the robust veterans of divisional concert parties, managed to give some well-earned entertainment to the forward troops.

John Cooper,[3] remembers vividly today, one such party at Castel Del Rio. He was then in the Lancashire Fusiliers of 78 Division which had battled through the cold and mud and craggy hills of Tunisia, the dust and heat of Sicily, and after very little rest, had been committed to battle again in Italy, fighting a succession of river crossings, the now legendary battles of the Sangro, and Cassino. By the October of 1944 they were in the thick of the worst yet encountered, the assaualt on Monte Spaduro.

These troops now really needed a few hours of rest, relaxation and entertainment. The Irish Fusiliers of the 78 Division had attacked this precipitous Spaduro ridge by night, hauling men up an almost impassable cliff to surprise and overcome the German defences. But at dawn, when the mist lifted, German machine-guns swept the Fusiliers' position prior to a fierce counter attack. Let the offical history of 78 Division give the reader a taste of what the audience at a subsequent concert party had just gone through, for it will perhaps explain more the events which followed.

'The Irishmen fought stubbornly but they were outnumbered: when they ran out of ammunition they flung rocks at the advancing Germans, battered at them with rifle butts, or grappled with their bare hands. Only a few got back from each company.'[4]

Two days later it was the turn of the Lancashire Fusiliers to attack Monte Spaduro. Once again it was a tough assignment but by one o'clock in the morning Monte Spaduro had fallen. There were counter attacks supported by four German machine-gun groups and German units armed with grenade discharging rifles, but the Fusiliers held the position, thanks to the support from the rest of the Brigade. John Cooper,[5] forty-seven years later, told the writer what happened during the next few days and the riotous night of the concert party which followed in Castel Del Rio.

> It was bitterly cold weather, lots of snow and ice. We had to wear white camouflage outfits and before the attack we were confined to our slit trenches which had about a foot of water in the bottom due to snow continually seeping in. We had a hot meal when the rations came up by mules, and a liberal rum ration to keep the cold out. (How did we survive?)

It was against this background that the forward units were sent for a short rest, no more than three or four days, to forward Division HQ at Castel Del Rio. To get there we had to tramp about eight miles through snow and mud carrying all our equipment and cross the dangerous San Clemente river, which the Germans shelled with their heavy artillery, frequently at irregular intervals. You just hoped you were not crossing it when it happened.

We arrived at our destination, wet and weary to find that we were billeted in a very large ancient castle in the centre of the village. The cooks had been very busy awaiting our arrival and we were rewarded with large helpings of stew and bread. Before retiring we were issued with American army sleeping bags. We had never known such luxury. (But they were taken off us when we left.)

The next afternoon we were given the opportunity of going to see the pantomime, *Cinderella* presented by the Divisional concert party. Albert Green and I – we had been called up together on the same day and had been together as C Company signallers all through the campaign and are still friends today – went together to see the show.

We are under the impression that the show was held in one of the very long rooms in the castle with quite a professional looking stage at one end. We were seated on forms running across the hall, with officers sitting in the front rows. The show was absolutely marvellous. Everyone had a really good time.

I don't know where all the props came from but they were most effective. The jokes were topical and about people we all knew. I remember too the female impersonators, or 'drag artists' as they are now known, were most impressive, but perhaps that was because we had been cut off from the real world for so long. I would say that the standard was somewhat better than the average amateur show and greatly appreciated. It was the talking point for some time after.

Then came the next memorable part of that day.

We had decided to have a party that evening. We were billeted in a very big room, and the new sleeping bags were laid out around the four walls, and we each claimed our patch. A huge vat of vino rosso appeared in the middle of the room by courtesy of my good friend Jack Fenwick who was then in charge of PRI funds (President of the Regimental Institute's money used for soldiers' comforts) and as usual our officers, warrant officers and NCOs donated bottles of whisky, gin and rum to our party. All these were emptied into the vat of red vino and into this too went much of our beer ration. It made, as you can well imagine, a lethal 'cocktail'. We sat around in our newly acquired sleeping bags, dipping our tin mugs into the Devil's Brew and singing our favourite songs: 'The White Cliffs of Dover', 'Roll out the Barrel', 'Bless 'Em All', 'Lili Marlene' and 'The D-Day Dodgers'. [Nancy Asquith, MP, had accused the Eighth Army of having a good time in Italy and dodging D-Day!]

There was the occasional solo, a few lewd jokes until one by one, we crawled into our sleeping bags and became unconscious. Soon, all that could be heard were grunts and groans and snores and all the other sounds that come from a group of sleeping, drunken soldiery.

Eventually silence fell over the inhabitants of the castle. Suddenly, in the middle of the night, a high pitched scream pierced the silence. Agitated voices began shouting: 'The castle's on fire!' The slumbering soldiers stirred in their sleeping bags, hoping the prankster would go to sleep. No one roused himself, murmurs came from the bags, 'Let the bugger burn' and 'Piss on it'. And everyone went back to sleep.

The next morning, bleary eyed and with splitting headaches, we were told that during the night, German heavy guns had shelled Castel del Rio and the castle itself had been on fire. Whilst we were sleeping, the officers, led by Captain Kevin Hill had spent most of the night trying to put the fire out with vino!

Soon we were back on the road to the hills, and to the snow, to the shells and death at short notice. But we set off with fond memories of hot food, the sleeping bags, the vino and the fire, but above all, the pantomime which had taken us back into a world that we used to know.

John Cooper's recollections must give a good deal of satisfaction to all those men and women from both the professional and amateur ranks who helped to remind those fighting men of a 'world they used to know'.

Eighth Army commander, General Sir Richard McCreery[6] recalled:

That winter of 1944-5 in Italy, really was a nightmare, because not only had the Eighth Army been fighting almost continuously since landing in Italy but the toll of those innumerabale river crossings all the way up could not only be measured in thousands of casualties and severe loss of equipment and supplies, but also in the numbing battle weariness of those who were left. It really was a ridiculous situation. We were battle weary, depleted, depressed, outnumbered and generally mucked about but we, who could least afford it, were asked to send formations to France and Greece!

The Army commander was not the only one feeling depressed and mucked about then. So too were many of the troops. There were murmurings of discontent and an increasing number of men being sent back to base rest centre, 'bomb happy', with battle fatigue.

One of these was a bombadier and part-time comedian, Spike Milligan. He had come through the assault landings at Salerno and the battles that followed. When his regiments telephone cables were cut by shell-fire it was his job to go out and repair them. The crunch came for him one day after he had been seventeen hours with the headphones on, and after a third night without sleep. Volunteers were called for to repair the line again. He recalled: 'I should never have volunteered. I was almost numb with fatigue. My piles were bleeding.[7]

On the way up the mountain carrying a fifty pound pack of batteries, spare cable and a transmitter, Spike and two other soldiers with him were caught in the open by a barrage of shelling.

The next thing that a dazed, wounded and jibbering Milligan remembers was having his wounded leg dressed and being handed two small white pills and a bowl of hot tea with which to swill them down. The doctors said; 'This man must be rested behind the lines for a period to stabilize his position.' Instead, he was sent back to the same gun position, the same shelling and to a battery commander who said: 'The noise of the guns will boost your morale.'[8]

It did not. It drove him into the psychiatric ward of Number 2 British General Hospital, Caserta.

Eventually he responded to treatment and was posted to a rehabilitation camp, north of Naples. There Gunner Milligan found his salvation. It was a huge camp, two thousand men, an enormous dance hall, a band, but no servicewomen. Wasting no time at all, trumpeter Milligan got himself in that band and quickly became involved in producing Leon Gordon's melodrama, *White Cargo*. In Milligan's production, the leading role of the 'temptress' was played by a former cellist, then a Welsh Guardsman, 'who took to drag like a duck to water.' He revelled in the part. It seemed to puzzle Milligan. He commented: 'I could never understand why the chap was all dressed up in his make-up and Hula-Hula skirt, hours before the curtain went up. Sometimes he went to bed wearing his make-up and still had it on in the morning. I suppose he was having a marvellous time for a change, poor chap.'

News of Milligan's talents soon reached the officer in charge of the Combined Services Entertainments Pool and he was invited to tour round units in Italy with one of its concert parties. Milligan was now home and dry. Safe for the duration.

By a strange coincidence, a man who was to appear with Milligan in many a successful post-war show, Lance Bombadier

Harry Secombe, was also at this time coming out of hospital and being sent to convalesce at the Eighth Army Rest Centre, Bari. Harry, who had come through some of the bloodiest fighting in North Africa, Sicily and Italy, with 132 Field Regiment Royal Artillery, was then in no condition to return to his unit. He had lost two stones in weight following a nasty bout of inflammation of the gall bladder and kidneys.[9]

He too found that once he arrived at the rest centre there was an opportunity for him to join a concert party. He gave his name to a sergeant and was put in a show for that very first evening. By this time he had accumulated some convincing concert party experience; he got a great reception from the troops who had been sent down from the line for a well earned rest. This gave Harry more confidence and his act got better and better. As a result he became part of the semi-permanent staff as a member of the concert party. He thrived and became convinced that this was the life for him after the war. With such an outfit and always a very responsive audience he was able to experiment and refine his act. He then got a further boost to his ambitions when, Carol Levis, then famous with the BBC *Discoveries* programme, complimented him on his act and invited him to go and see him in London once the war was over.

The future now looked rosy for Lance Bombadier Secombe.

Suddenly though, a black thunder cloud fell on that bright future. The camp was cleared of all superfluous personnel; the commanding officer was posted and other ranks were to be sent back up the line. The prospect pleased no one. Harry went to the Artillery training depot at Eboli, near Salerno. He recalled, 'I arrived wet and miserable. The place was a vast tented camp on the side of a hill and at first sight seemed very unpromising.'

But fate deemed otherwise. The camp boasted a well-equipped theatre and also a concert party of almost professional standard. By some strange stroke of serendipity, Harry was put in a tent supervized by a bombadier who had seen Harry's act in the Bari Rest Centre, and recommended Harry to the producer of the weekly 'Talent Night' show.

Now the whole of Harry Secombe's future seemed to depend upon the reception he got from this one performance. A poor response from the camp inmates and he'd be sent back up the line; an enthusiastic one and he would probably gain a place in the regular show. Nervously, excitedly and determinedly, he prepared for that most important performance.

What a relief it was when his jokes immediately provoked a roar of belly laughter. Troops loved to see authority sent up and their officers mimicked. Impersonation was one of Harry's strong points and he used it for all he was worth.

All went well. A big revue was planned for Christmas. New faces were needed and Harry was offered a place in the camp concert party.

Now he really did have to work hard at his act. He played the fairy queen in the pantomime, added to his impersonations, and even did a take off of Jeanette MacDonald and Nelson Eddy singing a duet! The experience he got in that training depot was invaluable. It was a very good place to learn the business of comedy and soon he was the principal comedian in the concert party. He too was home and dry. But there was a hard schedule of tours ahead and there were some tough assignments.

It was not all vino and tagliatelli for those concert parties then touring front line units. Travelling across war ravaged Italy then was difficult and dangerous. The Germans had blown every bridge over rivers and deep mountain gorges, in their retreat northwards. Hair-raising incidents were frequent.

Arthur Childs[10] could vouch for that! His service career in entertainment began when he was with a small RAF radar unit, invariably situated in remote locations where they were left to make their own entertainment. His concert party progressed so well that he was invited to join the RAF Entertainments Unit at Pozzuoli, near Naples, where he worked closely with Ronnie Taylor who had an outstanding musical talent as a pianist, singer and arranger of everything in the musical section. He was a man absolutely dedicated to entertainment and was convinced that his future lay in that direction, as indeed it did, after the war as Director of Variety with the BBC and writing for both BBC and ATV. At that time in Naples, Ronnie Taylor wrote and produced shows which the concert parties took on tour through the length and breadth of Italy. Those tours could at times be hazardous.

Arthur Childs recalls his close escape from what could have been a very nasty accident one dark night.

We had been directed to an RAF camp located in the heart of the wildest mountain region of the south of Italy. What on earth an RAF unit was doing there Heaven alone knew. When we got there, however, we found it to be a surprisingly large camp which had a good stage and theatre facilities. But it was the journey there which I remember most vividly for it brought us so close to disaster. On those narrow mountain roads, clinging to the edge of steep slopes, we got absolutely lost. There was no one to ask for directions, there were no signposts and the sketchy route given to us before we set off was useless.

We were late, it was February and dark early, pitch black darkness with not a light to be seen anywhere as we tried in vain to find the right route. When we turned onto a bridge, the driver stopped and we got out to have one more search for a signpost or some kind of clue as to where we were. I walked ahead with two companions towards the other side of the bridge thinking there might be a sign of some kind there. Suddenly my companion shot out his arm and stopped me in mid-stride. The road had ended in a jagged edge, from below came the roar of a torrent in a deep gorge, inches from our feet. Had our driver not stopped to look for signs we all could have finished in that gorge.

Never before had so many Bailey bridges been used, never had the Royal Engineers had to bulldoze so many buildings into piles of rubble to clear the roads to let the weight of the Allied offensive pass through as the enemy bitterly contested every mountain town and village.

For the entertainers, close on the heels of the forward troops, the devastation was a shocking experience. Emlyn Williams touring Italy with Kathleen Harrison arrived in Capua for a concert one night and found there were only two places untouched by shells and bombs – a brothel and a lunatic asylum.[11] The brothel was being used as a billet for American soldiers. They were ordered out so that Kathleen and other performers could move in. Later that evening though soldiers started queuing outside the building. Apparently, once the GIs had moved out and the ENSA women moved in, the word got round that the old business had started up again. Kathleen Harrison recalled,

> They somehow got the idea that a new 'Madame' was moving in with her girls and all the GIs lined up in readiness. In fact they even followed us into taxis and up to our rooms at first and made a general nuisance of themselves until it was sorted out and the commanding officer explained that our particular entertainment was on somewhat different lines ...

It was an interesting experience for Kathleen. She remembered well the décor and furnishings of that brothel in which the ENSA party was billeted. 'It had paintings, not on the walls but on the ceilings! There was no hygiene at all; the lavatory was simply a grill let into the marble floor and there were no baths so we had to stand to have a wash down at the basin.'

During that autumn of 1944 such discomforts were being experienced by a galaxy of stars arriving in Italy to entertain the Allied Forces. US General George C. Marshal had given full support to the United States Organization for Entertainment shows provided two stipulations were met. The first was that all shows should be open to all Allied troops and not just the US and secondly, all money raised should go to Service charities.

The first of the really big show companies to arrive in Italy was 'This is the Army'. Every performer in the company was an enlisted soldier, including its director, Irving Berlin. Before visiting Italy the show had a very successful run on Broadway and the film made of that show starred the future President of the United States, Captain Ronald Reagan, who was then playing second fiddle to a much greater celebrity, the World Heavyweight Boxing Champion, Sergeant Joe Louis.[12]

Perhaps by 1944 the well-known personalities of showbusiness were beginning to think of their post-war reputations and their answers to questions such as 'What did you do in the war?' Whatever the reason the stars began to forego their highly paid civilian contracts in the States and Britain to give concerts to the troops. Consequently by Christmas 1944, Naples was packed with entertainers from ENSA, USO, and the Services Central Pool of Artists.

It was from this central pool, commanded by Phillip Slessor, that the 'Stars in Battledress' show came, and into its ranks also came servicemen who before the war never even dreamed of going on to a stage. Now it was that the fruits of War Office discussions held in March 1941, were beginning to be enjoyed. Even in those early days of the war the War Office had seen that ENSA alone would never be able to satisfy all the Services' demands for entertainment and so units were instructed to appoint, whenever possible, an entertainments officer who would organize and maintain concert parties which would be supported by Army Welfare funds. So, despite what might have appeared in Naples to be a glut of performers, there were still not enough to go round units. Therefore appeals like the one below appeared again in unit routine orders:

> You may be only a Lance Corporal in your camp but in the Theatre you can be a Knight in shining armour one week and a flashing pirate the next. You've always wanted to act, haven't you? Come and try!

Peter Bevans,[13] then with the RAF Servicing Commando unit responded to such an appeal and before long he and fellow enthusiasts had stripped a hangar, made curtains from parachute material and put on a concert with 'a male voice choir' and an accordion. Rusty Russell, a girl with a good voice stationed at

Headquarters, Caserta, joined that 'Happy Hour' concert party and recently commented, 'Ropey though some of those shows were, they did raise laughs and gave plenty of fun to everyone. We made all our own costumes and wrote most of the material ourselves. Though my memory now fails me in many things I do remember one thing from those long-gone years – that everyone had a thumping good time!'[14]

David Clark[15] of the RAF who had started performing with small unit shows in North Africa now found himself appearing in sketches and compering big shows. The full weight of the War Office was now behind showbusiness in Italy. Nigel Patrick who, at twenty-nine had been told he was too old for a reinforcement officer when he arrived in North Africa, was put in charge of entertainment in Italy and Malta. 'At one time we had 34 theatres, 131 cinemas, and over 3,000 Italians employed,' he said. Working with him then was a bespectacled Army sergeant with a Groucho Marx style moustache who had started entertaining with the lads in his unit, Arthur Lowe, much better known today no doubt as Captain Mainwaring of that evergreen, popular comedy show, *Dad's Army*. With such official support many units were able to provide for their own entertainment needs, as well as benefiting from visits from the top stars.

There were times, though, when celebrities proved to be almost too hot to handle, as surely, for example, was the king of Warner Brothers himself, Humphrey Bogart. He flew to Italy to entertain the troops and based himself with his wife, Mayo Methot, at the Headquarters of US General Mark Clark in Caserta Palace. This palace had an opera house with seating for three hundred and with a number of boxes. Before each show began, a strange ritual was enacted. Novelist and thriller writer, Eric Ambler, then on a special assignment at the palace with the British Army Kinema Unit recalled what happened:[16]

'As we went in we were handed little slips of paper by a US warrant officer who muttered, as he gave out each slip, 'It's sung to the tune of "God Bless America" I think. Please give it all you've got." '

When he reached his seat, Ambler looked at the paper and saw the words:

THE SONS OF GENERAL CLARK

Stand up and sing the praise of General Clark,
Your hearts and voices raise for General Clark,
Red, white and blue, unfurled upon the field.
Its message flaunts Clark's sons will never yield.

We'll fight, fight, fight, with heart and hand.
As soldiers true embattled staunch will stand.
The Fifth's the best army in the land.
FIGHT! FIGHT! FIGHT!

Neither Bogart nor Ambler was impressed.

When entertaining with the forward units Bogart and Mayo alternated on stage. Bogart would give snippets of dialogue from some of his better known films and then Mayo would come on and sing anything the men requested which usually included 'I'll walk alone', 'You'll never know' and whether they asked for it or not, Mayo would always sing, 'Embraceable you'. Nine times out of ten this kind of programme went down well with the troops. But occasionally they were sceptical about this 'tough guy' from Hollywood, the 'big shot from gangland' and some of them were especially scornful of the US tank sergeant role Bogart had played in the film *Sahara*, where, virtually single-handed he had defeated Rommel's Afrika Korps. 'That kind of crap gives folks back home the wrong idea of what we're up against,' was the colourful comment made by one GI.[17]

It was in such a situation that Bogart, film producer John Huston and war correspondent Ernie Pyle found themselves in one day.[18] After a few drinks and more talk, a big sergeant suddenly picked up a sub-machine gun and tossed it at Bogart, saying, 'OK tough guy, show us how, huh?'

Bogart deftly caught the Tommy-gun and then with the Duke Mantee gangster lisp said, 'Thanks pal'. Suddenly he dropped into a half crouching position, tucked the gun close to his hip and barked, 'This is it' and pressed the trigger. To his horror a stream of bullets whammed out, narrowly missing Pyle, Huston and the others.

Not put out for a moment, Bogart went into his gangster character again, eyes narrowed, mouth twisted, teeth bared and fired two more bursts.

After that he became his normal self, tossed the smoking gun back to the wide-eyed sergeant and said mildly, 'Pal, I didn't know it was loaded.'

It was shortly after this incident that film director John Huston and his British Army Kinema counterpart, Eric Ambler, jeeped up into the hills to make a documentary film for the US War Department, which could be used for military studies and for including in news reels for public showing. Hitherto the War Department had deplored the lack of reality and truth in commercial war films. They wanted a film to show war how it really was and what actually happened. Or so they said.

Hollywood had mobilized all its best directors for such assignments, Frank Capra, Anatole Litvak, John Ford, and John Huston. They had already covered massive amounts of combat footage giving vivid coverage of the war. But nothing of all that was to come anywhere near what Huston was to film.

Originally the idea was simply to go to one of the forward areas, pick a small town and film what actually happened to the town and its people once the enemy had pulled out. But it did not work out that way at all.

San Pietro was the town they chose and after checking with Intelligence at Corps Heaquarters that the town had indeed been taken, Huston and his team set out. They arrived close to the hill town, left the jeeps and began to walk confidently up the narrow road towards the devastated buildings perched above them. On the way they passed a company of rangers, squatting under cover by the roadside, waiting to go into an attack. Ambler later recalled:

> They were from Texas, young, smiling and enjoying the sun that had just come through. When they saw our cameras they wanted to have their pictures taken for the news reels back home. Jules obliged by shooting a few close ups. John Huston used them later in the film about the fighting for San Pietro; it was the part of the film that moved me most when I saw it; I knew that all those smiling young men had long been dead.[19]

Still trusting Corps Intelligence's words that the town had been taken, Huston and his team walked on up the path towards San Pietro, cameras and kit on their shoulders. But they began to have some qualms when they came across an infantry section crouching in a ditch. Nevertheless, Huston still walked on, followed now only by Ambler and one or two of the original team. After a further two hundred yards German machine-guns and mortars opened up. Huston and film crew flung themselves into a ditch and crawled behind a low wall. Salvo after salvo of mortar bombs rained down as they crawled back towards the infantry. The reunion was not the friendliest. Now the enemy had been alerted.

There was, however, a man further back who was very pleased to see them, General Mark Clark. He was standing in an olive grove, map in one hand and pointing in the direction of San Pietro with the other. Photographs had to be taken of him in that pose. 'When the photographs had been taken,' wrote Ambler later, 'the General handed the map to an aide, and was driven away in the opposite direction.' So much for Clark's idea of leading from the front. And so much for the glorification of General Mark Clark.

Filming of the documentary then began in earnest. Some of the shoots had to be re-enacted the next day because it is very difficult to get good shots when the earth is erupting round the camera and the operator is trying to keep his head down. In such instances one tends to get shots of whirling sky and earth. But the rest of the film was real enough as US troops went into the attack. Death in action was plainly seen; all the human courage and carnage.

Few were ever permitted to see that film. And what stuck most vividly in the minds of the few who were able to see the whole film was the burial party sequence. It showed bodies being wrapped in white 'shrouds' and heaved about like sacks of flour, as Ambler recalled. 'With notable lack of ceremony, the dead men were bundled into GI body-bags and dumped in shallow graves. GI crosses were then hammered in to mark the spots.[20]

The scenes of slaughter, so descriptive of the true horrors of war caused the War Department to condemn the film as pacifist and demoralizing. It was cut from fifty minutes in length to thirty. Reality was not, after all, what the War Department wanted. That thirty minutes though, still stands today as a compassionate statement on the waste and futility of war.

Hutton's sombre voice on the soundtrack for the burial scene is unforgettable: 'These lives were valuable. Valuable to their loved ones, to their country, and to the men themselves.'

Soon though, the killing in Europe would be over. For the troops who had survived those campaigns there now came the anxiety of a posting to the Far East where battles were yet to be won.

12

Curtain Call

RAF Fitter, Fred Harvey,[1] had never seen anything like it before. Here was the film world of *Gunga Din*, and *King of the Khyber Rifles*. It was the north-west frontier of India. No longer visited by film stars. They were long gone. It was even twenty years since that insubordinate Flight Lieutenant, Arthur Harris, later to become the famous and controversial commander-in-chief of Bomber Command, had blotted his copy book there, complaining that his aircraft on those north-west frontier stations were held together by string and took off on wheels with naked rims because there were no tyres available.

But in the last years of the Second World War, the problems of life on the north-west frontier provinces were still the same as they had always been since the East India Company had attempted to control the area – heat, flies, boredom and aggressive tribes. Here was the Khyber Pass where in the mid-winter of 1841 only one man survived from the 20,000 of the British Army's Kabul garrison which attempted to withdraw to Jellalabad. The infamous Khyber Pass massacre.

It was to this barren, hostile land that fitter Fred Harvey and his concert party came. He was stationed at Risalpur, north of Peshawar, playing the trumpet in the small dance band of his unit, 27 Squadron RAF, and helping out in various ways with the concert party, when the surprising orders arrived.

He recalls:

> We had been performing in front of our own lads and visiting a few local Army and Air Force units with a show called, 'Over to you' and this had been a pleasant change from our usual routine of station duties. We had never dreamt of anything more than this until the morning our entertainments officer told us we were to set off on a three months tour of the North West Provinces. This seemed absolutely too fantastic to be true.

Hastily we had to get our show together and on the road. Three or four of the group who took female parts in the short plays and dance routines, dashed down to the local bazaar to buy make-up, material and dresses for their acts. Essential props were packed and within a few days we were ready to set off for a journey that would take in thousands of miles through some of the most inaccessible terrain imaginable.

That territory, in the north of Pakistan, is even now a wild region of tangled hill ranges, high plateaus and deep gorges breached by the Khyber Pass. It is a country with freezingly cold nights and terribly hot days reaching temperatures at times above 120°F; a place where violent thunderstorms can suddenly erupt. It was not a place for the inexperienced traveller.

We tried to use trains whenever possible even though they were primitive and with most uncomfortable slatted wooden seats. But when we could not travel by train, we used RAF Albion trucks which had a canvas canopy and wooden bench type seats with no back support. You can imagine what it was like to be driving for hour after hour up bumpy tortuous tracks in the hills above Peshawar near the Afghan frontier, with the dust billowing in from above the tailboard. To put it mildly, it was no picnic!

We got our reward, though, in giving the concerts to the lads on these outposts. They were most appreciative and we had a good many laughs afterwards at some of the escapades. There was one time in the middle of an open air show, when an alarm went off, and we saw Sikhs rushing down the hillside with bayonets fixed. Why they were coming in our direction, we had no idea but one thing we had to do quickly was hide our female impersonators who were in full dress and make-up to go on stage. Everyone knew what Sikhs could be like and there was no time for talk. We just pulled the drag artistes down and hid them with whatever was handy to save them from what could well have been a very nasty experience indeed!

In the most unlikely places now, ENSA artistes and concert parties were appearing, looking after the morale of the trops. About eight hundred miles south west from Risalpur, as the crow flies, if indeed it does fly there, lay Number 320 RAF Maintenance Unit, Drigh Road, in the Sind Desert near Karachi. It was a camp which assembled aircraft: Ansons, Oxfords, Spitfires, Thunderbolts and the Vultee Vengeance Dive Bomber. It was a camp where men felt quite apart from the rest of the world. Here it was that Lawrence of Arabia hid from the limelight after the First World War, taking the name and rank of Aircraftman Shaw. A little further down the road stood a solitary, and extraordinary high hangar built for the mooring of Britain's awe-inspiring, giant airship, the R101, seven hundred and seventy-seven feet long, with electric kitchen and blue and gold panelled smoke room, the last word in airships. In October 1930 it was to fly from London to India. It cruised for eight hours only and crashed in flames. But in that hangar until 1945 was a man paid to keep all the equipment greased and ready for the day when another mightier airship would take shape and fly to India from Britain. Perhaps someone had forgotten he was there.

Marjorie Sargeant,[2] of the Women's Auxiliary Corps (India), then stationed at Drigh Road with her RAF husband felt, that anything like that could have happened. They were in their own little world in the gritty wasteland where barrack blocks had woven wire mesh to keep out the sand when the wind whipped it up from the desert, and swarms of bugs infested the beds. But servicemen and camp followers made the best of it with their entertainment provided by 'The Drigh Road Players'.

Jack Lawrence[3] sang in the chorus and helped out wherever he was needed. Star of the show was 'a wee blonde rascal' called Johnny Rew accompanied by Trevor Francis.

Making his first appearance in front of a real audience with that concert party was a young RAF Physical Training Instructor, who could play the piano and sing, James Young, better known now as Jimmy Young of the BBC's long running programme. Telling how it all came about he said: 'I auditioned for the dance band and landed the singing bit. One of my party pieces was "Sierra Sue" which I learned from a Bing Crosby record. It went down well and became a must every time I sang.'[4]

The dance band and the concert party flourished. 'It played before packed houses,' said Jack Lawrenson, 'The Cookhouse was the Drigh Road theatre but soon we were playing in the real theatre and the 'Paradise' cinema of Karachi. Talent seemed to come out of the blue. It must have been a good show because the RAF top brass flew in from New Delhi for it!'

The commanding officer was very proud of the way his concert party was providing morale-boosting entertainment and soon he was inviting all the local dignitaries. Jimmy Young remembered that, 'They came resplendent in evening dress with bejewelled ladies – and they liked what they saw and heard. From then on our fame, if not our fortune, was made. Drigh Road concerts became the 'in' thing and Karachi merchants and businesses competed to take advertising in our programmes.'[5]

They did indeed. Karachi's smartest restaurant, 'Mexicano' and 'Karachi's Kosiest Kafe', 'Cumpers Cafe Grand' and 'The

Manhatten Soda Fountain' took as much space as they could get to attract custom.[6]

The old saying that nothing succeeds like success seemed to be proved by other benefits which spun off the concert party's success. Soon ENSA artistes began to arrive. In the early days they were not all up to the standards set by the 'Drigh Road Players' but they were the best that Colonel Jack Hawkins, the film star then organizing ENSA in India, could find. He explained how South East Asia Command was so badly served:[7]

> We called ourselves the arse-end Charlies, for we were at the end of a very long line. So far as the ENSA Headquarters in Drury Lane was concerned we were not only at the bottom of their catalogue of priorities, we were the bottom. It was a comic and sometimes depressing business. I don't suppose that even the most unsuccessful theatrical agent has ever had to handle quite so many dead-beat acts as were sent to me.

The situation was far worse for the fighting troops. The most bestial and bitter fighting of the whole war began in Burma with a Japanese offensive early in March 1944 and the battles being fought by Britain's Fourteenth Army must rank amongst the most blood-chilling in any war at any time. Then, the Army Commander, General William Slim was much concerned with the low morale of his men.

> These men were calling themselves a 'Forgotten Army' long before some newpaper correspondent seized on the phrase. In many ways they were right in thinking so. As far as the people in Britain were concerned, Burma was so remote and so far away from the war on their own doorstep, against the Germans, that the fighting in the Far East was beyond their imaginings.[8]

With no satellite television pictures, as we have today, to convey the horror of it all, people could not begin to picture what it was really like for their own men fighting a ferocious oriental enemy in steaming jungles at the same time as they were haunted with nameless fears and malignant malaria, dysentery, typhus and numerous other horrible diseases and skin eruptions. 'Worst of all,' wrote Slim, 'was the feeling of isolation, with all the heartsickness of long separation from home. The feeling of neglect, of being at the bottom of the priority lists, had sunk deep. There was a good deal of bitterness in the army.'

Even when these troops came out of the front line to rest areas, there was little or no entertainment for them. An irate General Slim could stand this state of affairs no longer. He wrote to the

War Office demanding some decent entertainment for his battle-weary fighting men. They were having an awful time, fighting a totally different kind of war to their regimental colleagues in Europe. It was a war too in which they had so far lost almost every battle. What was horrifying also was that in the aftermath of those battles, soldiers had seen grim evidence of Japanese cruelty left on the battlefield. A small British patrol, for example, came back with a gruesome report of their own troops found nailed to trees, beheaded before or after crucifixion.

Major Crawford, RAMC of 8th Mobile Surgical Unit, was lying on his camp bed one night when he woke to find two Japanese sentries at each end of his tent. Quietly he raised the side flap and silently rolled into the undergrowth. There, hidden, he lay all night listening to the sounds of brutal atrocities perpetrated on the helpless wounded, and the hospital medical staff. Dimly, in the half light he saw, 'Prisoners herded together and bayonetted to death, not swiftly but with gloating thrusts.'9

Small wonder that many of the forward troops were in a highly neurotic state known as 'jungle jitters'. Everyone lived in a stage of permanent apprehension. At any moment parties of infiltrating Japanese creeping through the jungle, were likely to hurl themselves suddenly upon defensive positions screaming, 'Banzai'. Then, ferocious and bloody hand-to-hand fighting ensued.

The Fourteenth Army had been split and surrounded. One force in Kohima was besieged and another in Imphal was cut off. Lines of communication and rear echelons were at risk. No one could be sure where or when the next attack might come. Haggard and weary troops at the perimeter of unit areas dreaded the coming of night. Their orders were clear. 'Do not move after dark under any circumstances. Any defender who leaves his trench must expect to be shot by his own comrades.'10

It was into such harrowing and hazardous situations that some of the top stars of showbiz then ventured. They were desperately needed and they were greatly appreciated.

One of the first of these to arrive was a man who had built up a great reputation on pre-war radio, Stainless Stephen. Under the light of a full moon, this bowler-hatted comedian, using two tank transporters as a stage, beguiled five thousand assorted fighting men near a certain Milestone on the Imphal-Kohima road. It was the first of a hundred shows he was to give before a hundred thousand of the 'Forgotten Army'. Recollecting his experience he wrote of the men he was entertaining:11

Exposure to sun and air has turned them the colour of teak, and they are as tough. It's an individual war out there; personal initiative counts more than anything. No overwhelming artillery barrage precedes the attack. The enemy must be winkled out of his bunkers by hand-to-hand fighting of the cloak and dagger variety. The Jap is a fanatical warrior whose ambition is to die for his Emperor; and with the co-operation of the Fourteenth Army, thousands of them have realized their ambition. And rather than surrender, the Nip commits hari-kiri by blowing himself up with one of his own grenades.

Audiences for those shows of Stainless Stephen in the Imphal sector were something to be remembered. 'There were no seats, the men arrived armed with rifles and Bren guns, they squatted on the mud and listened open-mouthed as we recalled memories of a dim, pre-war experience.'

From Imphal, Stainless Stephen sped in the Corps General's car via Palel to Tamu, along a road which must have been one of the outstanding engineering achievements of all times; there were hairpin bends every hundred yards and in fifty miles they climbed four thousand feet. 'Dust was three feet thick most of the way, I got grit in my gizzard and the continual swaying of the car round innumerable bends made me feel more dizzy than any blonde,' recalled Stainless.

After reaching Divisional headquarters at Tamu – a derelict Buddhist temple – he was given the inevitable mug of char, and shown the stage, an ammunition box. The audience appeared as if by magic from the dense tropical undergrowth, and the comedian began.

> What did I say to these men? What did they laugh at? I usually began with a gentle leg-pull describing the delights of India in general and the Burma front in particular; how I'd have to change my name from Stainless to Spineless if I did any more jeeping. I told them I'd eaten so many soya links [long oblong shaped sausages made from Soya beans] that I'd have to report sick with square tonsils.

As so many other comedians had found, gags on the personalities of the unit were sure to bring a roar of laughter.

For his final performance in Burma, Stainless Stephen drove up to the Khohima front – 7,000 feet up into the Chin Hills. Half the soldiers in his audience were convalescents from the rest camp who, with the Royal West Kents and the Assam Rifles had held out against vastly numerically superior Japanese forces for thirteen days in the fiercest hand-to-hand fighting on the whole front. Finding the right formula for that show was not easy. But he had a magnificent reception and then he was off again. This time to the Arakan front in south Burma.

There his stage was a three-ton truck and he stood in the light of the projector of a portable cinema. 'And did the insects buzz around me!' wrote Stainless on his return.

The high spot of his appearances on this part of the front was on one of the peaks of the Mayu mountains. To reach the troops there he had to drive up a jeep track with a gradient of one in two. 'On this part of the front, I lived in fox holes for five nights with plenty of rifle fire at night to remind me that there was a war on!' wrote Stainless Stephen ending the report of his trip.

What do you give the troops in the forward areas of such a battle ground as Burma? Presumably, if you were in a position such as Colonel Jack Hawkins then you can only send what you have. He was, however, pleased to relate that he found what he called 'the perfect entertainment for sex-starved troops' in the small cast of a play called *Love in a Mist*. It was a farce which had been a big success in London, about two young couples, one on honeymoon and the other on what used to be called 'a dirty weekend'. Both couples are trapped by fog in a lonely farmhouse on a bleak and isolated stretch of Dartmoor. These two couples are desperately trying to get to bed but are prevented by a series of absurd incidents and accidents. The soldiers enjoyed this little play so much that when ENSA Headquarters withdrew the cast from the forward area, General Slim sent an angry signal back to base: 'I protest in the strongest possible terms at the withdrawal of the play company *Love in a Mist*. I insist on its immediate return.'[12]

The cast was given a very short rest and went straight back to the forward areas. Travelling just behind the front line as fluid and fluctuating as that in Burma, was an ordeal in itself, apart from the risks of ambush by Japanese infiltrators but those stalwarts of showbiz that went to the Far East did a marvellous job.

During the battle for the river Irrawaddy, when an ENSA party was giving a concert near Allagappa, not far from the river-bank itself, Slim was to recall:

I thought what a tribute it was to our Air Force that in broad daylight we could collect several hundred men to watch a show almost within artillery range of the enemy. It was a good show too, and I was sorry I should have to leave before it was over to get back to the air strip. However, just when I was about to leave, it was whispered to me that a Japanese raiding party was across the road I should have to travel, so I was able, with a clear conscience, to continue my enjoyment while the intruders were chased away, and afterwards to thank the artistes, one of whom was a lady.[13]

One lady who was always keen to get as far forward as possible, arrived in Burma just a few days after the Japanese offensive of March 1944, the 'Forces Sweetheart' herself, Vera Lynn.

First of all she visited the three field hospitals at Dimapur, at the height of the Kohima battle and was shocked by what she saw of the terribly maimed and mutilated soldiers. 'Suddenly I was sickened by the smell of gangrene, disinfectants and the sense of desolation at the thought of life ebbing away all around me. I was overcome by it all, and sat down on somebody's bed feeling weary and ill, and futile.'[14] She asked for a glass of water but was told, 'We have no drinking water.'

For some of her shows in hospital there were men too ill to be moved into one big ward for the show, but these men were certainly not forgotten by Vera Lynn. She would go over to see them after the main performance was over. It was in such circumstances that she sang to the smallest audience in her long career, just two men. 'They were terribly wounded and they asked me to sing, "We'll meet again". I could see what they were thinking. In the end, only one got home.'

Travelling to units which had penetrated deep into the festering jungle was horrendous. Tracks became long ribbons of red mud and deep puddles. With torrential rain the temperature dropped so that troops and entertainers alike, shivered in thin cotton uniforms. And whenever a downpour stopped, the sun shone again sucking up steam from the sodden earth, which gleamed beneath incredibly thick, glistening jungle leaves.

Sweat would stream from everyone's hair, down the forehead and into smarting eyes. After what seemed an interminable time Vera Lynn's showbiz convoy would stop its jolting journey for a meal break. There was the usual obscene plague to contend with – fat flies.

Dame Vera Lynn later recalled some of these stomach-turning experiences. 'You'd get a bowl of some thickish soup, and the only way you could eat it was to get your spoon in quick and, with a sort of sideways movement, scoop it out from under the solid layer of flies which instantly settled on top of it.'[15]

Air travel was no picnic though. Small showbiz groups believing flying to be much easier than going by truck, would lurch down rutted tracks into a jungle clearing where close by the airstrip, an old Dakota would be sheltering beneath camouflage foliage. Already its fuselage would inevitably be piled high with sacks and crates. The few men and women would be helped inside and then, almost as an afterthought, be handed some old newspapers.

Take off was an experience never to be forgotten as they rose into air pockets which tossed the aircraft spasmodically up and down. Soon heads would be aching from the noise of the engines and stale air, mingling many odours. Some there were who were so ill they longed for death. Those who were not so air sick might look down through puffs of cloud onto the swollen green jungle, undulating as far as the eye could see. And beneath that dense green were men in jungle green merging with their background. Men waiting to be entertained, waiting for those brief moments when they could mentally sink into the luxury of a different world and forget the war altogether.

For those passengers in the Dakota, the evidence of that war came into focus as they approached Imphal, a small plain surrounded by hills, a shallow dish with a crinkly rim. Around the landing strip was all the wreckage of war; piles of mangled metal, bullet ripped Bren carriers, a staff car tilted on its side, riddled with bullet holes, five-gallon petrol tins and many burnt out aircraft.

The showbiz sleeping quarters were often little more than bamboo huts, unbearably hot, made hotter too with the warmth of the hurricane lanterns which attracted an incredible number of insects. Extraordinary large beetles flew straight into the light, stunning themselves and dropping like stones to the ground. Others, in their mad rush to the light got caught in women's hair.

Mosquito nets gave some protection in bed if they had been properly rolled up that morning but after a long day's travel, sleep was rarely disturbed, not even by the scurrying of rats in the roof, as Dame Vera Lynn recalled.

All this was a chastened experience for showbiz folk coming straight from the civilised world of London's theatreland and by the end of 1944 more and more of them were making the effort to visit Burma, showing the young servicemen they were not altogether forgotten. As one soldier in a field dressing station said to Vera Lynn, 'Home cannot be too far away, can it, if you can just appear among us.'

However, it is fair to say too, as one Burma Star veteran Peter Jackson[16] recently put it: 'They were a motley crew, but full marks to them. They came.'

And they came with odd requests from soldiers' relatives. George Formby, the star who said; 'Ah've enjoyed every minute of making millions of lads and lasses happy', was asked by a Glasgow woman if he would bring back from Imphal a photograph of her brother's grave. Somehow George found time to visit the military cemetery and there take a photograph of that soldier's final resting place.

George travelled far and wide in Burma. He even visited an RAF unit on Ramree Island off Burma's west coast. When the few men there heard he was coming, they set to and built an open-air theatre in two days from a damaged pagoda. Outside they hung a sign which read: RAF COCONUT GROVE THEATRE. Altogether George and Wee Georgie Wood, who accompanied him, played to over 250,000 troops.[17]

So beneficial were these showbiz visits deemed to be by the Commander of Allied Land Forces, South East Asia, General Sir Oliver Leese, that he wrote personal letters to fourteen stars chosen by his troops, asking them to visit Burma.[18] The troops, he said, would be most keen to see them in the monsoon period between the middle of May and the end of September. The response was disappointing. Four months later, only two of those fouteen requested, Donald Edge and Jack Daly, had arrived and then Lady Leese herself went into the attack, warning those stars who had failed to respond because of their more lucrative commercial contracts, that men would not forget how they had been treated so shabbily.

Lady Leese mentioned in this letter to *The Times* how much troops had really appreciated visits from such stars as Vera Lynn, Edith Evans, Joyce Grenfell, Kenway and Young, Forsythe Seaman and Farrell, Stainless Stephen, Elsie and Doris Waters, Wee Georgie Wood, George Formby and Noel Coward.

Units which were not favoured by ENSA-sponsored performers, had to rely upon whatever local talent was available and even then it was often a case of people volunteering in the time-honoured military fashion of – 'You, You and You!'

This is exactly what happened at Imphal Military hospital in December 1944. Sister Winifred Beaumont was there with the Queen Alexandra's and the Indian Army Sisters and those 'unsung heroines' of the nursing profession, Voluntary Aid Detachment nurses. In December 1944, the hospital was filled with casualties from the Imphal and Kohima sieges and the steady stream arriving daily from the fourteenth Army's attack on the Irrawaddy – the longest river crossing of the whole war.

Christmas was approaching. Matron called a meeting. Three senior sisters, the assistant matron, the home sister, and the sister in charge of the new wing, Winifred Beaumont. This was one of those typically brief military meetings of 'volunteers', as Winifred Beaumont later described in her fascinating book, *A Detail on the Burma Front*.[20]

> Matron waved us to be seated, handed round a packet of cigarettes and, when we were settled began: It wants a week or two to Christmas and I want you to give the boys a really good time.' She turned to her Assistant and said, 'You will be responsible for the Christmas dinner, and I know you will put on a good one.' To the Home Sister she said, 'You are responsible for the Boxing Day party in the mess. I want you to invite all the boys you can.' To me she said, 'You will produce a concert for Christmas Day.'
>   Matron waved her cigarette in dismissal. The whole meeting had taken less time than it did to smoke a cigarette.

That was the Army way of getting things done.

Operation Concert Party was on.

The logistics for the project, Sister Beaumont found, were formidable. 'The hospital had no players, no talent, no musicians, no singers, no musical instruments, no sheet music, no scripts, and no stage. Our one asset was a piano with no strings.'

But as the old saying goes, 'The show must go on!'

There was only one thing Winifred Beaumont could do. And she did it. She called a meeting, just a small one of only two people: an enthusiastic, handsome officer called Jack Robbins and an attractive Indian Red Cross officer called Sara, who had skin the colour of creamy white magnolia blossom, short golden hair which fluffed round her head like a halo and green eyes slanting upwards at the temples. It was whilst they were chatting over mugs of tea that the first glimmer of hope broke through the gloom. One of them remembered a character called 'Gentleman Jim' of the Royal Engineers, who lived in a tarpaulin cave on the perimeter of the hospital site. He had a reputation for being good with his hands. One of those rare types who could actually repair things instead of just sending for replacement parts. It emerged from subsequent talk that not only was he an expert rivalling Heath Robinson in improvization and repairs, but he could also play a tune on almost anything – on tables, bottles, and even bits of bamboo.

Forthwith, Sister Beaumont marshalled all her charms and persuasive spiel and advanced with determination written all over her face, upon the domain of the Royal Engineers and Gentleman Jim in particular.

From the start of her delivery it was clear that Gentleman Jim was interested. This was no run of the mill job of another wash-basin for the sisters' mess or reinforced guy lines for the larger tents. Here was a worthwhile challenge to his ingenuity, his very reputation, which he could not resist. Did not even want to resist. Making a piano out of a mere frame was a task he would enjoy taking on. But, nevertheless, he put up a token defence of his valuable time, which was all in keeping with the assumed, prickly part of his character, before surrendering on certain terms.

First of these was that Sister Beaumont should use her charm on what he called the 'Brylcreem Boys' of the RAF, who ran the air ferry service to Calcutta. She was to get them to go shopping for nuts and bolts, wire and a few other items which he scribbled down on the back of one of the R.E. worksheets.

The second of his terms was short but categorical. On no account should the medical colonel running the hospital be told. 'I don't want him breathing down my neck!'

Sister Beaumont though was not yet finished with Gentleman Jim. When the piano was mended and tuned would he please play it at the concert? He could, he would, but again on one condition – that the piano should go to the Royal Engineers' officers' mess after the concert.

Things looked brighter now. The ferry pilots were as obliging as ever and before the end of the week, Gentleman Jim had his wire and other paraphernalia.

As we have seen with other concert parties, once the idea began to move forward it gathered its own momentum. A corporal knew of a stage left behind by a regiment in a camp up Bishenpur road. He could arrange for transportation if Sister Beaumont would go with them one night. He needed the authority of her two pips just in case they were stopped and questioned.

That moonlit foray was a great success. Matron was delighted to see the stage in place the next morning. But the biggest problem was yet to be solved. Who was going to appear upon that stage? It would take no great feat of the imagination to guess that someone would suggest *Cinderella*, the Forces favourite panto.

Days were passing. A group sat sucking pencils ands scribbling down half-remembered lines from past productions, jokes and little sketches, which officers were to be lampooned and who were safe bets to be burlesqued? What could be done about the ball? Where were all the colourful dresses to come from in the middle of the jungle?

Problems, they told themselves, were there to be solved. One sister remembered she still had a sequinned evening gown in her box. Another dug out a pair of silver slippers. Yet another lent her precious diamante hair band. Excitedly now, men and women were searching for anything that might be useful. They vied with each other in their ingenuity and generosity. Somehow, by begging and borrowing from medical stores, the male parts of the panto were dressed in white trousers with cummerbunds sewn from yellow nylon cut from a parachute used to drop medical supplies. Even Matron was not above 'misusing' official equipment. She provided a roll of pure white mosquito netting with a few terse words to cover her rash offer: 'I want it back, intact.'

Well, apart from a piece cut off for Cinder's wedding veil and another piece dyed red for the Fairy Godmother's costume, whatever was left, did eventually go back.

Anyone who has ever had a job like Sister Beaumont's in organizing a concert will know that strange discoveries are made. Right there on the hospital site was a man who had actually sung in seaside concert parties! Jack Robbins heard him singing one day. He had a beautiful bass voice but there was a big snag. He was behind barbed wire, a prisoner in the 'special ward' patrolled by sentries. There was no time for formal requests to higher authority. Wire cutters were far quicker.

An attractive Indian nurse chatted up a sentry whilst Jack cut the barbed wire and freed the bass singer. He had very long legs. Another problem. No one on the unit had trouser legs to match his size. Except the medical colonel. It was another job for Winifred Beaumont. She asked the commanding officer for the loan of his trousers, not saying for whom they were needed.

Now, the day before Christmas, nearly everything was ready. The main tent was decorated with red, white and blue streamers made from bandages dyed in a mixture of Gentian Violet and red ink. A red blanket hung on the back wall bearing the message, 'MERRY CHRISTMAS' in tufts of snow white cotton wool.

The concert was a huge success. At one time the colonel, sitting of course in the front row, leant forward suddenly in his seat and stared at the bass singer's trousers, and then leant back with a smile, mouthing the words: 'My trousers!'

After the show, perhaps for the sake of good order and military discipline, he felt it was his duty to administer a mild rebuke to Sister Beaumont for the misuse of valuable medical stores, but, like Gentleman Jim, the 'Brylcreem Boys' of the ferry service and many others pressed into service for 'Operation Concert', he was no match for Sister Beaumont. She had a few succinct words of her own for the Colonel, too: 'I'm sure you agree Colonel, the wounds of a happy man heal faster than those of an unhappy man.'

A simple matter of morale.

By this time the morale of the whole Fourteenth Army was high. They had the Japanese on the run, a mortal blow had been struck at the fighting spirit of the Japanese army in Burma. Now it was the spirit of the 'Forgotten Army' that was in the ascendant bearing out the words of its commander that 'Morale is a state of mind, an intangible force which will move a whole group of men to give their last ounce to achieve something without counting the cost to themselves.'

Looking back now upon those critical years, many showbiz celebrities and those not so well known by the general public, must also feel a certain pride in the final victory, a part which has never been forgotten by the men and women who were there.

It was fitting that the great news of that victory was often delivered to the troops by showbiz stalwarts. Gracie Fields was in the Solomon Islands, the scene of so much heavy fighting, and was just about to go on stage when the general officer commanding the Force there stepped forward, took her by the hand, and led her forward. In front of the stage were twenty five thousand troops. The general held up his hand. All went quiet. Then he spoke, slowly and distinctly; 'Men, at last I can tell you the only thing you want to know. The Japs have surrendered.' In the second's silence of wonderment and before the cheering could start, he held up his hand again and said, 'I have England's Gracie Fields here. I am going to ask her to sing the Lord's Prayer.'[21]

Gracie remembered, 'There was a movement as of a great sea – every man had taken off his cap. The matted green of the tall dark jungle surrounded us, but above our clearing the noon sun seared down from the brilliant sky onto twenty-five thousand bowed heads. I started to sing. 'Our Father which art in Heaven ...'

The Andrews Sisters were on board a troopship taking eight thousand unhappy soldiers to the South Pacific. They had already served in Europe and had not been home for four years. Maxine recalled the next few dramatic moments:[22]

> It was just their bad luck. We were trying to get them into good spirits. During the show, however, something happened which lifted their spirits more than anything we could have done. I was standing waiting for my turn to go out to Patty, when a soldier thrust a note into my hand. 'It's from the commanding officer. Take it out for Patty to read.' I took it out without reading it myself and shoved the note in front of Patty. She read it aloud without glancing at it herself first. 'The war is over.' Patty started to cry and then shouted to the soldiers still disbelieving the note. 'You don't have to go, fellas! This is the end. This is the end!'

References

For the published works cited below, see Bibliography for publisher and date.

Prologue
1. Clifton, James, *I was Monty's Double* and *Secrets and Stories of the War*
2. Ibid.
3. James Leasor, *The Experiences of Sir Leslie Hollis, The War at the Top*
4. Michael Korda, *Charmed Lives*

1. War on the Air Waves
1. Kenneth More, *Happy Go Lucky*
2. Rex Harrison, *Rex*
3. *The Times*, 9 September 1939
4. *The Times*, 12 September 1939
5. Arthur Marshall, *Life's Rich Pageant*
6. Ted Kavanagh, *Tommy Handley*
7. Ibid.
8. Ibid.
9. Correspondence with the author
10. *Daily Telegraph*, 9 January 1992
11. Ted Kavanagh, *Tommy Handley*
12. Jack Warner, *Evening All*
13. Geoffrey Talbot, *Ten Seconds From Now*
14. Arnold Haskell, *Since 1939*
15. *BBC Year Book 1946*
16. Ibid.
17. Lord Moran, *The Struggle for Survival*
18. *BBC Year Book 1946*
19. Robert Hewison, *Under Siege*
20. Ronald Howard, *In Search of My Father*
21. Kenneth More, *Happy Go Lucky*
22. Sir John Wheeler Bennett, *Special Relationships*
23. Robert Dougall, *In and Out of the Box*
24. R. Ingersoll, *Report on England*
25. Ibid.

2 *Not a Dry Eye in the House*

1. Author's interview with Pat Ford in Charlottesville, June 1992
2. Michael Korda, *Charmed Lives*
3. Ibid.
4. William Stevenson, *A Man Called Intrepid*
5. Morella, Epstein and Griggs, *Films of World War Two*
6. Michael Korda, *Charmed Lives*
7. Ibid.
8. Brian Connell, *Knight Errant*
9. Ibid.
10. Barry Norman, *Talking Pictures*
11. Ronald Howard, *In Search of My Father*

3 *Burlesque and Barbarism Behind the Wire*

1. Roderick Grant, *51st Highland Division at War*
2. Ibid.
3. In conversation with the writer
4. Roderick Grant, *51st Highland Division at War*
5. Rheinhold Eggers, *Colditz: The German Story* and P.R. Reid, *Colditz*. The two accounts vary slightly in detail.
6. See also, Airey Neave, *They Have Their Exits*
7. John Dominy, *The Sergeant Escapers*
8. Ibid.
9. See M.R.D.Foot, *S.O.E.* and *Resistance* and Parker Dodds, *Setting Europe Ablaze*
10. *Daily Telegraph*, 6 May 1944
11. Airey Neave, *They Have Their Exits*
12. See also, Alan Burgess, *The Long Tunnel*
13. Rheinhold Eggers, *Colditz: The German Story*

4 *Carmen Miranda Saved My Life*

1. Alan Moorehead, *The End in Africa*
2. Sir Harry Secombe, *Arias and Raspberries*
3. James McGrath in conversation with the author
4. Vernon Scannell, *Argument of Kings*
5. Neil McCallum, *Journey with A Pistol*
6. Sir Harry Secombe, *Arias and Raspberries*
7. David Clark in correspondence and conversation with the author
8. Hubert Haines in correspondence with the author
9. James McGrath in conversation with the author
10. Sir Harry Secombe, *Arias and Raspberries*
11. Spike Milligan's war service is covered in six volumes of his memoirs which include: *Adolph Hitler, My part in his downfall, Rommel, Gunner Who?, Monty, His part in my victory, Mussolini, His part in my downfall* and *Where have all the bullets gone?*
12. Richard Roberts in correspondence with the author
13. Arthur Clements in correspondence with the author

14. Rey Gill in correspondence with the author
15. Jim Whitehorn in correspondence with the author
16. Cyril Risbridger in correspondence with the author
17. John Harris, *A Funny Place to Hold a War*
18. Thomas Booth in correspondence with the author
19. David Clark in correspondence with the author
20. Jack Blades in correspondence with the author
21. Marlene Dietrich, *My Life*
22. John Graven Hughes, *Grease Paint War*
23. Gracie Fields, *Sing As We Go*
24. Pamela Trescott, *A Comic Life*
25. Joe Hyams, *Bogie*
26. Christopher Buckley, *Road to Rome*

5 The Best Medicine
 1. Roderick Grant, *The 51st Highland Division at War*
 2. Dwight D. Eisenhower, *Crusade in Europe*
 3. Sir Harry Secombe, *Arias and Raspberries*
 4. Ibid.
 5. Marlene Dietrich, *My Life*
 6. Arthur Marx, *The Nine Lives of Mickey Rooney*
 7. Harry Finchley, tape recording to the author
 8. Joyce Grenfell, *Entertaining the Troops and Requests the Pleasure*
 9. Anna Neagle, *There's Always Tomorrow*
10. Noel Coward, *Middle East Diary*
11. Dr Ray James in correspondence with the author
12. Naomi Jacob, *Me Over There*
13. Ralph Martin, *The GI War*

6 Hollywood Waves the Flag
 1. Report by Bosely Crowther of the *New York Times*, December 1942
 2. Report by Howard Barnes, *New York Herald Tribune*, December 1942
 3. Morella, Epstein and Griggs, *The Films of World War Two*
 4. Ibid.
 5. Arthur Clements in correspondence with the author
 6. Hugh Berry's report and letters to the author
 7. David Clark, in correspondence and conversation with the author
 8. Freddie Smith, letters and tape recordings
 9. Ibid.
10. Report by Bosely Crowther, December 1984
11. See Maurice Sellar, *The Best of British*
12. *Time* Magazine, May 1942
13. *The Films of World War Two*

7 All Change
 1. Philip Purser and Jenny Wilkes, *The One and Only Phyllis Dixie*
 2. John Costello, *Love, Sex and War*

3. *The One and Only Phyllis Dixie*
4. Donald Sinden in the foreword to *From Drags to Riches*
5. Rebecca Bell-Metereau, *Hollywood Androgyny*
6. Jeremy Pascall, *50 Years of the Movies* and Rebecca Bell-Metereau *Hollywood Androgyny*
7. Dietrich, *My Life* and Leslie Frewin, *Dietrich*
8. Jeremy Pascal, *50 Years of the Movies*
9. Alf Lewis in correspondence with the author
10. Peter Selby in correspondence with the author
11. Regina May in correspondence with the author
12. Sergeant Baker in correspondence with the author
13. W.A. Lovett in correspondence with the author
14. *Daily Telegraph* report, December 1991
15. Danny La Rue, *From Drags to Riches*
16. Ibid.
17. *The Independent*, 19 December 1991
18. *Theatre World*, November 1944
19. Haskell, Powell, Myers, Ironside, *Since 1939*
20. Lynn Booth Hilliard in correspondence with the author
21. Haskell, Powell, Myers, Ironside, *Since 1939*
22. Hewison, *Under Siege*
23. Ibid.
24. Ibid.
25. Sir Anthony Quayle, *Time to Speak*
26. Hewison, *Under Siege* and Angus Calder, *The People's War*

8 *A Moment or Two of Forgetfulness*

1. Dwight D. Eisenhower, *Crusade in Europe*
2. On 5 November, Eisenhower's personal assistant, Kay Summersby, recorded in her diary, 'General Betts reports that disciplinary conditions in the army are becoming bad.' There were numerous cases of desertion, rape, murder and pillage. For rape and murder cases Eisenhower held public executions. The immediate family of the victims and civic officials of the towns were present to see the execution. See *The War Between the Generals*, David Irving, Chapter 16
3. Dwight D. Eisenhower, *Crusade in Europe*
4. Marlene Dietrich, *My Life*
5. Ibid.
6. Dwight D. Eisenhower, *Crusade in Europe*
7. Leslie Frewin, *Dietrich*
8. Sergeant Woodford in conversation with the author
9. Dr Roland Winfield, *The Sky Belongs to Them*
10. See Max Hasting's *Bomber Command*
11. *Daily Telegraph*, 26 January 1991
12. A. Randall & R. Seaton, *George Formby*
13. Robert Hewison, *Under Siege*
14. Hughes, John Graven, *The Grease Paint War*

15. Roger Wilmut, *Kindly Leave the Stage*
16. Roger Key, tape recording and letters to the writer
17. William Collins, *The Memoirs of Field-Marshal Montgomery*

9 Strike Up the Band

1. See David Irving's *The War Between the Generals*
2. Geoffrey Butcher, *Next to a letter from home – Glen Miller's Wartime Band* and Chris Way, *The Big Bands Go to War*
3. Mollie Urquart in conversation and correspondence with the author
4. According to research carried out by the BBC Radio 5 presenter, Frank Wappat
5. Ibid.
6. Frank Wappat in conversation with the author
7. Geoffrey Butcher, *Next to a letter from home*
8. Chris Way, *Big Bands Go to War*
9. Geoffrey Butcher, *Next to a letter from home*
10. Ibid.
11. Ibid.
12. Ian Maclean, *Ministry of Morale*
13. Albert McCarthy, *The Dance Band Era*
14. Ibid.
15. Dame Vera Lynn, *Vocal Refrain*
16. Chris Way, *Big Bands Go to War*
17. Ibid.
18. Account from former Flight Lieutenant Gary Beasley to the author
19. Chris Way, *Big Bands Go to War*
20. Ibid.
21. Ibid.
22. David Niven, *The Moon's a Balloon*, and Albert McCarthy, *The Dance Band Era*
23. Peter and Letitia Bedford in conversation and correspondence with the author

10 ENSA Revives a Battered Army

1. Sir Dirk Bogarde, in Part Two of *By Myself*, Channel 4 Television, 12 January 1992
2. Ibid. and *Sunday Telegraph*, 12 January 1992
3. Doug Kneale in correspondence with the author
4. Naomi Jacob, *Me Over There*
5. Gertrude Lawrence, *A Star Danced*
6. Gay Clark in correspondence and conversation with the author
7. *Daily Telegraph*, 26 January 1991
8. Gertrude Lawrence, *A Star Danced*
9. Ibid.
10. Bert Woodfield in correspondence and conversation with the author
11. *The Scotsman*, 9 August 1944
12. Gertrude Lawrence, *A Star Danced*
13. Peter Fawcett in conversation with the author

14. Tom Taylor in correspondence with the author

11 *Yes, They're Still Fighting in Italy*
1. *News Review*, 1 February 1945
2. Ibid.
3. John Cooper in correspondence and conversation with the author
4. Cyril Ray, *History of the 78th Division – Algiers to Austria*
5. John Cooper in correspondence and conversation with the author
6. Brian Harpur, *The Impossible Victory*
7. Spike Milligan, *Mussolini, His part in my downfall*
8. Ibid.
9. Sir Harry Secombe, *Arias and Raspberries*
10. Arthur Childs in correspondence with the author
11. John Graven Hughes, *The Grease Paint War*
12. Morella, Epstein,Griggs, *The Films of World War Two*
13. Peter Bevans in correspondence with the author
14. Rusty Russell in correspondence with the author
15. David Clark in correspondence and conversation with the author
16. William Collins, *Here Lies Eric Ambler*
17. Joe Hyams, *Bogie*
18. Ibid.
19. William Collins, *Here Lies Eric Ambler*
20. Ibid.

12 *Curtain Call*
1. Fred Harvey, in correspondence and conversation with the author
2. Marjorie Sargeant in correspondence and conversation with the author
3. Jack Lawrence in correspondence and conversation with the author
4. Jimmy Young, *J.Y. An Autobiography*
5. Ibid.
6. Drigh Road concert party programme
7. Jack Hawkins, *Anything for a Quiet Life*
8. Field Marshal Sir William Slim, *Defeat into Victory*
9. Anthony Cotterell, *RAMC*
10. *Defeat into Victory*, Ibid.
11. *The War Illustrated*, May 1944
12. Jack Hawkins, *Anything for a Quiet Life*
13. Field Marshal Sir William Slim, *Defeat into Victory*
14. Vera Lynn, *Vocal Refrain*
15. Ibid.
16. Conversation with the author
17. Randall, A. and Seaton, R., *George Formby*
18. Jack Hawkins, *Anything for a Quiet Life*
19. Ibid.
20. Winifred Beaumont, *A Detail on the Burma Front*
21. Gracie Fields, *Sing As We Go*
22. Ralph Martin, *The GI War*

Bibliography

Ambler, Eric, *Here Lies Eric Ambler* (William Collins, 1985)
BBC Year Book 1947
Beaumont, Winifred, *A Detail on the Burma Front* (BBC Books, 1977)
Bell-Metereau, Rebecca, *Hollywood Androgyny* (Columbia University Press, 1985)
Bennett, Sir John Wheeler, *Special Relationships* (Macmillan, 1975)
Buckley, Christopher, *Road to Rome* (Hodder and Stoughton, 1945)
Burgess, Alan, *The Long Tunnel* (Bloomsbury, 1990)
Butcher, Geoffrey, *Next to a letter from Home – Glen Miller's Wartime Band* (Mainstream, 1986)
Calder, Angus, *The People's War* (Jonathan Cape, 1969)
Connell, Brian, *Knight Errant* (Hodder and Stoughton, 1955)
Costello, John, *Love, Sex and War* (Collins, 1985)
Cotterell, Anthony, *RAMC* (Hutchinson, 1945)
Coward, Noel, *Middle East Diary* (The Right Book Club, 1945)
Dietrich, Marlene, *My Life* (Weidenfeld and Nicolson, 1989)
Dodds, Parker, *Setting Europe Ablaze* (Springwood, 1983)
Dominy, John, *The Sergeant Escapers* (Ian Allan, 1974)
Dougall, Robert, *In and Out of the Box* (Collins and Harvill Press, 1973)
Eggers, Rheinhold, *The German Story of Colditz* (Robert Hale, 1961)
Eisenhower, Dwight D., *Crusade in Europe* (William Heinemann Ltd, 1948)
Fields, Gracie, *Sing As We Go* (Frederick Muller Ltd, 1960)
Foot, M.R.D., *Resistance* (Eyre Methuen, 1961)
——*S.O.E.* (BBC, 1984)
Frewin, Leslie, *Dietrich* (Leslie Frewin, 1967)
Grant, Roderick, *51st Highland Division at War* (Ian Allan 1977)
Grenfell, Joyce, *Entertaining the Troops* (Macmillan, 1990)
——*Requests the Pleasure* (Macmillan, 1976)
Harpur, Brian, *The Impossible Victory* (William Kimber 1980)
Harris, John, *A Funny Place to Hold a War* (Hutchinson, 1984)
Harrison, Rex, *Rex* (Macmillan, 1976)
Haskell, Arnold, *Since 1939* (Longmans Green & Co.Ltd, 1947)
Haskell, Powell, Myers, Ironside, *Since 1939* (Reader's Union, 1948)
Hastings, Max, *Bomber Command* (Michael Joseph, 1979)
Hawkins, Jack, *Anything for a Quiet Life* (Elm Tree Books, 1973)
Hewison, Robert, *Under Siege* (Weidenfeld and Nicolson, 1977)

Howard, Ronald, *In Search of My Father* (Kimber, 1981)

Hughes, John Graven, *Grease Paint War* (New English Library, 1976)

Hyams, Joe, *Bogie* (Mayflower Books, 1973)

Ingersoll, R., *Report on England* (Right Book Club, 1941)

Jacob, Naomi, *Me, Over There* (Hutchinson, 1947)

James, Clifton, *I was Monty's Double* (Popular Book Club, Odhams 1957) and *Secrets and Stories of the War* (Reader's Digest, 1963)

Kavanagh, Ted, *Tommy Handley* (Hodder and Stoughton, 1949)

Korda, Michael, *Charmed Lives* (Random House, 1979)

La Rue, Danny, *From Drags to Riches* (Viking, 1987)

Lawrence, Gertrude, *A Star Danced* (W.H. Allen, 1945)

Leasor, James, *The Experiences of Sir Leslie Hollis, The War at the Top* (Michael Joseph, 1959)

Lynn, Dame Vera, *Vocal Refrain* (W.H. Allen, 1975)

McCallum, Neil, *Journey with A Pistol* (Corgi, 1953)

McCarthy, Albert, *The Dance Band Era* (November Books 1971)

Maclean, Ian, *Ministry of Morale* (Allen and Unwin, 1979)

Marshall, Arthur, *Life's Rich Pageant* (Collins, 1986)

Martin, Ralph, *The GI War* (Little Brown, Boston, 1967)

Marx, Arthur, *The Nine Lives of Mickey Rooney* (Berkley, 1986)

Milligan, Spike, *Adolph Hitler, My part in his downfall*

——*Rommel, Gunner Who?*

——*Monty, His part in my victory*

——*Mussolini, His part in my downfall*

——*Where have all the bullets gone?*

Moorehead, Alan, *The End in Africa* (Hamish Hamilton, 1943)

Moran, Lord, *The Struggle for Survival* (Constable, 1966)

More, Kenneth, *Happy Go Lucky* (Robert Hale, 1959)

Morella, Epstein and Griggs, *Films of World War Two*

Neagle, Anna, *There's Always Tomorrow* (W.H. Allen, 1974)

Neave, Airey, *They Have Their Exits* (Hodder and Stoughton, 1953)

Niven, David, *The Moon's a Balloon* (Hamish Hamilton, 1972)

Norman, Barry, *Talking Pictures* (BBC Books, Hodder and Stoughton, 1987)

Pascall, Jeremy, *50 Years of the Movies* (Hamlyn Publishing Group, 1981)

Purser, Philip and Jenny Wilkes, *The One and Only Phyllis Dixie* (Futura, 1978)

Quayle, Sir Anthony, *Time to Speak* (Barrie and Jenkins, 1990)

Randall, A. & Seaton, R., *George Formby* (W.H. Allen, 1974)

Ray, Cyril, *History of the 78th Division – Algiers to Austria* (Eyre and Spottiswoode, 1952)

Reid, P.R., *Colditz* (Hodder and Stoughton, 1952)

Scannell, Vernon, *Argument of Kings* (Futura, 1987)

Secombe, Sir Harry, *Arias and Raspberries* (Robson Books, 1989)

Sellar, Maurice, *The Best of British* (Sphere 1987)

Slim, Field Marshal Sir William, *Defeat into Victory* (Corgi, 1965)

Stevenson, William, *A Man Called Intrepid* (Macmillan, 1976)

Talbot, Godfrey, *Ten Seconds From Now* (W.H. Allen, 1985)

Trescott, Pamela, *A Comic Life* (W.H. Allen, 1988)
Warner, Jack, *Evening All* (W.H. Allen, 1975)
Way, Chris, *The Big Bands Go to War* (Mainstream, 1991)
Wilmut, Roger, *Kindly Leave the Stage* (Methuen, 1985)
Winfield, Dr Roland, *The Sky Belongs to Them* (William Kimber, 1976)
Young, Jimmy, *J.Y. An Autobiography* (W.H. Allen, 1974)

Index